national STATISTICS

Labour Market Review 2006

Office for National Statistics

palgrave macmillan

First published 2006 by
PALGRAVE MACMILLAN
Houndmills, Basingstoke, Hampshire RG21 6XS and 175 Fifth Avenue, New York, NY 10010, USA
Companies and representatives throughout the world.

PALGRAVE MACMILLAN is the global academic imprint of the Palgrave Macmillan division of St. Martin's Press, LLC and of Palgrave Macmillan Ltd. Macmillan® is a registered trademark in the United States, United Kingdom and other countries. Palgrave is a registered trademark in the European Union and other countries.

ISBN 1-4039-9735-7

This book is printed on paper suitable for recycling and made from fully managed and sustained forest sources.
A catalogue record for this book is available from the British Library.

10 9 8 7 6 5 4 3 2 1
15 14 13 12 11 10 09 08 07 06

Printed and bound in Great Britain by
William Clowes Ltd,
Beccles, Suffolk.

Cover picture: Getty Images

A National Statistics publication

National Statistics are produced to high professional standards set out in the National Statistics Code of Practice. They are produced free from political influence.

About the Office for National Statistics

The Office for National Statistics (ONS) is the government agency responsible for compiling, analysing and disseminating economic, social and demographic statistics about the United Kingdom. It also administers the statutory registration of births, marriages and deaths in England and Wales.

The Director of ONS is also the National Statistician and the Registrar General for England and Wales.

Contact points

For enquiries about this publication, contact the Labour Market Statistics Helpline.

Tel: 020 7533 6094
E-mail: labourmarket@ons.gsi.gov.uk

For general enquiries, contact the National Statistics Customer Contact Centre.

Tel: 0845 601 3034 (minicom: 01633 812399)
E-mail: info@statistics.gsi.gov.uk
Fax: 01633 652747
Post: Room 1015, Government Buildings,
Cardiff Road, Newport NP10 8XG

You can also find National Statistics on the Internet at:
www.statistics.gov.uk

Contents

List of figures and tables

3: Employment

4: Unemployment

Foreword

As National Statistician I welcome the publication of *Labour Market Review 2006*. This publication comes in the tenth anniversary year of the foundation, in 1996, of the Office for National Statistics (ONS), and celebrates a decade of advances in labour market statistics.

Statistics relating to people's activity in the workplace feature in the national and local news media almost every day. The latest indicators of employment, unemployment and earnings are followed closely by economic analysts for what they reveal about the state of the UK economy. And there is widespread interest in the range of statistics published by ONS at both national and local levels, and for numerous sub-groups of the population, which illustrate the roles and actions of people, employers and government in the world of work.

As with other topic areas, it is crucial that the labour market statistics published by ONS are trusted by both experts and the general public. I believe that the statistical improvements described in this volume have considerably enhanced this trust. Particularly significant has been the introduction of an internationally recognised basis for the UK's official employment and unemployment statistics.

Together with the new online guide described in the introduction to the volume, *Labour Market Review 2006* should provide an ideal reference source for everyone who has an interest in using ONS's labour market statistics to gain insights into an important aspect of life in 21st-century Britain.

Karen Dunnell

Karen Dunnell
National Statistician
March 2006

Guide to Labour Market Statistics

Recently launched on the National Statistics website, this online guide provides explanation of many labour market concepts, sources and methods.

Keywords highlighted throughout the Labour Market Review 2006 by this symbol (Topic) feature in the Guide.

The Guide can be found at:
www.statistics.gov.uk/labour_guide

Introduction

Advances in labour market statistics, 1996–2006

Almost certainly, the most significant development in the UK's labour market statistics during the last ten years was the introduction in 1998 of the monthly publication by ONS of unemployment, and related labour supply statistics, from the Labour Force Survey (LFS) on the basis of internationally recognised definitions. The presentation of these statistics as the UK's official measures in an integrated monthly publication together with other labour market statistics, defused the controversy which had previously surrounded the issue of the public's trust in the UK's measurement of unemployment.

Building on this much stronger foundation for the UK's official labour market statistics, four wide ranging strategic National Statistics Quality Reviews have been carried out and published since 2002. The conclusions of these reviews have led to the development of significant new labour market statistics outputs and surveys. They have also created a blueprint for further improvements which can be implemented, as resources permit, over a number of years to come.

Some of the new and improved labour market statistics outputs which have been introduced since 2002 are:

- The monthly Average Earnings Index (AEI) excluding bonuses, Average Weekly Earnings (AWE), and the Index of Labour Costs and Hours (ILCH)
- More reliable statistics of low pay and of numbers of people earning below the National Minimum Wage
- Job vacancy statistics covering the whole economy
- A much enhanced set of statistics relating to public sector employment
- Regular analyses of adults and children in workless households
- Modelled employment, unemployment and other time series back to 1971 on the basis of consistent ILO definitions
- Local area labour market profiles, including new local area indicators such as residence based claimant count proportions, job densities and modelled unemployment rates on the ILO definition
- A new set of consistent series of historical labour market data became National Statistics in 2004. These tables are included after Chapter 6 in this publication.

Some examples of newly introduced ONS labour market surveys underpinning these outputs are:

- The monthly survey of job vacancies (VS)
- The quarterly public sector employment survey (QPSES)
- The annual survey of hours and earnings (ASHE)
- Local area sample boosts to the LFS, which greatly improve the quality of sub - national labour market statistics.

Online Guide to labour market statistics

Launched with this publication is ONS's Guide to Labour Market Statistics. This online guide provides a comprehensive reference source to all aspects of labour market statistics. It is designed to follow the framework, described in the following section, which has been now been adopted by ONS for the analysis and presentation of labour market statistics sources and outputs.

The online guide describes, and provides guidance about:

- The concepts which underpin the labour market statistics compiled and published by ONS
- The sources used to provide the data from which the statistics are compiled
- The methods used to generate the statistics
- The means of dissemination of the statistics via web-based and paper publications, data releases, publication schedules, and analytical/ methodological articles available
- The strengths and weaknesses of each data source, and the most suitable source to use for each particular purpose

The aim of the Guide is to act as an easily accessible reference source helping users and analysts of all types to improve their understanding of the extensive range of labour market statistics now published by ONS.

The guide can be found at: www.statistics.gov.uk/labour_guide

The Framework for Labour Market Statistics

Labour Market Review 2006 presents a selection of labour market statistics in the context of a framework based on the concepts of labour supply and labour demand (Figure A).

This framework reflects the range of roles in the labour market: of employers, in creating labour demand; of currently employed people, in creating labour supply; and of people, not currently working or seeking work, in creating a potential future labour supply. The framework also reflects the potential for the government benefits system to influence the behaviour of people in the labour market. An example of this is when the conditions for receipt of a benefit are tightened, requiring recipients more actively to seek work, there may be a consequent rise in labour supply.

Figure A
Framework for labour market statistics

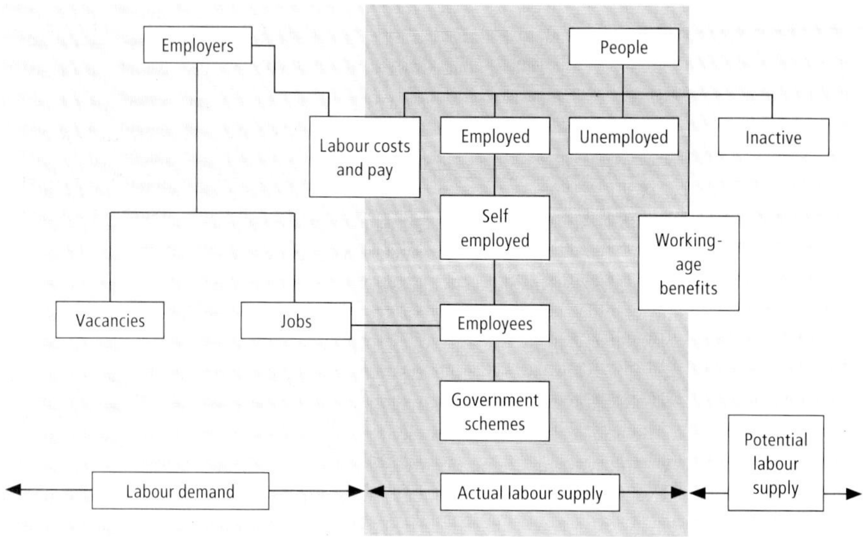

While the labour market framework is helpful for understanding the roles of the different participants in the labour market, it should not be over-interpreted to imply that all labour market statistics may be unambiguously classified as supply or demand. Statistics of actual hours of work, for example, provide valuable information both about labour demand but also about the aggregate level of labour supply.

Uses of Labour Market Statistics

Labour market statistics provide the basis for the quantitative understanding of an aspect of life in the UK in the 21st century that is of great interest across a wide spectrum of society. For this reason, ONS has an important role in publishing labour market statistics in order to inform public understanding and debate.

In parallel to this public information, there are a number of specific areas of policy and analysis where labour market statistics meet clear needs of central and local government. The following are some examples.

Macroeconomic policy

Labour market statistics have a key role in providing some of the information which is important for macroeconomic policy in both the short term and the longer term.

In the short term, labour supply figures from the Labour Force Survey (LFS), together with statistics of labour demand and changes in earnings, are closely watched by analysts in order to assess the extent of inflationary pressures arising from labour costs. In recent years, for example, a key focus of interest has been the extent to which incoming migration to the UK from the EU accession countries has increased aggregate labour supply and hence helped to alleviate demand pressures.

In the longer term, macroeconomic analysis reflects the understanding that both the quantity and quality of the nation's supply of people and their skills, as measured by statistics from the LFS and elsewhere, are key determinants of national output and performance. In a UK economy dominated by the services sector, this statistical measurement of people and their skills is increasingly important.

For the interpretation of the labour market statistics for both these short and longer term purposes, macroeconomic analysts place great emphasis on the importance of consistent long time-series of key labour market indicators. For example, such series of employment, hours of work, unemployment and inactivity back to 1971 are an essential input for the Treasury's and the Bank of England's economic models which are used, respectively, for the assessment of fiscal and monetary policy.

Employment policy

Government policy, relating to the promotion of employment opportunities for all, requires good quality statistics showing the extent of employment among different groups of people within the community, and the extent of the skills these groups have acquired. This information, as well as broader labour supply information showing the extent of unemployment and inactivity, is needed both for local areas of the UK and population sub-groups such as ethnic minority groups, the disabled and lone parents. There is also a strong policy interest in the impact of future demographic trends on the age structure of the working population.

Statistics of educational qualifications and skills already obtained by people, as well as the extent of the job related training being undertaken to develop improved skills, are important for understanding the quality of available labour supply and for formulating training policies designed to improve the prospects for employment. In the context of industrial relations policy, statistics are needed relating to working time arrangements, trades union membership and the extent of labour disputes.

Statistics relating to the distribution of earnings are also needed in connection with the National Minimum Wage policy. Most recently, in the context of the government's policy for public services reform, there has been a surge of high-level policy interest in the improvement of statistics relating to public sector employment.

Regional policy

Labour market statistics support economic planning at sub-national level and the devolved administrations in Scotland, Wales and Northern Ireland have a distinct interest in all aspects of labour market statistics applying to their countries. More generally, labour market statistics are needed in the context of formulating policies to enhance the efficiency of regional economies across the UK.

Differences between the labour markets of local areas within regions are often greater than the differences between regions, and there is also a strong interest, from both central and local government, in statistics for local areas to help inform neighbourhood renewal and other locally focussed policies.

Chapter 1

The labour market in the wider economy

- Towards the end of 2005 there was a mixed global economic picture, with the US economy still strong, and signs of a gradual pick-up in Europe. However, both the Japanese and the UK economies appeared to have weakened.

- Growth in the UK was below trend in 2005, and there were signs of an easing in the strong consumer demand which had supported recent growth. Consumer expenditure, retail sales, and house price growth all slowed.

- The UK labour market remained strong, despite the wider economic slowdown. There were tentative signs of some easing, with the claimant count rising, but employment remained historically high.

The labour market is a key part of the economy. The share of national income that goes to labour is around 55 per cent (measured as compensation of employees divided by Gross National Income at market prices). This has fallen over the last 30 years, having been around 60 per cent for most of the period 1950–1973, and having peaked at 66 per cent in 1975.

Longer-term trends in the labour market have major implications for the wider economy. Labour demand has been increasing over the past decade, reflecting the ongoing growth in the economy. By comparison, labour supply has also been rising, affected by population growth, largely driven by net incoming international migration since the early 1990s, and by the rise in female participation in the labour force over recent decades. Offsetting this, there has been a marked fall in male participation and a tendency for the average hours worked by individuals to decline.

The levels of demand and supply within the labour market are important because labour market tightness, arising when demand is not sufficiently met by supply, can lead to rising earnings growth. Earnings growth and the consequent upward pressure on overall labour costs is the key mechanism through which inflationary pressure may be transmitted from the labour market to consumer prices.

One of the key changes in recent years has been that earnings growth has been more benign. There is a wide range of possible reasons for the more settled wage growth position, which include factors such as changes in the labour market and industrial structure and the drivers affecting changes in the behaviour of the unemployed and the economically inactive.

For example, industrial structure has seen a continuing switch from manufacturing to services. Service sector jobs may be generally more flexible (in terms of hiring and firing); similarly, they are often seen as being less unionised. Both of these factors may reduce wage pressures within the labour market. More generally there is the question of the non-accelerating inflation rate of unemployment (NAIRU), that is the rate of unemployment consistent with sustainable or trend output growth. Put simply, it is the rate of unemployment below which inflation will start to accelerate. During the early 1980s the UK NAIRU was widely perceived as being around 7 per cent. However, with unemployment below 5 per cent and no sign of significant inflationary pressure, the NAIRU would appear to have fallen. This could be a result of the factors above and the labour market reforms of the 1980s and 1990s increasing labour market flexibility.

Any assessment of wage pressures also needs to take account of the effect of the economically inactive on total labour supply, because a significant proportion of people entering employment do so directly from inactivity rather than passing through the pool of unemployment. An increase in the potential labour supply, resulting from either growth in the number of inactive through demographic changes or an increase in the numbers among them who are most likely to seek work, can reduce pressures within the labour market. Contrary to the perception that seems to be commonplace in the media, the overall inactivity rate has not changed much over the last 30 years. The rate peaked at 23 per cent in the early 1980s but was around 21 to 22 per cent for much of the 1970s – the rate it is now.

Another factor affecting wage pressures may have been an impact from the monetary policy framework introduced in recent years, initially with the move to direct inflation targeting in the early 1990s and then the introduction of the independent Monetary Policy Committee in 1997. If these measures have affected individuals' expectations of inflation, they may have in turn affected wage claims. Greater credibility for policy should lead individuals to expect lower, more stable, inflation, thereby tending to encourage lower pay settlements in line with those expectations.

The economic background to 2005

Turning to look at the specific economic position in 2005, there was a mixed global economic picture in the period up to the July–September quarter of 2005 (Figure 1.1).

Looking back, growth in 2002 had been modest in all of the main economies. However, there had been a pick-up in 2003 in the United States, Japan, and the UK, though the Eurozone remained subdued.

This stronger picture continued into 2004 and 2005 for the United States with growth consistently running at around 1 per cent per quarter. However, in the other two countries the picture weakened; in Japan, growth weakened markedly in 2004, and though there was a pick-up in early 2005, it had fallen back to 0.2 per cent in Q3 2005. In the UK, quarterly growth was 0.5 per cent or less throughout the year.

Meanwhile, Eurozone growth, which was sluggish in 2003 and 2004, has seen a gradual pick-up in 2005. While still modest in the first half of the year, quarterly growth had risen to 0.6 per cent in July–September (Q3).

Figure 1.1
Quarterly GDP growth for the United States, United Kingdom, Eurozone and Japan, July–September 2003 to July–September 2005

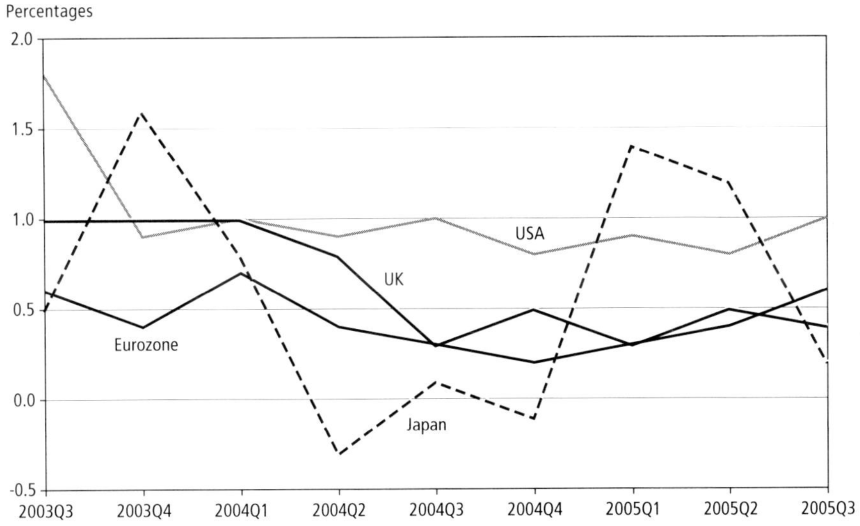

Source: UK, National Accounts; Eurozone, Eurostat; USA and Japan, OECD

The general output picture fed into the labour market performances of the different countries in 2005. The United States labour market continued to improve marginally: unemployment fell from 5.4 in December 2004 to 5.0 per cent in October 2005 (Figure 1.2), and the employment rate for those aged 16 and over was up from 62.4 to 62.8 per cent. Similarly, the labour market performance of the European Union improved slightly, reflecting the improvement in the output figures: unemployment remained high but fell from 8.8 to 8.3 per cent. By comparison, Japan saw its unemployment rate fall from 4.5 to 4.2 per cent in September 2005, before bouncing back, up to 4.5 per cent.

Figure 1.2
Unemployment rates for the United States, United Kingdom, Eurozone and Japan, December 2003–October 2005

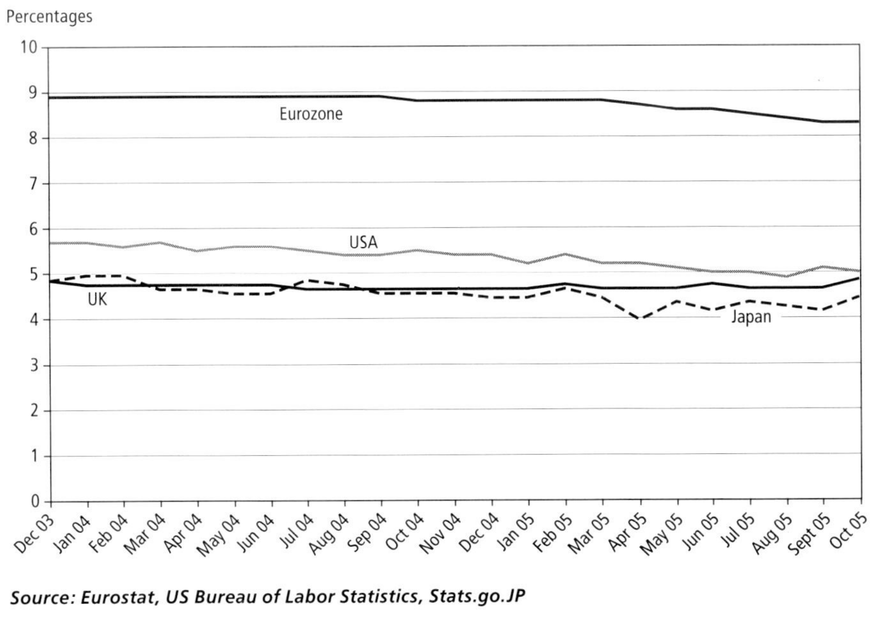

Source: Eurostat, US Bureau of Labor Statistics, Stats.go.JP

Unemployment in the UK was up from 4.7 per cent in October–December 2004 to 4.9 per cent in August–October 2005 and the working-age employment rate went fell from 74.9 to 74.7 per cent. The overall labour market position remains strong, but this easing reflects the slowdown in the UK economy and the fact that growth was below trend for five consecutive quarters.

Signs of the slowdown can be seen in a number of areas. For example, there have been signs that growth in consumer demand has eased. Quarterly growth in UK household final consumption expenditure has slowed from 1.3 per cent in the first quarter of 2004 to 0.5 per cent in the third quarter of 2005. Meanwhile, around the start of 2004 the volume of retail sales was increasing by around 2 per cent per quarter; this declined over the year to -0.1 per cent in the final quarter. It has recovered since but remained down at 0.7 per cent in the third quarter of 2005.

Another sign of the easing in the economy and the labour market is that wage growth remained relatively benign. Average earnings growth did pick up from around 3.5 to 4.5 per cent between mid-2003 and early 2005, but the rate excluding bonuses has since eased back to around 4.0 per cent. This is markedly lower than the 10 per cent earnings growth seen the last time the employment rate was as high (1990), or the 30 per cent (nominal) growth seen when the unemployment rate was as low. Real wage growth has been even more subdued, consistently below 3 per cent since 2001, and often well below, compared with 10 per cent growth in early 1975.

Other economic factors in 2005

Alongside the general economic background to 2005, there were a number of specific events or factors that had an impact on the labour market during the year.

- The most obvious was the ongoing situation in the Middle East and strong global demand for oil. Oil prices were pushed above $30 a barrel in 2003 following the coalition invasion of Iraq, and given the continuing uncertainty about the situation in the region, prices continued to rise in 2005, peaking at $64 per barrel in September, before dropping back slightly to around $55 in November.
- Government policy developments are also likely to have had an impact on the labour market.
- In October 2005, the main rate for the National Minimum Wage increased from £4.85 per hour to £5.05 per hour. The development rate, mainly covering youths aged 18–21, increased from £4.10 per hour to £4.25 per hour. Similarly, the accredited training rate (for workers aged 22 and over who are receiving accredited training in the first six months of a job with a new employer) was also raised to £4.25 per hour, from £4.10.
- In 2005 the roll out of the Department for Work and Pensions' Jobcentre Plus continued. Jobcentre Plus integrates social security offices and job centres with the aim of fully integrating work and benefit services. The rollout of 1,000 Jobcentre Plus offices started with a Pathfinder exercise in 2001 and is due to be completed by 2006.

Labour demand

- In the second quarter of 2005, there were 30.8 million jobs in the economy, one of the largest numbers ever recorded. Of these, 26.7 million (87 per cent) were employee jobs.
- Employment in service sector jobs grew from 61 per cent of the total in 1978 to 82 per cent in 2005. Over the same period employment in manufacturing fell from 28 per cent to 12 per cent.
- People are increasingly choosing to work fewer hours and the level of part-time working has grown. As a result, the average hours worked by individuals has had a downwards trend since a peak at the end of 1994.
- In the three months to May 2005 there were 639,100 vacancies in the economy. The industry with the largest number of vacancies in this period was distribution, hotels and restaurants with 188,100 vacancies.
- The redundancy rate has declined since the latest peak observed in the winter quarter of 2001. In the summer quarter of 2005 it stood at 6.1 per thousand employees, having reached 5.2 per thousand in spring 2005, a record low since comparable records began in 1995.
- Overall, the proportion of employees receiving job-related training has increased from 26 per cent in 1995 to 31 per cent in 2005.

The concept of labour demand is directly linked to employers. Labour is a key input to the production process, because firms require workers in order to produce goods and services. The demand for labour refers to employers' demand for this input.

Statistics of labour demand are designed to illustrate the need for labour from employers for producing their output. The statistical picture is complicated as employers may fill vacancies with people who have more than one job, either with them or with another employer, or with people who share the same job. Moreover, in the case of some enterprises, part or all of the labour demand of an employer may be met by his or her own work as a self-employed person.

This chapter starts by looking at the labour input that is actually employed by firms, namely the number of jobs in the economy and the number of hours worked by people in employment. However, at any point in time, part of an employer's requirements for labour may remain unmet. Unmet labour demand is captured through statistics on vacancies, which are discussed in the following section. In addition, this chapter looks at other issues relating to the demand for labour, namely job separations and re-employment, skills, and the relationship between labour demand and the economic cycle.

Jobs and hours of work

Employers are interested in labour as an input to the production of goods and services. This input can vary in two ways: first, through the number of people that a firm employs, which is captured by statistics on the number of jobs in the economy and second, through the number of hours that employed people work, which is captured by statistics on hours of work.

Jobs

The number of jobs in the UK economy has been following an upward trend since 1959, when the current series first became available. There have been significant fluctuations around this trend, which are closely linked to the economic cycle. In the second quarter of 2005, there were 30.8 million jobs in the economy, following a record high in the first quarter of 2005, when the number of jobs in the economy was the largest since comparable records began in 1959 (Figure 2.1).

Employee jobs represent the majority of all jobs in the UK. The number of employee jobs has grown from 22.8 million jobs in the second quarter of 1959 to 26.7 million in the second quarter of 2005, equivalent to an increase of 17 per cent. However, there has been a decline in the proportion of all jobs which are employee jobs from 90 per cent in 1959 to 86 per cent in 2005. This reflects the growth in self-employment during the period.

Jobs by industry

Figure 2.2 shows the number of employee jobs by industry in 1978, when a breakdown by industry first became available, and 2005. The largest increase in employee jobs has been in the finance and business services industry, where the number of employee jobs more than doubled between 1978 and 2005. Large increases were also observed in public administration, education and health (up by 40 per cent) and distribution, hotels and restaurants (up by 38 per cent). In contrast, the extraction and production industries, made up of agriculture and fishing, energy and water, manufacturing and construction, showed a combined fall of approximately 50 per cent, from 9.4 million employee jobs in 1978 to 4.7 million in 2005. Manufacturing alone accounted for around 81 per cent of this decline, with the number of employee jobs in this sector falling from 6.9 million in 1978 to 3.1 million in 2005.

Figure 2.1
Workforce Jobs, 1959 (Quarter 2)–2005 (Quarter 2)[1]
United Kingdom

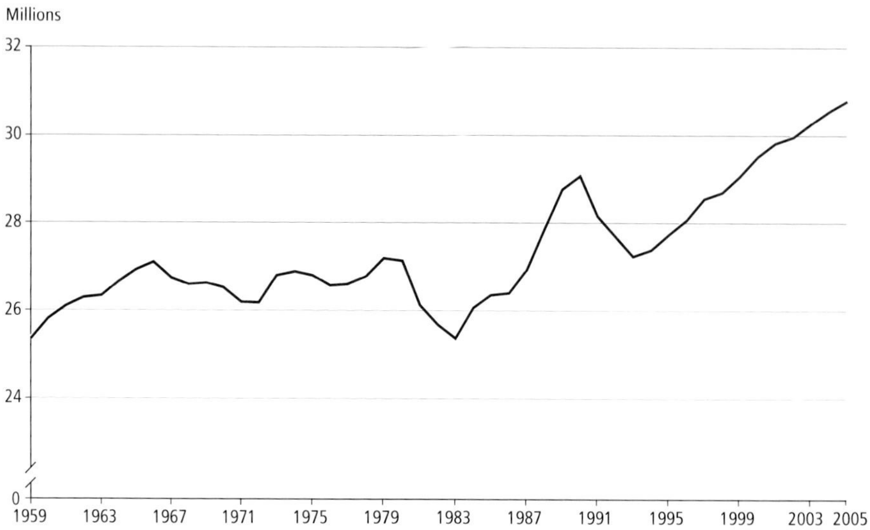

1 *Seasonally adjusted.*
Source: Workforce Jobs

Figure 2.2
Employee Jobs: by industry, 1978 (Quarter 2) and 2005 (Quarter 2)[1]
United Kingdom

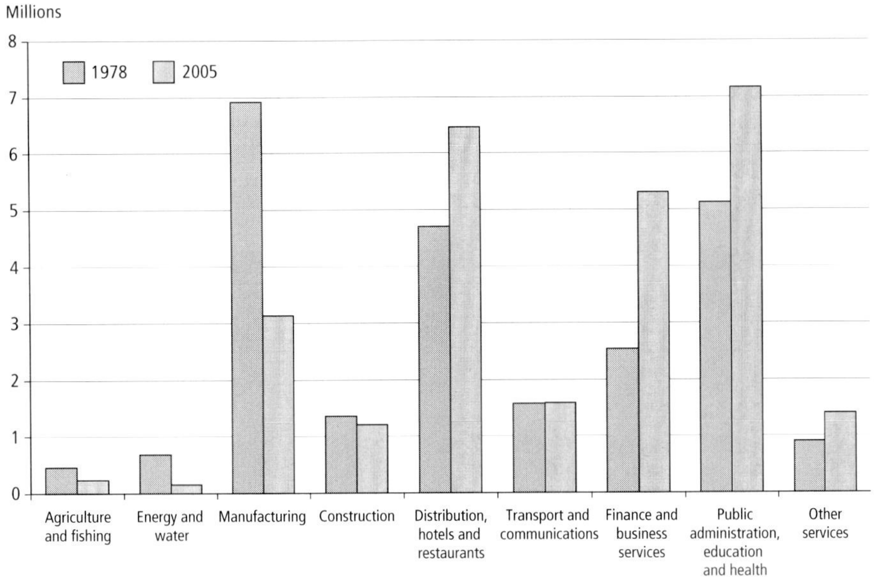

1 Seasonally adjusted.
Source: Employee Jobs

These job figures reflect the structural changes that have prevailed in the UK economy, with a declining proportion of total output produced by the extraction and production industries, and an increasing proportion of total output produced by the service sector. Employee jobs in the service sector comprised 61 per cent of all employee jobs in 1978, compared with 82 per cent in 2005. Over the same period, the percentage of employee jobs in manufacturing fell from 28 per cent to only 12 per cent (Figure 2.3).

Industry Jobs

Figure 2.3
Composition of Employee Jobs: by broad industry group, 1978 (Quarter 2) and 2005 (Quarter 2)[1]
United Kingdom

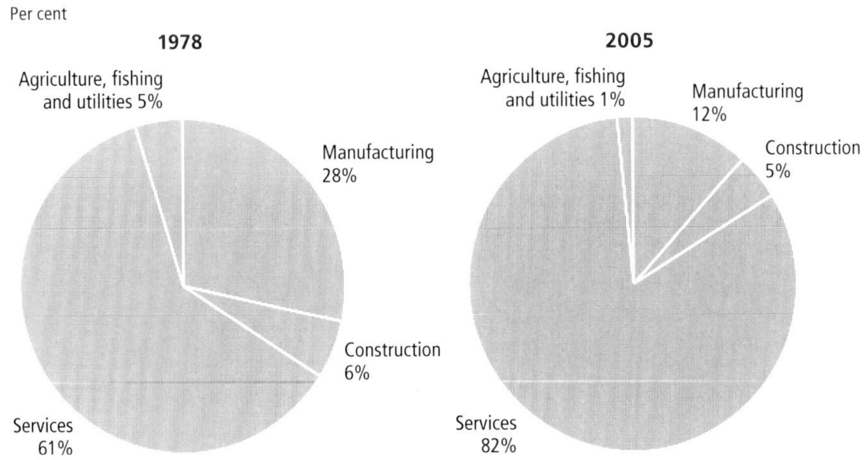

1 Seasonally adjusted.
Source: Employee Jobs

Job densities

Estimates of the number of jobs in local authority areas in the UK can be compared with the population of working age to produce estimates of job densities (Map 2.4 overleaf). These provide an indication of the level of labour demand from employers in an area (number of filled jobs), against the potential labour supply (resident population of working age in an area). The main data sources for estimates of the number of jobs are employer surveys. These are then compared with the official mid-year population estimates for people of working age. The working-age population is made up of all males aged between 16–64 and all females aged between 16–59. This reflects the different ages at which males and females currently become eligible for the state pension.

Areas where job density is greater than one indicate more jobs in an area than residents of working age, and can signify the presence of inward commuting (although care needs to be taken in interpretation as an individual can have more than one job). Estimates of less than one show that there are fewer jobs in an area than residents of working age, and are a possible sign of outward commuting (although, again, caution needs to be used as not all residents of working age in an area would want or be able to work).

Hours of work

As mentioned earlier, employers may vary the labour input to their production process by adjusting the number of hours that employed people work. In the short run, a firm is more likely to respond to a shock in the demand for its product by adjusting hours worked rather than the number of people employed. This is because firms face costs in adjusting the size of their workforce, such as training,

Map 2.4
Job density: by unitary authorities and local authority districts, 2003
United Kingdom

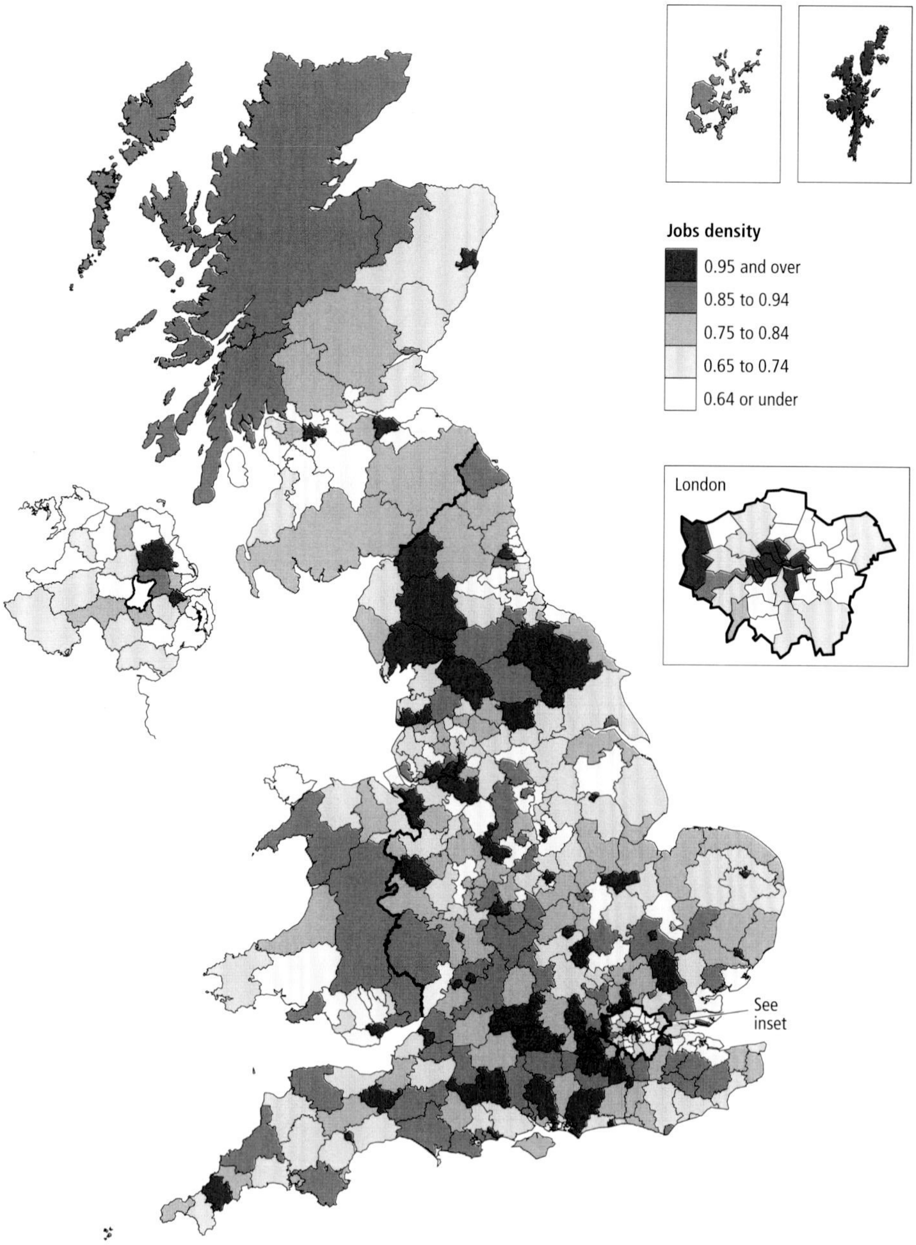

Source: Office for National Statistics; Department of Enterprise, Trade and Development

administration and search costs. In the presence of such costs, firms may find it more profitable to adjust hours of work rather than number of jobs.

Variation in hours worked is viewed as a more responsive indicator of labour demand. For example, consider a firm that faces an unexpected increase in the demand for its product. In the short run, in order to meet this increased demand, it may require its workers to work overtime. Statistics on the number of jobs will not capture this change in labour demand, as the number of people employed has remained unchanged. Statistics on hours, however, will capture the change in labour demand, by reporting an increase in total hours worked.

Figure 2.5 shows total weekly hours of work in the UK since 1971. Total hours of work have seen large cyclical variations, which relate closely to the economic cycle. In spring 2005, total actual hours of work stood at 917.7 millions, exceeding the previous peak in total hours observed in 1989.

Figure 2.5

Total actual weekly hours of work,[1] 1971–2005[2]

United Kingdom

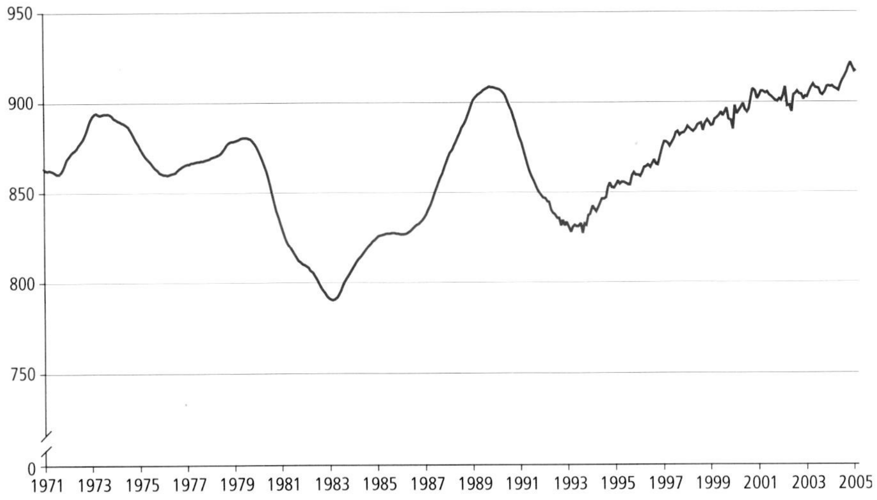

1 Main and second job.
2 Seasonally adjusted.

Source: Labour Force Survey

Figure 2.6

Average weekly hours of work and total number of people in employment,[1] 1992–2005[2]

United Kingdom

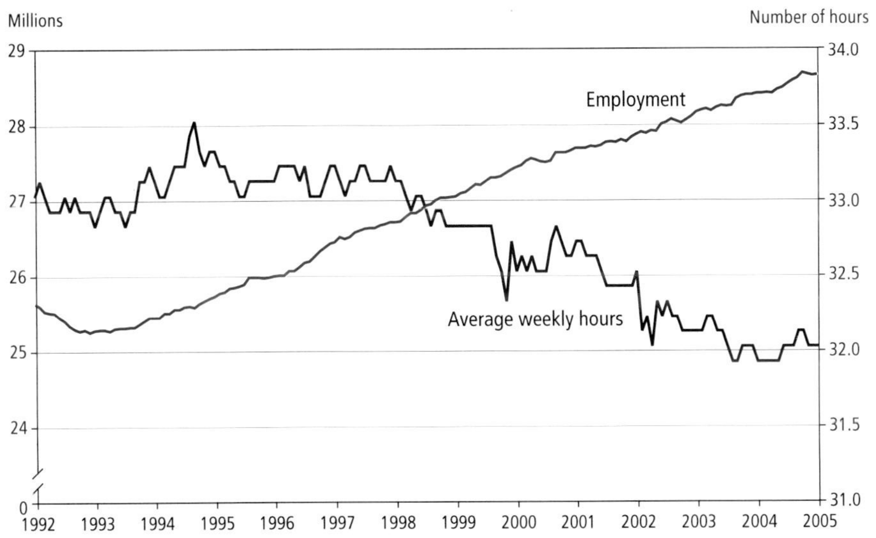

1 Aged 16 and over.
2 Seasonally adjusted.

Source: Labour Force Survey

Movements in total hours of work arise as the combined effect of two forces: movements in average hours worked by individuals and movements in the number of people in employment.

Average hours worked by individuals have generally been trending down since a peak at the end of 1994 (Figure 2.6). This trend reflects mostly supply-side factors as people increasingly choose to work fewer hours and the level of part-time working has increased.

The downward trend in average hours of work implies that the growth in total hours of work observed throughout the 1990s was driven by gains in employment. Indeed, although average hours remain well below the levels seen in the early 1990s, employment growth has more than compensated for the decline in average hours.

Hours

Vacancies

At any point in time, part of an employer's requirements for labour may remain unmet. Unmet labour demand is captured through statistics on vacancies. Vacancies arise when new posts are created or former jobholders leave a post. These are an outward sign that employers are acting to recruit new employees. Vacancies also provide some insight into employers' behaviour and can act as an indicator of changes in employers' perceptions of economic conditions or outlook.

In the three months to May 2005 there were 639,100 vacancies in the economy. Looking at vacancies by industry, these tend to fluctuate around different levels, broadly reflecting the industry size and turnover levels. The industry with the largest number of vacancies during this period was distribution, hotels and restaurants with 188,100 vacancies (Figure 2.7 overleaf). Education, health and public administration also showed a consistently higher level of vacancies than most other industries, recording 153,000 vacancies in the three months to May 2005. Since 2001, the finance and business service sector has shown a significant fall in the number of vacancies up to the middle of 2003, followed by a sustained increase through to 2005.

Vacancy survey

Job centre vacancies

Figure 2.7

Number of vacancies by industry, April–June 2001 to March–May 2005[1]

United Kingdom

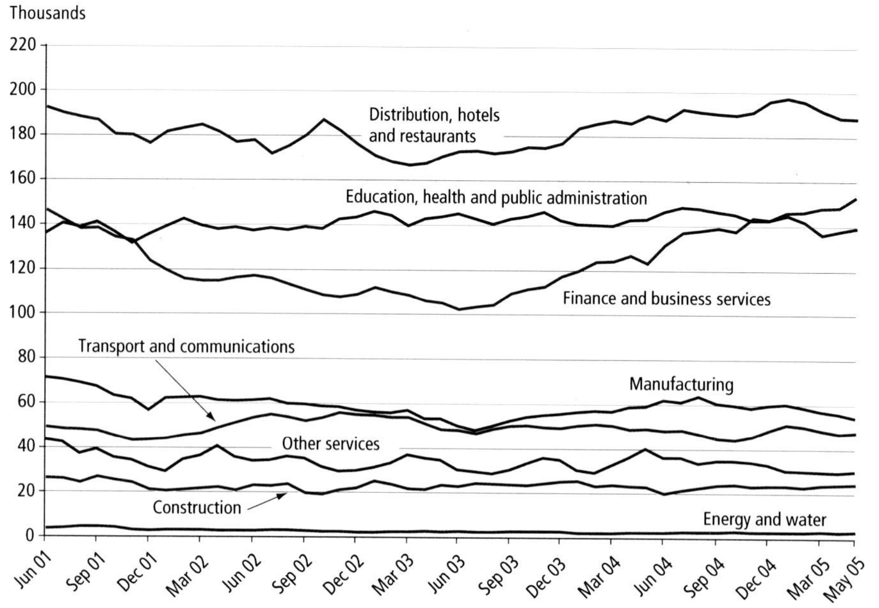

1 Seasonally adjusted.

Source: Office for National Statistics Vacancy Survey

Job separations and re-employment

Job separations occur when an employee leaves a paid job or when an employee's job is removed. Increasing frequencies of job separation can be an indicator of changes in the labour market and the economy. In periods of economic growth, it is common to see employees leaving their job to seek better ones, while in periods of downturn, redundancies may increase.

Job separations can be *voluntary*, when an employee leaves a job of their own accord or *involuntary*, when an employer initiates the separation. Redundancies, dismissals and temporary jobs ending are classified as involuntary redundancies. All other reasons are classified as voluntary job separations. These include resignations and retirement. There are about twice as many voluntary job separations as there are involuntary ones.

The position of job separations within the labour market framework is unclear. Job separations may arise as a result of demand side forces, for example companies facing reduced demand for their products and, as such, requiring a lower labour input. However, they may also arise as a result of supply side forces, for example due to individuals' decision to exit the labour market and enter retirement.

Job separations can be presented as levels or rates. Separation rates are calculated as the number of working-age people who separated from a paid job in the three months before interview divided by the number of people who said they were in employment for more than three months, plus those who had separated from a paid job. This number is expressed as a percentage.

Figure 2.8 shows voluntary and involuntary job separation rates for all people of working age from spring 1995, the earliest period available, to summer 2005. Involuntary separations show the least change over the time period, the lowest being 1.0 per cent in the spring quarter of 2005 and the highest being 1.9 per cent in 1995 and 1998. The involuntary separation rate has not risen above 1.5 per cent since autumn 2001. Voluntary job separation rates have shown more movement in

Figure 2.8

Job separation rates,[1] March–May 1995 to June–August 2005[2]

United Kingdom

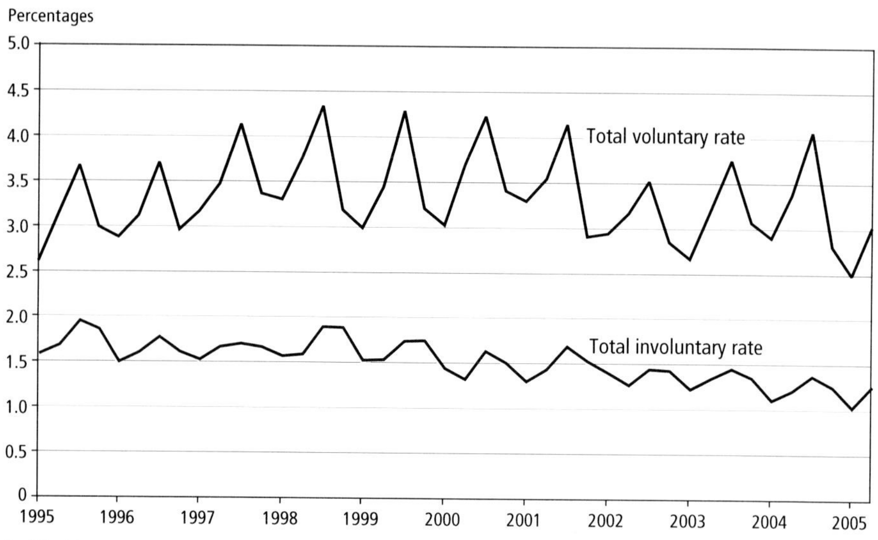

1 Working age.
2 Not seasonally adjusted.

Source: Labour Force Survey

Table 2.9
Job separations: by reason, 1995–2005[1]
United Kingdom Millions and percentages

	Involuntary separations				Voluntary separations						
Autumn to summer	Dismissed	Made redundant voluntary redundancy	Temporary job ended	Total Involuntary separations (millions)	Resigned	Gave up work for health reasons	Retired (early and at or after statut. ret. age)	Gave up work for family personal reason	Left for some other reason	Total voluntary separations (millions)	Total (millions)
1995–96	*3.0*	*14.2*	*17.6*	1,650	*25.0*	*4.3*	*1.8*	*9.8*	*24.3*	3,091	4,741
1996–97	*3.0*	*12.4*	*17.2*	1,588	*28.9*	*3.7*	*2.2*	*10.3*	*23.1*	3,290	4,879
1997–98	*3.1*	*11.6*	*15.6*	1,595	*36.8*	*3.3*	*1.9*	*8.6*	*22.5*	3,656	5,251
1998–99	*2.9*	*13.7*	*15.8*	1,696	*37.5*	*3.3*	*1.8*	*8.5*	*20.1*	3,546	5,242
1999–2000	*2.7*	*12.7*	*14.6*	1,563	*38.6*	*3.0*	*1.6*	*8.3*	*22.1*	3,653	5,216
2000–01	*2.4*	*12.6*	*13.3*	1,480	*38.0*	*3.2*	*1.6*	*7.3*	*25.3*	3,758	5,238
2001–02	*2.4*	*14.8*	*13.2*	1,528	*35.6*	*3.5*	*1.8*	*7.4*	*23.4*	3,510	5,039
2002–03	*2.6*	*14.0*	*13.6*	1,430	*34.2*	*3.3*	*1.7*	*7.0*	*23.6*	3,307	4,737
2003–04	*2.9*	*11.9*	*12.8*	1,312	*34.7*	*3.7*	*1.9*	*7.7*	*24.7*	3,455	4,767
2004–05	*2.8*	*12.1*	*13.0*	1,271	*34.5*	*3.6*	*2.1*	*6.9*	*23.7*	3,293	4,564

1 Not seasonally adjusted.
Source: Labour Force Survey

the time period with a low of 2.5 per cent in the spring quarter of 2005 and a high of 4.3 per cent in the autumn quarters of 1998 and 1999.

There is a strong seasonal pattern in job separations, with rates peaking in the autumn quarter of every year. Typically the rate in the autumn quarters is between 0.5 and 1 percentage point higher than in the other quarters. As a result of this the four quarters from each year of the labour force survey (autumn to summer) have been averaged to provide an annual estimate shown in Table 2.9. The table shows levels of job separations by reason for leaving.

Two reasons stand out in terms of their effect on the overall movements in job separations: resignations and temporary workers. During the time series available, resignations have increased from 1.2 million in 1995–96 to 1.6 million in 2004–05, driving the increase in overall voluntary separations from 3.1 million to 3.3 million over the same the period.

The number of temporary jobs ending has decreased from 836,000 in 1995–1996 to 591,000 in 2004–2005, driving the fall in the involuntary job separations from 1.7 million to 1.3 million over the same period.

The redundancy rate has seen a significant decline since the latest peak observed in the winter quarter of 2001. In the summer quarter of 2005 it stood at 6.1 per thousand employees, having reached 5.2 per thousand in spring 2005, a record low since comparable records began in 1995. Redundancy rates by industry are available since 1997. In recent years, redundancy rates have been highest in the manufacturing sector, followed by the construction industry. In the summer of 2005, the redundancy rate for manufacturing stood at 15.5 per thousand and for construction at 8.1 per thousand. Historically, the industry showing the lowest redundancy rates has been public administration, education and health, with the rate not exceeding three redundancies per 1,000 employees at any point since 1997.

Table 2.10 overleaf shows re-employment rates broken down by industry. Re-employment rates show the proportion of people made redundant in the three months before their Labour Force Survey interview who were in employment again at the time of their subsequent interview. The respondent's new industry category is not necessarily the same as the industry they were made redundant from, which is the one shown by the figures. There appears to be little relationship between redundancy rates and subsequent re-employment. Years with high redundancies do not necessarily show high re-employment as a large number of redundancies in a year suggest that the economy is weak and jobs may not be available. The overall re-employment rate has increased from 43.9 per cent in 1998–1999 to 46.7 in 2004–2005, reflecting an increasing healthy labour market. As the data are only available since 1997, it is not possible to compare the current re-employment rate with that observed during a period of economic recession.

Table 2.10

Re-employment rates in the three months after redundancy: by previous industry, 1998–2005[1]

United Kingdom Percentages

Autumn to summer	Agriculture, fishing, energy and water (A–C, E)	Manufacturing (D)	Construction (F)	Distribution, hotels and restaurants (G–H)	Transport and communication (I)	Banking, finance and insurance (J–K)	Public administration, education and health (L–N)	Total services (G–Q)
1998–99	*43.7*	*41.9*	*40.2*	*48.2*	*52.1*	*44.6*	*46.3*	*46.5*
1999–2000	*49.2*	*40.6*	*44.0*	*46.3*	*58.1*	*49.9*	*35.2*	*46.3*
2000–01	*52.9*	*42.6*	*48.4*	*47.9*	*50.9*	*51.1*	*44.2*	*49.2*
2001–02	*43.1*	*45.0*	*40.8*	*44.9*	*46.3*	*41.7*	*37.3*	*43.0*
2002–03	*46.1*	*41.3*	*41.6*	*42.9*	*40.6*	*41.8*	*41.4*	*42.2*
2003–04	*51.8*	*45.7*	*43.3*	*48.9*	*45.1*	*48.9*	*38.7*	*45.9*
2004–05	*31.4*	*41.8*	*59.0*	*52.5*	*49.7*	*40.2*	*51.9*	*47.7*

1 Not seasonally adjusted.

Source: Labour Force Survey

Looking at the industry breakdown, in 2004–2005 the highest re-employment rates were in construction, distribution, hotels and restaurants and public administration, education and health. The lowest re-employment rate was in agriculture.

Redundancies

Redundancy data

Skills

The level of skills in the workforce is of particular importance to employers and, as such, an important parameter in terms of the demand for labour. This is because a rise in the level of skills of the people employed by a firm is associated with an increase in productivity. In addition, investment in skills has been found to be linked to innovation and flexibility. As a result, skills and skill shortages have a significant impact on a range of economic measures such as productivity, GDP growth, employment and earnings.

Over the past century, the UK has experienced dramatic changes in the structure of the economy with a shift from an economy based on manufacturing to one where the service sector is dominant. The labour market has had to adjust in response to the changing demand for certain skills to avoid a mismatch between demand and supply. Employers may face skill shortages or skill gaps if a balance is not met.

Skill shortages and gaps

Skill shortages are defined as recruitment difficulties caused by a shortage of individuals with the required skills in the accessible labour market. Skill gaps are deficiencies in skills of an employer's existing workforce, both at the individual level and overall, which prevent the firm from achieving its business objectives. Skill gaps generally arise from inadequate training.

The 2004 National Employers Skills Survey (NESS) found that 8 per cent of establishments reported having hard-to-fill vacancies (HtFV) and 4 per cent spontaneously cited skills shortages among applicants as part of the reasons why these vacancies were proving hard to fill. Once prompted, 6 per cent of establishments reported skill-shortage vacancies (SSV). Comparison with previous surveys in 2001 and 2003 indicates that, while the proportion of all employers facing HtFVs and HtFVs caused by skills shortages has remained stable since 2001, the number of SSVs as a proportion of total employment fell from 2001 to 2003 and again from 2003 to 2004.

The pattern of recruitment difficulties by occupation shows that there is a particular concentration of skills shortages among 'skilled trades'. This occupational group accounts for 20 per cent of all SSVs and only 9 per cent of total employment. Conversely, 'professionals' and 'managers and senior officials' account for around 29 per cent of total employment and only 14 per cent of SSVs.

At a regional level, London faces the least acute problem in terms of skill shortages, accounting for 18 per cent of total employment and only 11 per cent of SSVs. The highest number and concentration of SSVs is found in the South East, which accounts for 16 per cent of total employment and 20 per cent of all SSVs.

Looking at the nature of skills lacking in connection with SSVs, technical and

Figure 2.11

Distribution of skills gaps and employment: by occupation, 2004

England

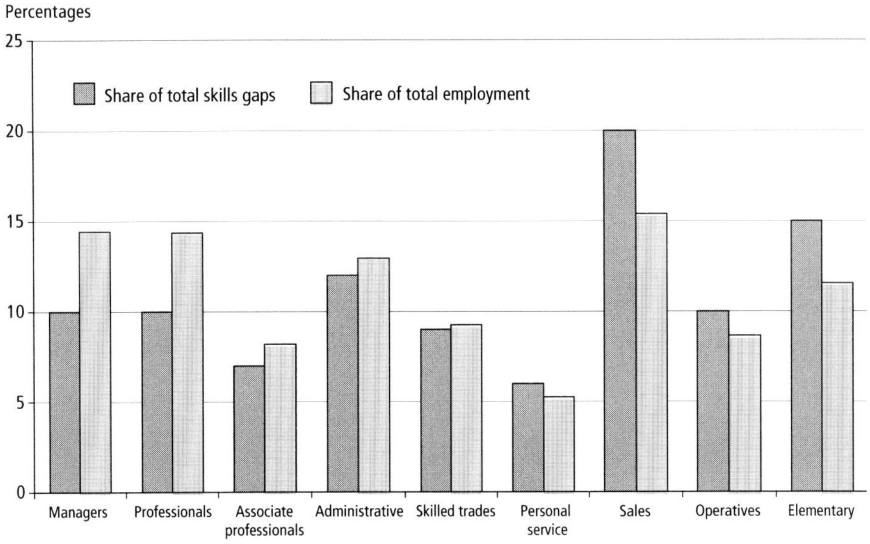

Source: National Employers Skills Survey 2004

practical skills (excluding IT skills) were the most commonly cited problem by employers. This was followed by communication, customer handling and team working skills.

Skills gaps are recorded by employers as being present when members of staff are not thought to be fully proficient to meet the requirements of the job. Data from the 2004 NESS shows that one in five establishments (20 per cent) reported skills gaps in their workforce and 1.5 million workers were described by employers as not being fully proficient. This equates to 7 per cent of the workforce in England. As such, the volume of skill gaps far exceeds that of recruitment problems.

Looking at the distribution of skills gaps by occupation (Figure 2.11), 'sales and customer service' and 'elementary' occupations account for 35 per cent of all skills gaps, much higher than their share of total employment (27 per cent). In density terms, that is, the number of skills gaps as a percentage of total employment, these two occupational groups record the highest density of skills gaps (9 per cent). Density is lowest among managers and professionals, with only 5 per cent of staff in these occupations described as not being fully proficient.

Looking at the causes of skill gaps, the main reasons employers give as to why their staff are not fully proficient in their job is lack of experience or have recently been recruited. This may indicate that the majority of these gaps in skills are temporary as over time staff become more familiar with the tasks required of them. In around a quarter of cases where staff were deemed not to be fully proficient, employers attributed this partly to their own failure to train and develop these staff properly.

One of the most common ways of dealing with internal skill deficiencies is for employers to provide training for their staff. Overall, the proportion of employees receiving job-related training has increased from 26.0 per cent in 1995 to 31.1 per cent in 2005 (Table 2.12). Levels of job-related training vary significantly over both industry and occupation but on a more individual level, training appears to be concentrated among those employees who already have the highest level of qualifications. However, there has been an increase from 8.7 per cent in 1995 to 12.0 per cent in 2005 of the proportion of people who hold no qualifications receiving job related training.

Table 2.12

Job-related training received by employees: by highest level of qualification, 1995, 2000 and 2005[1,2]

United Kingdom Percentages

	1995	2000	2005
Degree or equivalent	*42.8*	*44.1*	*42.3*
Higher education	*42.9*	*43.2*	*42.9*
GCE A level or equivalent	*25.8*	*29.1*	*30.5*
GCSE grade A–C or equivalent	*25.8*	*28.9*	*28.0*
Other qualifications	*18.0*	*20.0*	*22.5*
No qualification	*8.7*	*10.3*	*12.0*
Total	*26.0*	*29.8*	*31.1*

1 Spring quarters.
2 Not seasonally adjusted.

Source: Labour Force Survey

Figure 2.13

Year on year growth rates for output, total hours worked and workforce jobs, 1971–2005[1]

United Kingdom

Percentage change

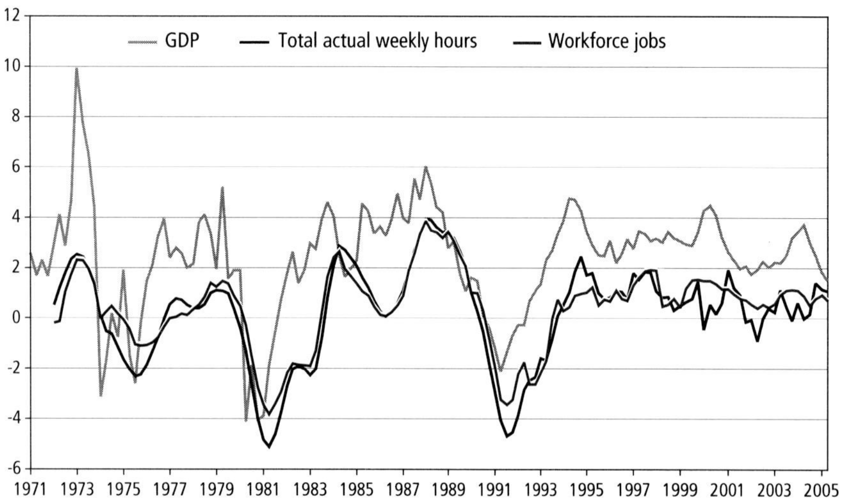

1 Seasonally adjusted.

Source: National Accounts; Labour Force Survey; Workforce Jobs Productivity

Labour demand and the economic cycle

As explained earlier, labour is a key input to the production process, because firms require workers in order to produce their output. As such, labour demand is derived demand, in that it is only sought as a means to producing goods and services demanded by consumers. This link between the demand for labour and the demand for goods and services in the economy is fundamental to understanding the cyclical variations observed in the labour market.

There is a strong relationship between growth in gross domestic product (GDP) and several labour market indicators, such as the number of jobs and the number of total hours worked, with a one or two quarter time lag between the two (Figure 2.13). Historically, the cyclical pattern observed in the labour market appears to be closely related to the economic cycle. This occurs due to the link between the demand for labour and the demand for goods and services in the economy.

When demand for goods and services in the economy is strong, firms attempt to meet this demand by producing more output. In order to achieve this increase in production, a firm may increase its labour input, either in terms of hours of work (for example, through paid and unpaid overtime) or in terms of the number of people employed. As such, cyclical variations in the labour market can be attributed to changes in the demand for labour, which is closely linked to the demand for goods and services in the economy.

Productivity

Labour productivity measures the economy's output in relation to its labour input. High productivity of labour generally indicates efficient production of goods and services and a competitive economy. Changes in labour productivity may result from a number of factors, such as the level of capital investment, the organisational structure of firms and the level of skills in the workforce. Three measures of productivity are produced: output per worker, output per filled job and output per hour worked.

Productivity is generally increasing over time (Figure 2.14). This reflects primarily technological growth but also other factors such as

Figure 2.14

Growth in whole economy output per worker and output per hour,[1] **1961–2005**[2]

United Kingdom

Percentage change

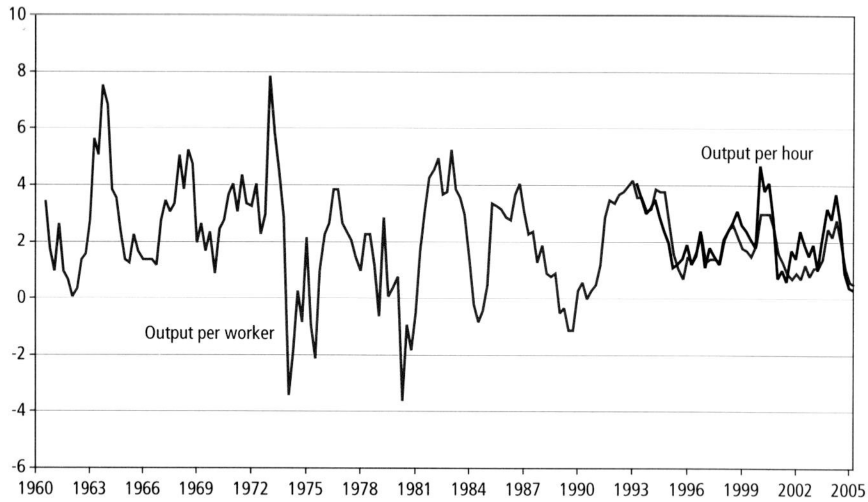

1 Since 1992.
2 Seasonally adjusted.

Source: Productivity Release, Office for National Statistics

organisational change, higher human capital through education and increased competition in the economy. The last decade has seen the longest period of unbroken productivity growth since the early 1970s. The 'per worker' and 'per hour' series have followed similar paths over the last ten years. There are occasional differences, such as the higher spike in 2000 in the 'per hour' series. This reflected strong employment growth over the year, but a fall in average hours worked, leading to slower growth in total hours worked.

In the second quarter of 2005, output per worker and output per filled job grew at an annual rate of 0.5 per cent, while output per hour grew at an annual rate of 0.3 per cent. This represents a significant slowdown in productivity growth and is the lowest rate of growth recorded since the early 1990s. It is due to a slowdown in output growth that was not reflected in the employment and hours figures. As growth in employment and hours of work was sustained, labour productivity declined.

Measuring productivity

Chap
3

Labour supply – employment

- UK employment levels have been rising generally over the last three decades, increasing from 24.6 million in 1971 to 28.8 million in 2005.
- The employment rate for people of working age rose from 71 per cent in 1995 to 75 per cent in 2005. For men the rate rose from 76 per cent to 79 per cent and, for women, from 66 per cent to 70 per cent.
- Employment rates among parents have increased: in the ten-year period to spring 2005 the employment rate for couple mothers, couple fathers and lone parents increased by 6 percentage points, 4 percentage points and 14 percentage points respectively.
- 'Managers and senior officials' is the largest occupational group in the UK with 15 per cent of people employed in this group. Twenty per cent of males are employed in skilled trades compared with only 2 per cent of females.
- The proportion of people in employment who are self-employed remained steady, at just under 13 per cent throughout 2005.
- Employment in the public sector rose by 95,000 in the year to June 2005 to stand at 5,846,000.
- The percentage of teleworkers has doubled between spring 1997 and spring 2005, from 4 per cent to 8 per cent of the total workforce.

Labour supply statistics are designed to illustrate to what extent the population of the country is engaged in paid work; and the extent to which people would be engaged in such work if their personal circumstances were different or if jobs that attracted them were available.

Figure 3.1 is adapted from the Labour Market Framework and shows the structure of actual and potential labour supply in terms of the main forms of employment, unemployment and inactivity.

Labour market framework

Economic activity

Economic inactivity

Demographic trends

Demographic trends have a key impact on labour market supply. Latest population projections, produced by the Government Actuary's Department suggest that the population of the UK is likely to increase by 7.2 million over the period 2004–2031. This increase is equivalent to an annual growth rate of 0.42 per cent or 12 per cent over the 27 years.

This relative stability in terms of overall size disguises marked changes in age structure. It is well known that the population of the UK is steadily ageing with the mean age predicted to rise from 39.5 years in 2004 to 43.3 years in 2031. In 2004 there were just over 0.5 million (5 per cent) more children aged under 16 than people of state pensionable age. However, from 2007 the population of state pensionable age is projected to exceed the number of children and by 2031 is projected to exceed it by almost 4 million (34 per cent). These projections mean that the number of people of working age is expected to rise by around 3.1 per cent from 37.1 million in 2004 to 38.2 million in 2010. Given that the increase in women's state pension age from 60 to 65 is due to be introduced between 2010 and 2020, the population of working age is predicted to rise to

Figure 3.1
The structure of actual and potential labour supply

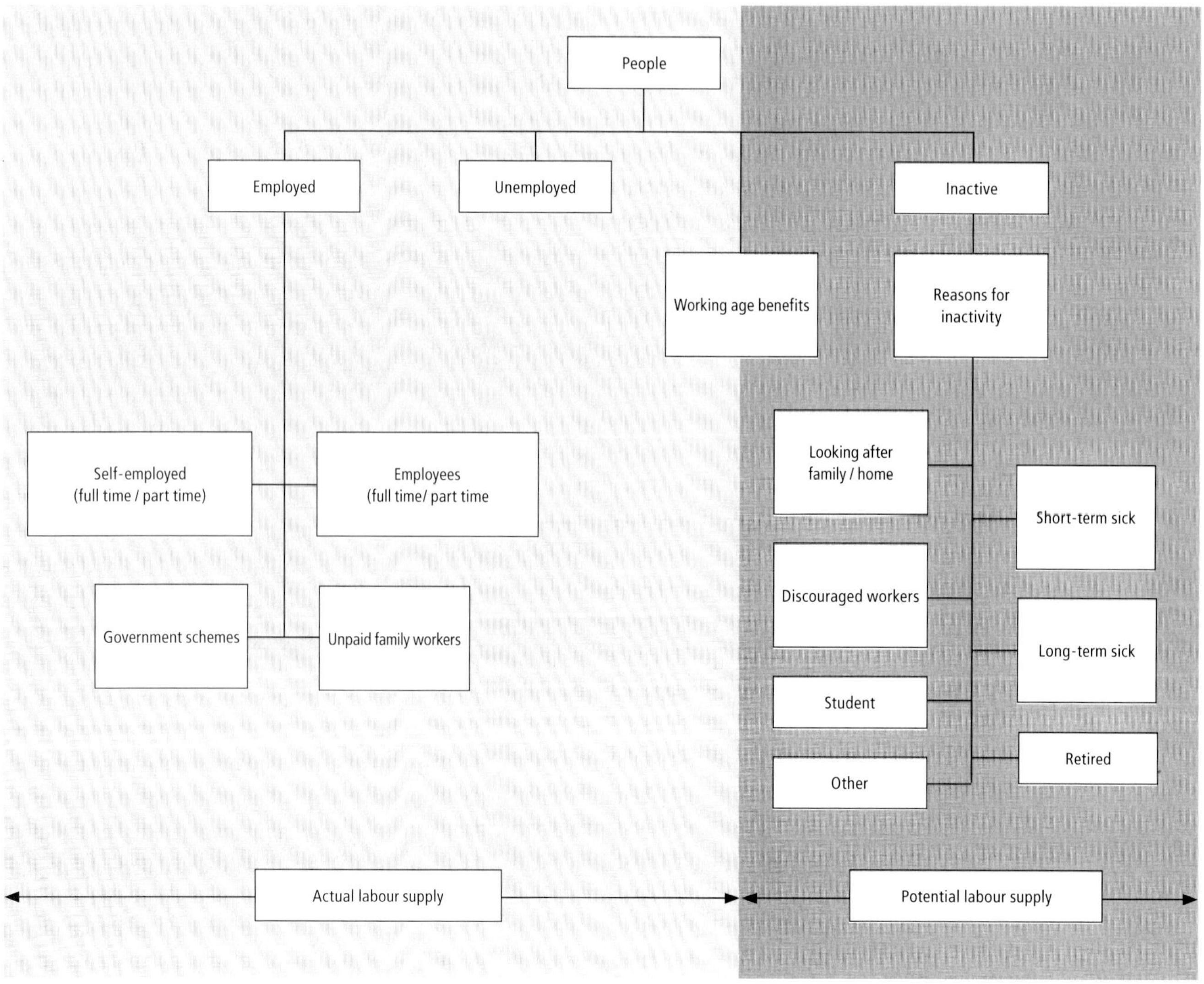

Figure 3.2
Population Structure: by age, sex and economic activity, autumn 2005[1]

United Kingdom

Thousands

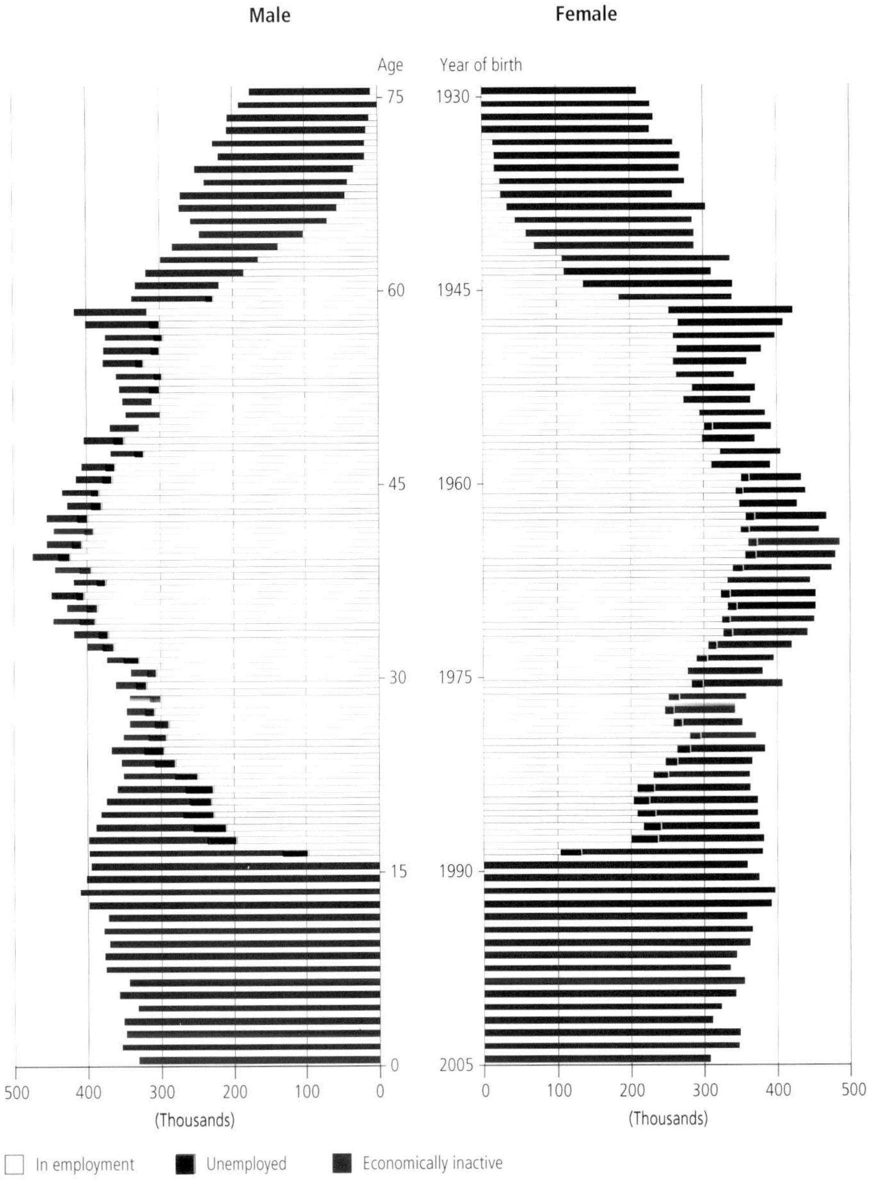

1 Not seasonally adjusted.

Source: Labour Force Survey

40.5 million by 2020. Although the size of this group is projected to increase only slightly, the composition is expected to alter. The working-age population will become much older: in 2004 there were 2.1 million more working-age adults aged below 40 than were aged 40 and above, but by 2010 there will be just 1.0 million more and by 2020 there will be 0.9 million fewer working-age people below 40 than aged 40 and over.

Figure 3.2 shows the impact of changes to the UK population on economic activity. For further information on the new labour force projections, see section A.10 of Appendix A.

Employment

Changes have been occurring over recent decades in the structure and composition of the workforce. In terms of how individuals supply their labour, influences on the changing composition of the workforce include the ageing of the population and its increasing diversity, such as the growth in the numbers of women working, students in employment and foreign workers. Structural changes encompass a number of well documented trends, such as the growth in the service industry, decline in manufacturing and improved technological capacity. These wide-ranging changes in the nature of employment are the response from employers trying to address changing employee and consumer demands, individuals trying to achieve a work-life balance and governments trying

How employment is measured

The Labour Force Survey (LFS) provides the preferred measure of the number of people in employment. Using the standard International Labour Organisation (ILO) definition, people are classed as employed if they are aged 16 or over and have done at least one hour of work in the reference week or are temporarily away from a job (for example, on holiday). In addition to standard measures of employment, statistics on hours worked are also required to understand and interpret the nature, quality and volume of employment in the labour market.

Employment

What is employment?

Figure 3.3

Levels of employment,[1] January–March 1971 to July–September 2005[2]

United Kingdom

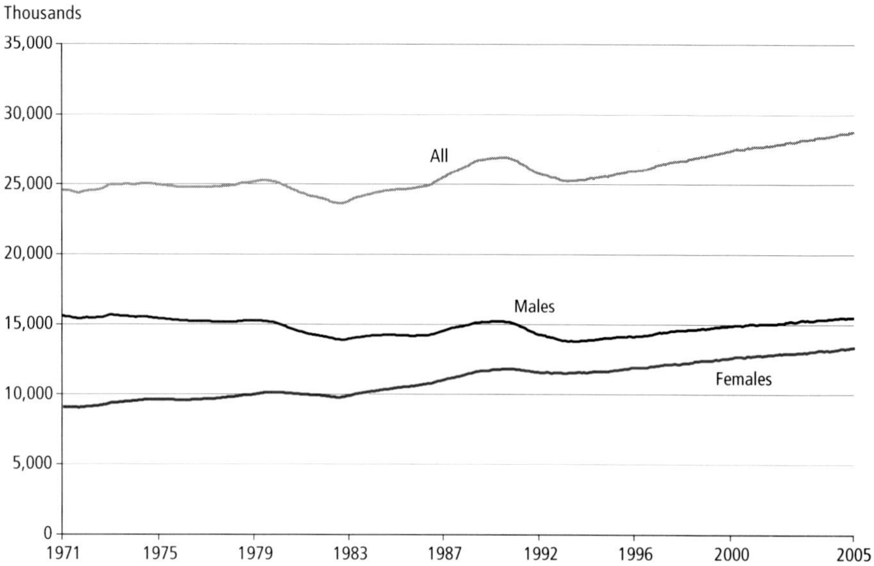

1 All aged 16 and over.
2 Seasonally adjusted.

Source: Labour Force Survey

to reduce economic inactivity and absences from work.

The *level* of employment in the UK has been rising generally over the last three decades from 24.6 million in 1971 to 28.8 million in 2005 and was at its lowest level, 23.6 million, in 1983 (Figure 3.3).

Figure 3.4 shows the employment *rate* for the working-age population for the same period. The two graphs show different patterns of employment change as the employment rate, the proportion of the population of working age who are in employment, takes changes in the size of the population into account.

Figure 3.4

Employment rate,[1] by sex, January–March 1971 to July–September 2005[2]

United Kingdom

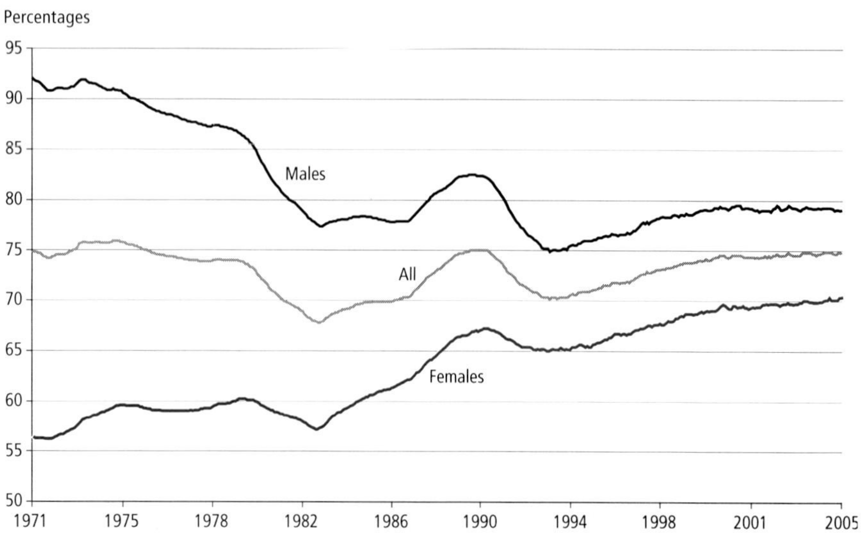

1 Working age.
2 Seasonally adjusted.

Source: Labour Force Survey

Figure 3.4 indicates that although the pattern of employment rates broadly follows that for employment levels (Figure 3.3), some of the increase in levels since the early 1990s can be accounted for by a change in the size of the working age population. This means that although the level of working-age employment increased from 24.5 million in February to April 1993 to its current level of 27.7 million, the employment rate only increased from 70 per cent to 75 per cent over the same period.

Characteristics of people in employment

Employment rates vary among different sub-groups of the population in terms of sex, age, disability status, ethnic origin, qualification levels and type of employment.

The overall employment rates for working-age males and females have shown a similar pattern over the last ten years. The employment rate rose from 76.5 per cent in July to September 1995 to 79.1 per cent in July to September 2005 for males and from 66.1 per cent to 70.4 per cent over the same period for females. Before 1993, different trends in the employment rate can be seen between the sexes. For the ten years after 1971, the male employment rate fell, while the female employment rate rose until these differing trends were halted by a steep drop in the employment rate for both sexes in the early 1980s. The drop was more pronounced among males. The employment rate then recovered and increased for both sexes until the beginning of the 1990s, with the increase being more evident for females.

In addition to differences in employment rates for males and females, variations exist by age. Only the 50 and over age group has shown a continued increase in the employment rate since 2000.

Families

There were 12.9 million working-age parents with dependent children in spring 2005 which accounted for 35 per cent of the working-age population. This can be broken down into three main sub-groups: married and cohabiting mothers (5.5 million); married and cohabiting fathers (5.5 million) and lone parents (1.9 million).

- Couple mothers and lone parents have historically had lower employment rates than both couple fathers and working-age people without dependent children.
- Employment rates among parents have increased steadily in recent years and the gaps between different types of parents have narrowed. Over the ten-year period to spring 2005, the employment rate for couple mothers, couple fathers and lone parents increased by six percentage points, four percentage points and 14 percentage points respectively. These upward trends reflect increases in both full-time and part-time employment.
- The employment rates of couple mothers and lone parents vary according to both personal and family characteristics.
- Personal characteristics include educational qualifications. Employment rates are highest among graduates and lowest among those with no qualifications.
- Family characteristics include the number and ages of children within the family. Couple mothers and lone parents with three or more dependent children were much less likely to be in employment than those with one or two children. They were also less likely to be in full-time employment.
- Couple mothers and lone parents with children of pre-school age were much less likely to be in employment than those whose youngest child was of school age. However, employment rates have increased steadily in recent years among both couple mothers and lone parents with pre-school age children, and the gap between them has narrowed.

Families and work
Workless households
Work and worklessness data

Aside from the 16–17 age group, all other groups have remained at a broadly constant employment rate since 2000. The employment rate of the 16–17 age group has decreased gradually from 49.7 per cent in the period September to November 1997, the highest rate in the time series, to 38.8 per cent in July to September 2005.

There has been a gradual increase in the employment rate of the long-term disabled from 45.1 per cent in autumn 1998 to 49.9 per cent in autumn 2005, an increase of 4.8 percentage points.

Employment rates can be compared across ethnic groups. It should, however, be noted that care must be taken when using ethnicity data as the different ethnic groups often have different demographics, such as differing proportions of people within the age ranges, which can affect employment rates. In winter to autumn 2005, the White, Mixed and Black or Black British had employment rates above the average for the UK, while

Figure 3.5
Employment rate:[1] by ethnic group, winter 2004 – autumn 2005[2]
United Kingdom

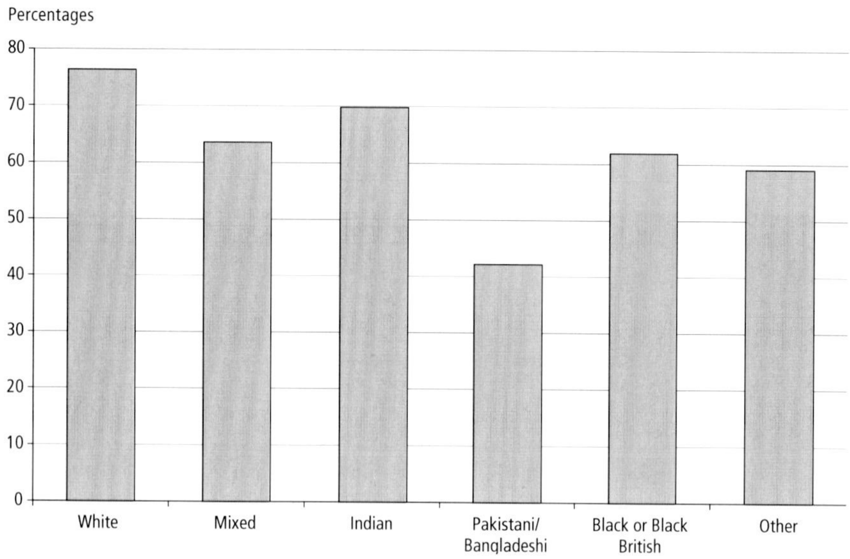

1 Working age.
2 Not seasonally adjusted.
Source: Labour Force Survey

all other groups were the same or below (Figure 3.5).

The skill level of those in employment is measured using the highest level of qualification held. This allows differentiation between those in employment who have progressed to further and higher education and those who have not. The employment rate varies according to qualification level and those with no qualifications are less likely to be in employment than those with higher qualifications (Figure 3.6). Only 50 per cent of those with no qualification were in employment in 2004 compared with 88 per cent of people with a degree or equivalent.

Qualifications

Type of employment

The largest occupational group in the UK is 'managers and senior officials' with 15 per cent of people employed in this group (Figure 3.7). This compares with only 8 per cent employed in the personal service occupations. There are clear differences in the choice of occupation by sex: 20 per cent of males in employment name their occupation as being a 'skilled trade' compared with only 2 per cent of females. In contrast, females are more likely to be employed in the 'sales and customer service' occupation: 12 per cent in 2005 compared with 5 per cent of men.

Occupation

Usual hours

The pattern of usual hours worked by those in employment has changed over the last decade with more people working less than 45 hours (Figure 3.8). The percentage of people working over 45 hours has decreased from 25.7 per cent in 1995 to 20.9 per cent in 2005. This reduction was mainly a result of fewer males working these hours. While there are a smaller proportion of women working over 45 hours, this proportion has shown little change over the last decade. Correspondingly there has been an increase in people in employment usually working between 16 and 45 hours.

Figure 3.6
Employment rate:[1] by highest qualification, spring 2004[2]
United Kingdom

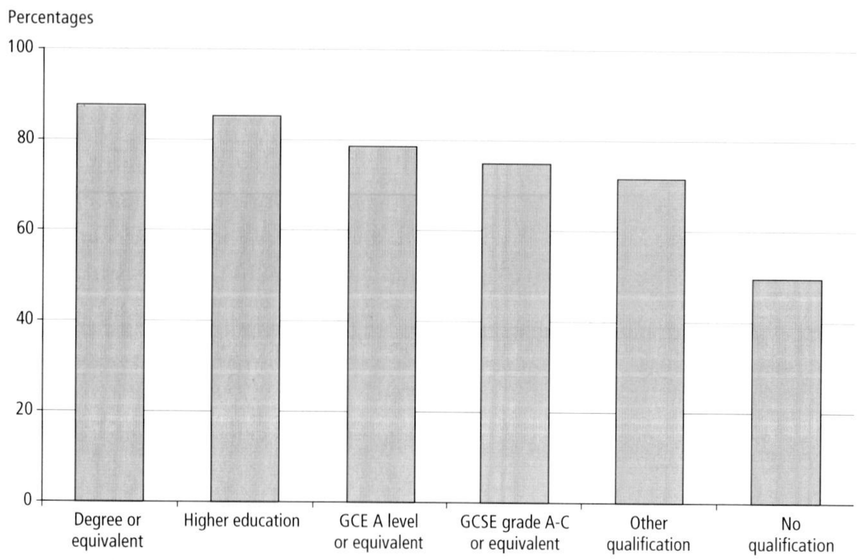

1 Working age.
2 Not seasonally adjusted.
Source: Labour Force Survey

Figure 3.7
Distribution of occupations among employees:[1] by sex, spring 2005[2]
United Kingdom
Percentages

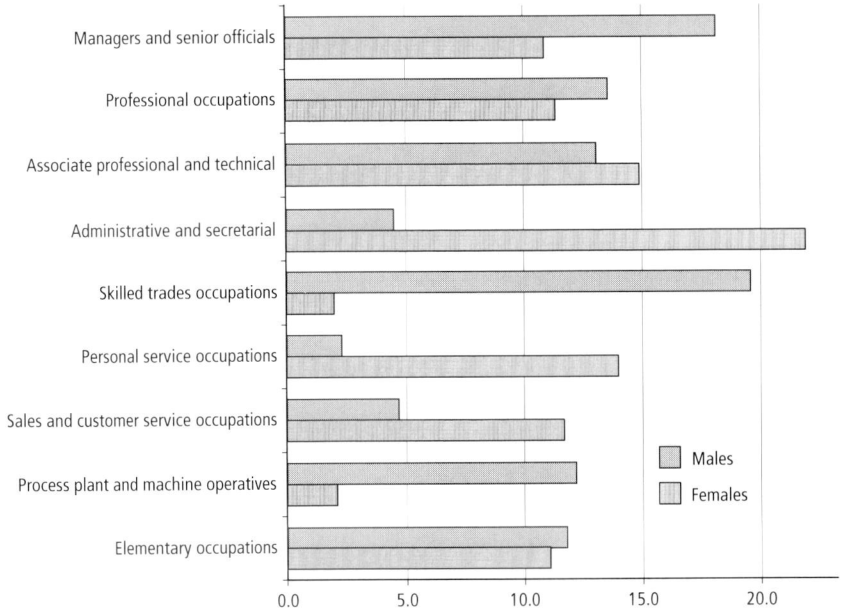

1 *Working age.*
2 *Not seasonally adjusted.*
Source: Labour Force Survey

Figure 3.8
Distribution of usual hours worked,[1] July–September 1995 and July–September 2005[2]
United Kingdom
Percentages

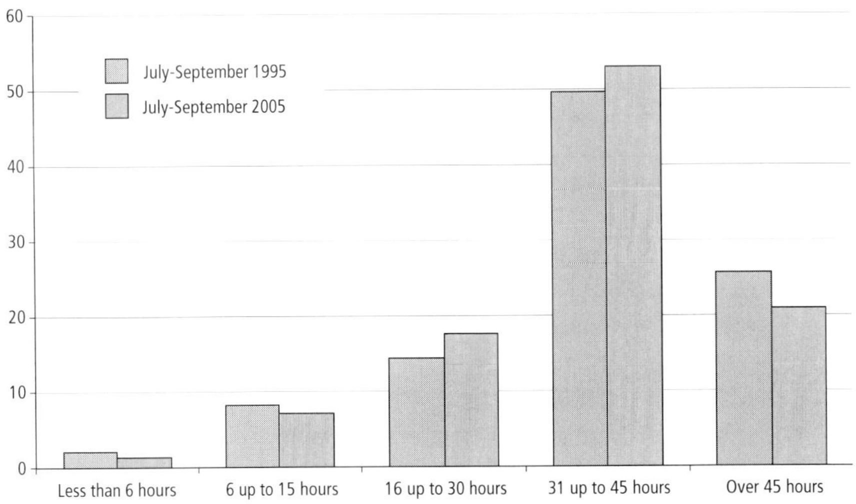

1 *Main job only.*
2 *Seasonally adjusted.*
Source: Labour Force Survey

Self-employment

There are signs of increasing flexibility within the UK labour market. One example of this is the growth in the number of self-employed people. The proportion of people in employment who are self-employed remained steady at just under 13 per cent throughout 2004 and 2005.

While the proportion of the self-employed people working over 45 hours has decreased, it is still high compared with all employees who work over 45 hours. In the three months to October 2005, 34 per cent of the self-employed were working over 45 hours, 16 percentage points more than the average for those in employment. Comparing males and females, 40 per cent of self-employed males and 19 per cent of self-employed females were working for over 45 hours, and 43 per cent of self-employed males and 26 per cent of self-employed females were working between 30 and 45 hours.

Self-employed

Among those in employment, the proportion working part time has been increasing. In the three months to May 1984, the beginning of the time series, 21 per cent of people in employment worked part time. This rose to 26 per cent for the three months to May 2004, an increase of five percentage points. Since then, there has been a slight decrease in the rate of part-time work. In the three months to October 2005 the proportion of people working part time was 25 per cent.

Part-time employment has traditionally been dominated by females and this is still the case. In 2004, 44 per cent of female employees were working part time compared with 11 per cent of males (Figure 3.9 overleaf). However, the gap between the percentage of females and males

Figure 3.9

Percentage of people in employment working part time: by sex,[1] March–May 1984, 1994 and 2004

United Kingdom

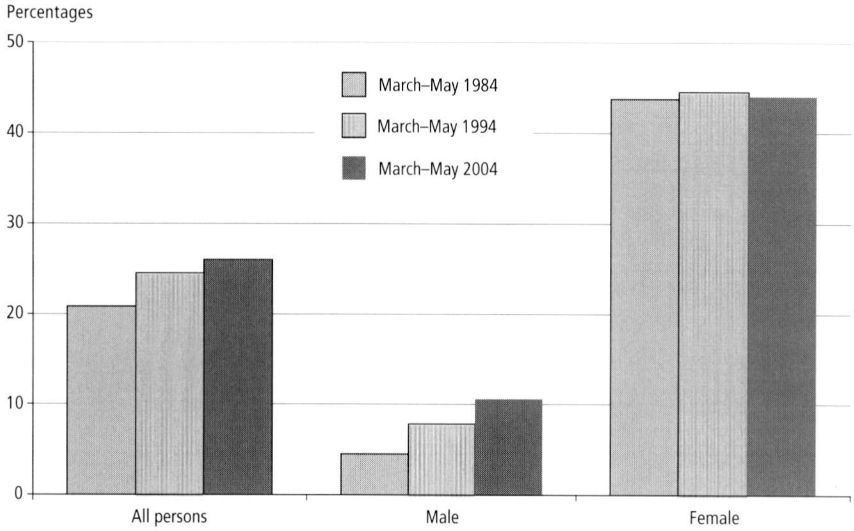

1 Not seasonally adjusted.

Source: Labour Force Survey

Teleworking

Teleworking generally includes people who work mainly in their own home or in different places using home as a base, who use both a telephone and a computer to carry out their work at home. The proportion of teleworkers in the total workforce has doubled between spring 1997 and spring 2005 (4 per cent to 8 per cent respectively).

- Most teleworkers were self-employed (62 per cent). Some 41 per cent of self-employed people, but only 4 per cent of employees, were teleworkers in spring 2005.
- Teleworking appears to be more prevalent among male workers than among female workers. In spring 2005, the teleworking rate for males was 11 per cent, compared with 6 per cent for females.
- Teleworking is more common, and is growing at a faster rate, among older workers than among younger age groups.
- There are teleworkers in each occupation group. The teleworking rate is highest in skilled trades occupation. This occupation group has seen the biggest increase in the teleworking rate, mainly due to an increase in teleworking in the building and construction trades. In line with this teleworking is most common in the construction industry.

Home-based teleworking

working part time has been decreasing over the last 20 years. The percentage of males working part time has increased by six percentage points since 1984 whereas the percentage of females has remained almost constant.

The predominant reason given for working part time remains, for both males and females, that a 'full-time job is not wanted'. This reason accounted for 49 per cent of males and 81 per cent of females working part time in the three months to November 2004. The only reason for working part-time that has shown a change in the proportion of people citing it over the last decade is the 'unavailability of a full-time job'. For males this has dropped from 23 per cent in the three months to November 1994 to 15 per cent in the three months to November 2004, a decrease of eight percentage points. For females the decrease is lower, a fall of four percentage points from 9 per cent to 5 per cent. This probably reflects an improvement in the economic climate over this period.

Full-time/part-time status

A reduction in the number of temporary workers is another sign of labour market improvement. The level of temporary workers has gradually fallen from a high of 1.8 million in the three months to June 1997 to 1.4 million in the three months to October 2005. The rate of temporary workers has shown a similar pattern with the proportion of temporary workers out of all in employment at 5.6 per cent in the three months ending October 2005, a record low since the beginning of the series in 1992.

Moreover, the reasons for undertaking temporary work have changed (Figure 3.10). In 1992, around 36 per cent of temporary workers had undertaken

Figure 3.10
Reasons for temporary working, 1992–2005[1]
United Kingdom
Percentages

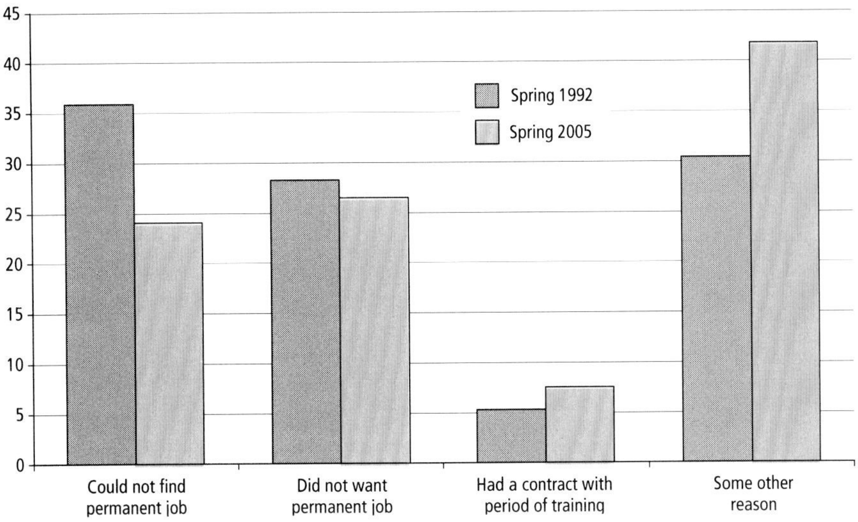

1 Seasonally adjusted, spring quarters.
Source: Labour Force Survey

Figure 3.11
Government supported trainees rate: by sex,[1] March–May 1992 to July–September 2005[2]
United Kingdom
Percentages

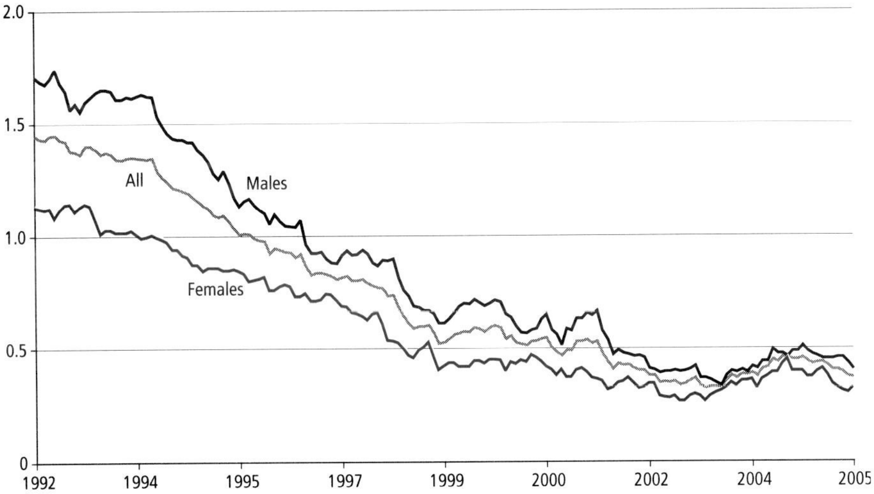

1 All aged 16 and over.
2 Seasonally adjusted.
Source: Labour Force Survey

temporary work because they were ‘unable to find a permanent job’. This proportion has fallen with approximately 24 per cent of temporary workers ‘unable to find permanent work’ in 2005. The group showing the largest increase over the period were those who stated that they were doing temporary work for some other reason, increasing from 30 per cent in spring 1992 to 42 per cent in spring 2005.

Government-supported trainee levels fell to a low at the end of 2002 and the beginning of 2003 but have started to increase since then (Figure 3.11). This follows a decade of decline in which the number of government-supported trainees fell from around 371,000 in the three months to May 1992 to 106,000 in the three months to May 2002. In the three months leading up to May 2005, there were 116,000 government-supported trainees.

Government training schemes

Another change in employment patterns in recent years has been the increase in the proportion of people who are working from home. Home workers can be spilt into three groups:

- Those who work predominately in the home
- Those who work and live in the grounds or premises of their work, for example a landlord of a public house who lives on the premises
- Those who use home as a base and travel to their work, for example a plumber with their office in their home who travels to carry out work

Employment status tends to affect which of these groups an individual falls into with employees being the least likely to work from home in any capacity and the self-employed being the most likely. In spring 2005 there were around 3.1 million people in the UK who worked mainly in their own home, or in a different place using the home as a base. The number of homeworkers has risen from 2.3 million in spring 1997.

In spring 2005, 64 per cent of employees and self-employed people ‘working at home’ were women. The opposite is true for those who use their ‘home as a base’. This sector is dominated by men with 79 per cent of those who used their 'home as a base' being men. This can be partly explained by the different occupations of those who work at home.

Public sector employment

Employment in the public sector fell every year between 1991 and 1998, reducing by 816,000 from the 1991 total of 5,982,000. For the 12 months to June 2005 it rose by 95,000 to stand at 5,846,000. This followed several years of increases and as a result, employment in the public sector was 680,000 (13.2 per cent) higher in June 2005 than in 1998, but still below those levels seen in 1991 and 1992 (Figure 3.12).

Between June 2004 and June 2005 central government employment increased more than local government with central government up by 55,000 on the year to 2,533,000 while local government employment increased by 40,000 to 2,929,000 (around 2.2 per cent and 1.4 per cent respectively). This fits with the longer-term picture where central government has been expanding more quickly than local government; central government increased by 21.4 per cent since June 1998 compared with 8.1 per cent for local government.

In the year to March 2005 civil service employment remained flat. Overall, civil service numbers have expanded broadly in line with wider government over the past year, and slightly faster over a longer time scale, increasing by 10.5 per cent since 2000.

When looking at estimates by industry the largest annual increases in the year to June 2005 were in the health and social services sector (up by 60,000 employees to 1,937,000) and in education (SIC division 80 – up 19,000 to 1,361,000). It should be noted that this definition of education is broader than the school workforce estimates published by Department for Education and Skills and therefore are not directly comparable. There was also a rise within the public administration sector, with an increase of 17,000 employees to 1,255,000, and in the police service (including civilians and community support officers), up by 12,000 employees. **Figure 3.13** shows that since June 1998 employment levels in the health and social services sector and education increased by 300,000 and 224,000 respectively (18.3 and 19.7 per cent). There were also rises of 128,000 (11.4 per cent) in public administration and 45,000 (19.7 per cent) in the police service.

A public/private sector split is produced by taking the whole UK economy employment level from the LFS and deducting the public sector employment estimates to produce a private sector series. Looking at the public/private sector employment split there has been larger growth in the public sector in recent years, although

Figure 3.12

Public sector employment: level and annual change, 1991–2005[1]

United Kingdom

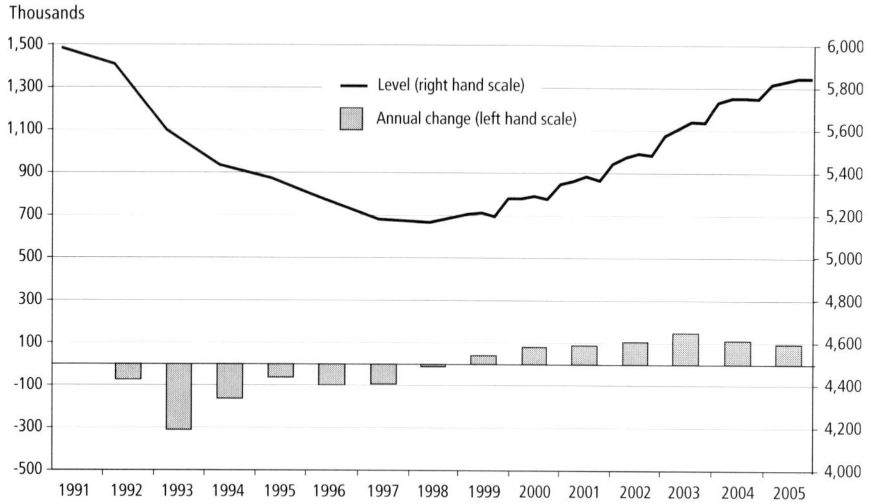

1 *Not seasonally adjusted.*

Source: Returns from public sector organisations, Office for National Statistics

Public sector employment in the LFS

Although the LFS is the preferred measure for UK employment figures as a whole, better estimates of public sector employment are derived from data supplied by public sector organisations themselves. The LFS overestimates the number of people working in the public sector because respondents unknowingly classifying themselves in the public sector when in reality they are part of the private sector according to National Accounts principles (employees working at a university for example).

Estimates from public sector organisations are based on a multiplicity of sources and often have different definitions, reference dates and geographical coverage, which has led to inconsistencies between sources. ONS has been leading cross-departmental work to improve the quality of these statistics.

For further information see section A.9 of Appendix A.

Figure 3.13

Public sector employment growth: by industry, 1998–2005[1]

United Kingdom

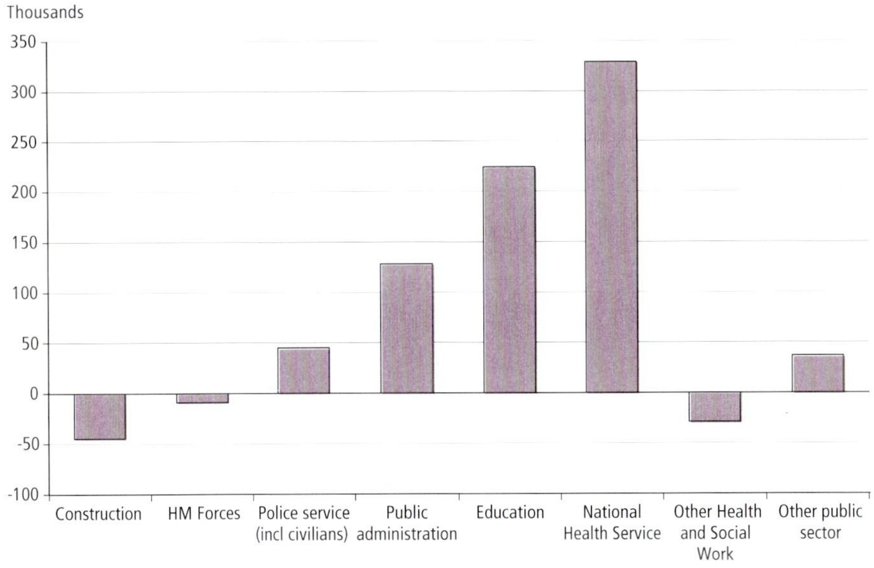

1 *Not seasonally adjusted.*

Source: Returns from public sector organisations, Office for National Statistics

employment has increased in both sectors. In the year to June 2005, employment in the private sector rose by 216,000 (1.0 per cent), compared with a rise of 95,000 (1.7 per cent) in the public sector. The public sector has expanded to represent around 20 per cent of total employment in 2005, compared with around 19 per cent in 1999.

Further detailed analysis and the latest PSE estimates are available on the National Statistics website.

Public sector and private sector

Public sector employment

Underemployment

The standard ILO definitions of employment and unemployment (see Glossary) are useful in terms of measuring headline figures but are less effective at capturing the diversity that exists in the UK labour market. An example of this is underemployment. Someone who is working for at least one hour a week is, in ILO terms, classified as employed. In reality, this individual may be overemployed, fully employed or underemployed, and this will have an impact on their future labour market behaviour.

Underemployment is usually defined as when someone wants to work extra hours, is available to start within two weeks and has worked less than the average sex-specific constructed hours. Figure 3.14 shows the percentage of people of working age who would like to work additional hours in their current job at their normal base rate in an attempt to separate out the people who would like to work more hours for more money, but are not underemployed. The majority of people would not like to work more hours (93 per cent), and this percentage has increased slightly over the past five years.

International comparisons of employment

Due to the seasonality of the employment data, year-on-year changes are used to monitor changes in the employment rate internationally. Like the UK, the employment rates of the United States and Japan have shown slight increases.

Figure 3.14

Percentage of people wanting to work more hours in their current job,[1] 2000–2004[2]

United Kingdom

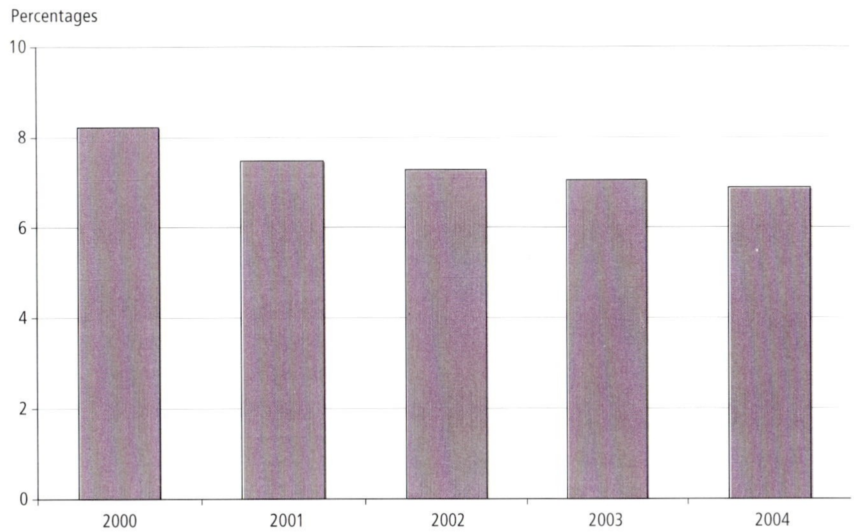

1 *As a percentage of all people of working-age in employment*
2 *Not seasonally adjusted.*

Source: Labour Force Survey

The employment rate for the United States increased by 0.3 percentage points from 71.3 per cent in the three-month period ending December 2004 to 71.6 per cent in the same three month period in 2005. For Japan, the employment rate increased by 0.3 percentage points from 68.9 per cent to 69.4 per cent over the same period as the United States. The Eurozone showed the greatest increase in the employment rate. Data are only available up to the three-month period ending June 2005, when the employment rate reached 63.6 per cent, an increase of 0.6 on the same period in 2008.

Employment data for the European Union is collated centrally by Eurostat on a different basis to the recognised UK employment rate. Employment rates are not seasonally adjusted and are based on a population aged 15–64 rather than the seasonally adjusted working-age employment rate used in the UK. The United States employment rate is based on a population aged 16–64.

Labour supply – unemployment

- Unemployment fell from a peak of 3 million in 1993 (just under 11 per cent) to 1.5 million (around 5 per cent) in 2001. Since then there has been a further and more gradual decline, although unemployment rose slightly in the three months to September 2005 when the unemployment rate was 4.7 per cent.

- In the three months to September 2005 the male unemployment rate was 5.2 per cent while the female rate was 4.2 per cent.

- In the three months to September 2005 the unemployment rate for those aged 16–17 was 22.4 per cent, compared with rates of 10.9 per cent for those aged 18–24, 3.4 per cent for those aged 25–49, and 2.9 per cent for those aged 50 and over.

- In the 12 months to November 2005, the lowest unemployment rates were for people of White ethnic origin (4.4 per cent) and those of Indian origin (6.8 per cent). Unemployment rates were highest for people of Pakistani or Bangladeshi origin (15.0 per cent).

- In the 12 months to November 2004 the unemployment rate among long-term disabled people was 7.2 per cent, down by 3.2 percentage points from five years earlier.

The number of unemployed people in the UK is measured through the Labour Force Survey (LFS) following the internationally agreed definition recommended by the ILO.

Unemployed people are those who are:

- Without a job, want a job, have actively sought work in the last four weeks and are available to start work in the next two weeks, or
- Out of work, have found a job and are waiting to start it in the next two weeks.

How unemployment is measured

The ONS publishes two different measures of people who want to work but do not have a job: LFS unemployment and the claimant count.

The LFS provides estimates of both the unemployment level and the unemployment rate. The rate is the best indicator because it measures the proportion of the economically active population who are unemployed and so it takes account of changes in the size of the population over time, as well as changes in the level of unemployment.

The claimant count is a count of claimants of unemployment-related benefits, which is based on the administrative records of people claiming these benefits. These are currently Jobseeker's Allowance (JSA) and National Insurance (NI) credits.

The claimant count is directly affected by changes to the rules governing entitlement to unemployment related benefits. This means that comparisions over time are affected by changes to the benefit system. Using the two sources together provides a more comprehensive picture of the labour market.

Unemployment

How is unemployment measured

JSA

Unemployment trends

There will always be a certain level of unemployment even within a healthy economy as people enter or re-enter the labour force or move between jobs. This is known as 'frictional unemployment'. Labour Force Survey data, which are available back to 1971, show that unemployment follows a cyclical pattern. During the early 1970s unemployment was relatively low at around 1 million or around 4 per cent of the economically active population aged 16 or over (Figures 4.1 and 4.2). Unemployment

Figure 4.1
Unemployment levels: by sex,[1] January–March 1971 to July–September 2005[2]
United Kingdom

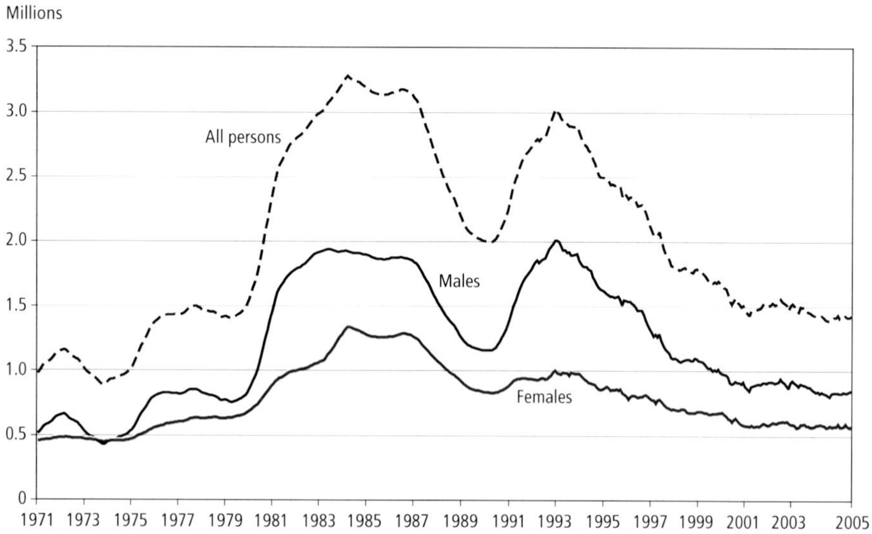

1 All aged 16 and over.
2 Seasonally adjusted.

Source: Labour Force Survey

Figure 4.2
Unemployment rates: by sex,[1] January–March 1971 to July-September 2005[2]
United Kingdom

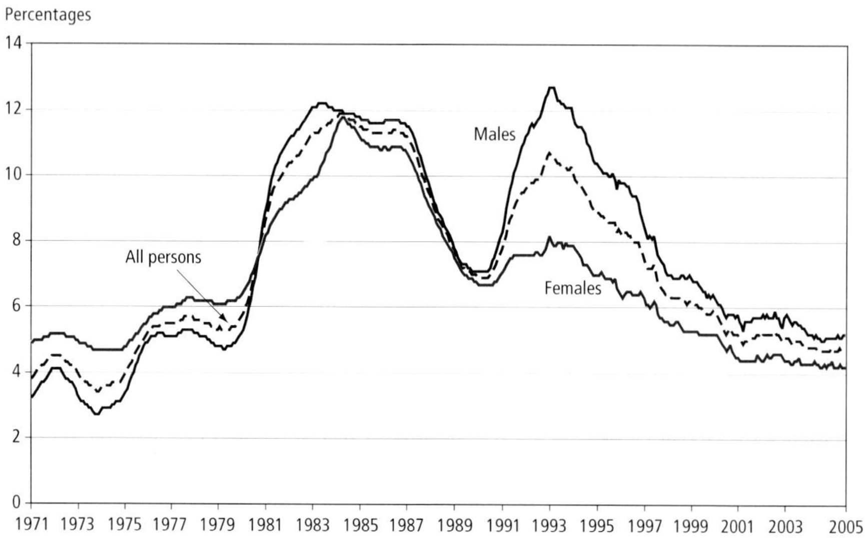

1 All aged 16 and over.
2 Seasonally adjusted.

Source: Labour Force Survey

increased in 1975–76 following a recession, before levelling off at around 1.5 million (5 per cent) in the late 1970s. It remained largely unchanged until 1980, when it rose sharply, peaking at over 3 million (just under 12 per cent) in 1984. The late 1980s saw an economic recovery, with unemployment falling to around 2 million (7 per cent) before the recession of the early 1990s drove it back up to 3 million (around 10 per cent). Since this peak in 1993, unemployment has decreased gradually to reach levels and rates similar to those last seen in the late 1970s and this trend continued for much of 2005. The unemployment level and rate for the three months to September 2004, at 1.39 million and 4.7 per cent respectively, were the lowest on record since 1976. Since this time, unemployment levels and rates have risen slightly. In the three months to September 2005, the unemployment level stood at 1.43 million (up by 41,000 from a year earlier) and the unemployment rate was 4.7 per cent (up by 0.1 percentage point from a year earlier).

A breakdown of unemployment by duration is available on a seasonally adjusted basis back to 1992. Since then, long-term unemployment, when a person has been unemployed for over 12 months, has followed a similar pattern to overall unemployment levels, rising to a peak of 1.3 million (44 per cent of the unemployed total) in the early 1990s and decreasing since then. This downward trend in long-term unemployment continued during 2004. In the three months to August 2004, the number of people unemployed for more than 12 months was the lowest on record, at 272,000 (19.5 per cent of the unemployed total). In the three months to September 2005 long-term unemployment stood at 293,000.

Duration of unemployment

Figure 4.3
Unemployment and the claimant count,[1] 1980–2005
United Kingdom

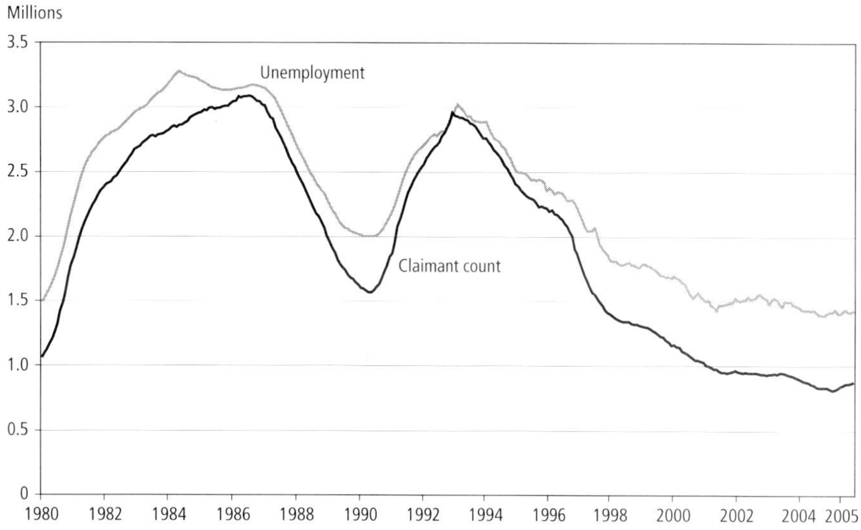

1 All aged 16 and over.
Source: Labour Force Survey, Office for National Statistics; administrative data, Jobcentre Plus

In addition to the LFS measure of unemployment, the claimant count measures the number of people claiming unemployment-related benefits.

Trends in the number of people claiming unemployment-related benefits have followed a similar pattern to the LFS measure of unemployment, although there are periods of divergence and convergence. The claimant count reached two peaks of around 3 million during the recessions of the mid-1980s and 1990s and has been falling over the last decade (Figure 4.3). In January 2005 the claimant count was 813,800, the lowest level since 1975. Since then, the level has increased slightly to reach 878,000 in September 2005.

One of the major reasons for the divergence between the unemployment rate and the claimant count over the past few years has been that many people, who were previously inactive in the labour market, have been encouraged by the improvement in the economy to begin actively to seek work. This means that they have become defined as unemployed under the ILO definition but as they have not been claiming Jobseeker's Allowance they are excluded from the claimant count.

Claimant count

Characteristics of unemployed people

Unemployment rates vary among different sub-groups of the population in terms of sex, age, disability status, ethnic origin, qualification levels and previous occupation.

Unemployment rates for men and women have followed similar cyclical trends, but the recessions of the 1980s and 1990s had a greater impact on male unemployment (Figures 4.1 and 4.2). The 1980s recession resulted in a particularly sharp increase in the male unemployment rate, which overtook the female rate in the latter half of 1980 and has stayed above it ever since. In the three months to September 2005 the male unemployment rate was 5.2 per cent while the female rate was 4.2 per cent.

Sought occupation of JSA claimants

Jobseeker's Allowance (JSA) is one of the benefits received by unemployed people. JSA claimant count data are based on information provided monthly to ONS from the JSA payments system run by Jobcentre Plus.

Figure 4.4 shows that in September 2005 the majority of female claimants were seeking work in sales and customer service, administrative and secretarial, elementary or personal service occupations. Men concentrated their search more in elementary, skilled trades and process, plant and machine operative occupations.

Figure 4.4
JSA Claimants: by sought occupation and sex, September 2005
United Kingdom

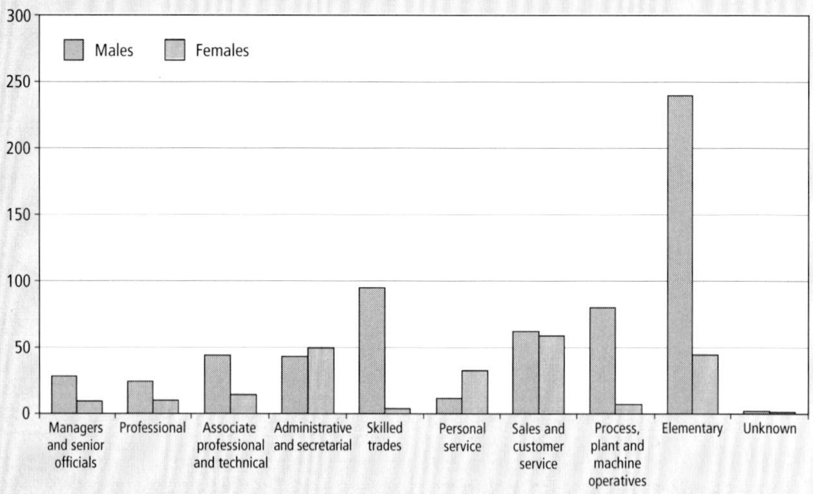

Source: Jobcentre Plus administrative system

More information on sought and usual occupation of JSA Claimant data is available on the National Statistics website: www.statistics.gov.uk/cci/article.asp?id=1231

Information about unemployment rates by age is available on a seasonally adjusted basis back to 1992.

Unemployment rates for young people have been consistently higher than for those in older age groups and have not followed the overall downward trend (Figure 4.5). Throughout the past decade, about one fifth of the economically active population aged 16–17 was unemployed. In the three months to September 2005 the unemployment rate for this age group was 22.4 per cent, compared with rates of 10.9 per cent for those aged 18–24, 3.4 per cent for those aged 25–49, and 2.9 per cent for those aged 50 and over.

Figure 4.5
Unemployment rates: by age group, March–May 1992 to July–September 2005[1]
United Kingdom

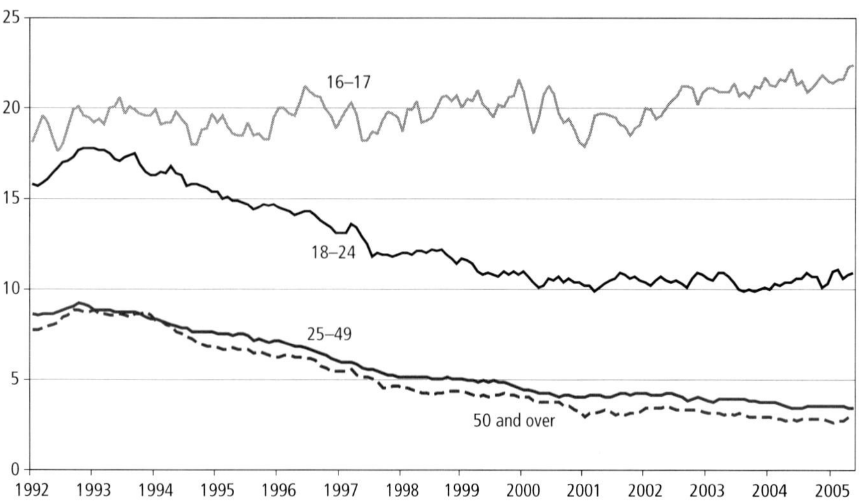

1 *Seasonally adjusted.*

Source: Labour Force Survey

Young people account for an increasing proportion of the unemployed total. In the three months to September 2005 some 42 per cent of unemployed people were under 25 years old, compared with 31 per cent in 1992. The 16 to 17 year old age group increased from 5 per cent of the unemployed total to 13 per cent over the same period (Figure 4.6).

As with employment, care must be taken when using ethnicity data for analysis. The different ethnic groups often have different demographics, such as differing proportions of people within the age ranges. Unemployment rates vary by ethnic group (Figure 4.7). In the 12 months to November 2005, the lowest unemployment rates were for people of 'white' ethnic origin (4.4 per cent) and those of Indian origin (6.8 per cent). Unemployment rates were highest for people of Pakistani or Bangladeshi origin (15.0 per cent) and for the Black or Black British group (12.8 per cent).

Figure 4.6
Unemployment proportions: by age group, March–May 1992 to July–September 2005[1]
United Kingdom
Percentages

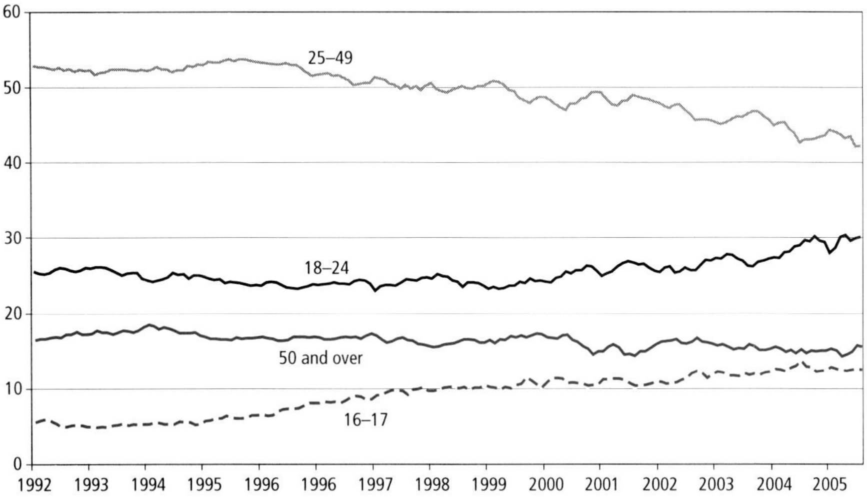

1 *Seasonally adjusted.*
Source: Labour Force Survey

Figure 4.7
Unemployment rates: by ethnic group,[1] **2004–2005**[2]
United Kingdom
Percentages

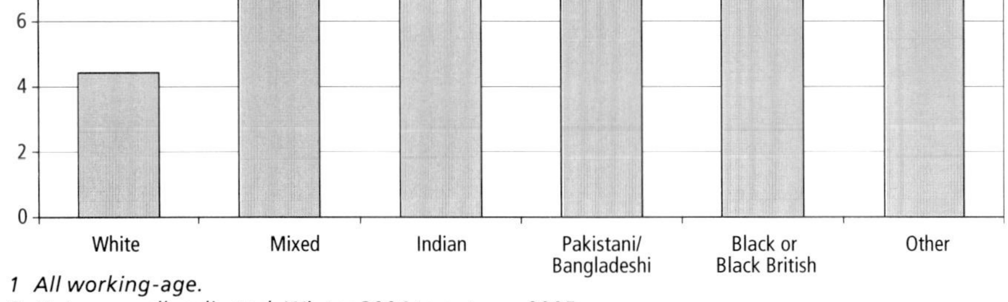

1 *All working-age.*
2 *Not seasonally adjusted. Winter 2004 to autumn 2005.*
Source: Labour Force Survey.

The LFS estimates of unemployment rates for the working-age population by disability status are available back to 1998. These show that unemployment rates are higher among working-age people with a long-term disability than they are for people who are not long-term disabled. The unemployment rates for both groups have decreased over the past five years, and so has the gap between them. In the 12 months to November 2004 the unemployment rate among long-term disabled people of working age was 7.2 per cent (down by 3.2 percentage points from five years earlier) compared with 4.5 per cent for those without a long-term disability (down by 1.0 percentage point from five years earlier). Nearly a fifth of the unemployed population of working age had a long-term health problem or disability (19.7 per cent).

People with no qualifications are more likely to be unemployed than those with qualifications, particularly if the qualifications are at higher levels of educational attainment. In the 12 months to November 2004 the unemployment rate for working-age people with no qualifications was 9.8 per cent, compared with rates of 5.7 per cent for those qualified to GCE A-Level or equivalent, and 2.7 per cent for graduates. One-fifth of the unemployed population of working-age had no qualifications (20.9 per cent).

Qualifications

The LFS asks unemployed respondents who have worked within the last eight years, questions about their last job. This information can be used to calculate unemployment rates by previous occupation (Figure 4.8 overleaf). In the 12 months to November 2004 unemployment rates were highest among those who previously worked in the elementary occupations (7.7 per cent) and lowest among those who previously worked in professional and managerial occupations (1.6 and 1.9 per cent respectively).

The LFS also asks unemployed respondents about the type of work they have been looking for and their main method of job search. In the 12 months to November 2004 most unemployed people were looking for work as an employee (87.0 per cent), while 2.9 per cent were seeking self-employment, 1.3 per cent were seeking a place on a government employment or training programme and the remaining

Figure 4.8

Unemployment rates: by previous occupation,[1] 2003–2004[2]

United Kingdom

Percentages

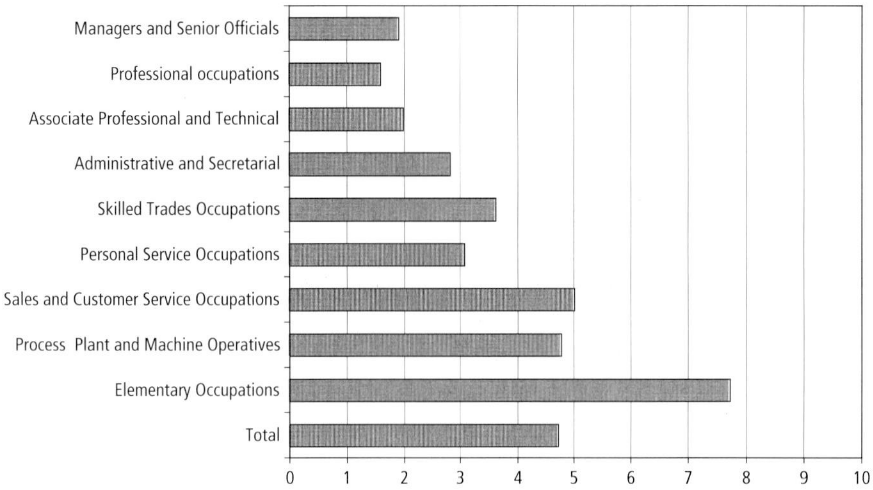

1 Standard Occupational Classification 2000.
2 December 2003 to November 2004. Not seasonally adjusted.

Source: Labour Force Survey

8.8 per cent had no preference. Of those who were looking for work as an employee, most (71.1 per cent) were looking for full-time work or had no preference, while 28.9 per cent were looking specifically for part-time work. Unemployed women were more likely to be looking for part-time work than unemployed men (46.4 per cent and 15.6 per cent respectively).

The most common method of job search was studying or replying to advertisements in newspapers, journals or on the Internet. This was used by 41.5 per cent of unemployed people, while 28.5 per cent visited Jobcentres as their main method, 10.5 per cent applied directly to employers, and 7.2 per cent mainly sought work through friends and relatives.

Job search

International comparisons of unemployment

Data for the last decade show that in contrast to the downward trend in the UK, the trends in other countries have varied. The unemployment rate in Japan has increased steadily from 3.0 per cent in 1994 and has begun to level out at 4.7 per cent in 2004 (**Figure 4.9**). In the United States, the unemployment rate followed a downward trend between 1994 and 2000 (from 5.8 per cent to 3.9 per cent) but took an upward turn in 2001, exceeding the rate for both the UK and Japan and reaching over 6 per cent before levelling off at 5.5 per cent in 2004.

The UK unemployment rate has been 3 to 4 percentage points lower than the average for the Eurozone-12 and the EU-25 countries over the past five years. It has also been 2 to 3 percentage points lower than the rate in Canada over the same period.

These international variations reflect the fact that unemployment is affected by the interaction of many factors, in addition to the global economic cycle. These include cultural and institutional factors, and employment legislation.

Figure 4.9

Unemployment rates in the United Kingdom and selected countries, 1993–2005[1]

Percentages

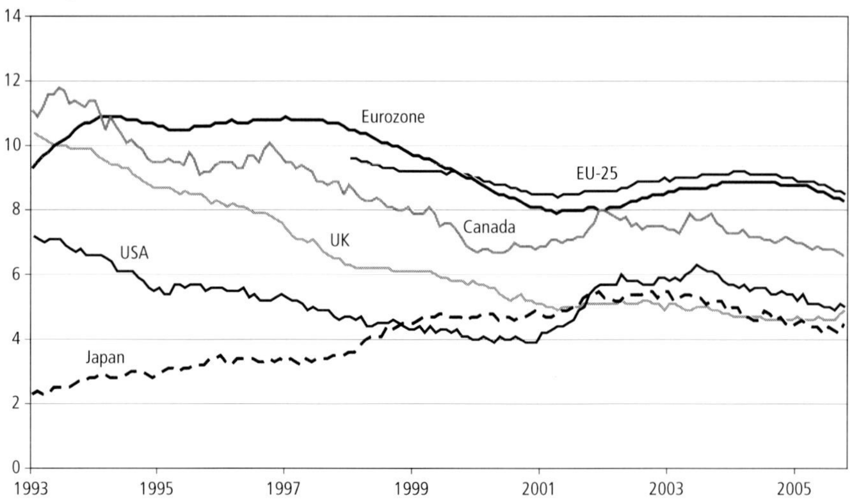

1 January 1993 to October 2005. Not seasonally adjusted.

Source: Labour Force Survey, Office for National Statistics; Eurostat; StatsBLS; StatCan; Stat.go.JP

Chapter 5

Labour supply – economic inactivity

- There were 7.89 million people of working age in the UK in the three months to September 2005 who were neither working nor seeking work, the economically inactive.
- Despite relative stability in overall inactivity rates there have been different trends for men and women. Among men the inactivity rate has grown from 4.9 per cent in 1971 to 16.6 per cent in 2005. In comparison the female inactivity rate has declined from 40.6 per cent in 1971 to 26.4 per cent in 2005.
- The largest group among the economically inactive is those looking after the family and home. The size of this group has, however, declined over recent years as more women, particularly those with children enter the labour market.
- In autumn 2005, 2.1 million people were inactive due to long term sickness, 27 per cent of all those who were inactive.
- The inactive student group has increased over the past decade so that in autumn 2005 they represented 23 per cent of all working-age inactive people.
- Economic inactivity rates are highest among those with no qualifications and lowest for those with a degree, or equivalent.

People who are neither in employment nor unemployed are classified as economically inactive. International standard definitions have been agreed that differentiate between the unemployed and the economically inactive by whether or not the individual is looking for and available for work. The economically inactive include those who want a job but have not been seeking work in the last four weeks, those who want a job and are seeking work but not available to start work, and those who do not want a job.

In recent years there has been increasing recognition of the need for macroeconomic analysis to consider the size and composition of the inactive group. This analysis is used in assessing potential labour supply and the likelihood of people in the inactive group moving into the labour market at some point in the future. In addition, there has been a greater policy focus on the scope for reducing inactivity, as well as unemployment, as a means of boosting economic performance.

It is therefore, important to try to understand the various groups within the inactive category to build a fuller picture of the reasons why these people are not economically active. The characteristics of people who are economically inactive and the reasons why they are in this group are described in more detail after looking at trends for economic inactivity.

Economic Inactivity

Economic inactivity trends

Data from the Labour Force Survey (LFS) back to 1971 show that the overall inactivity rate has remained fairly stable over the period, even though there have been considerable fluctuations in the economic cycle.

Figure 5.1

Economic inactivity rates: by sex,[1] January–March 1971 to July–September 2005[2]

United Kingdom

Percentages

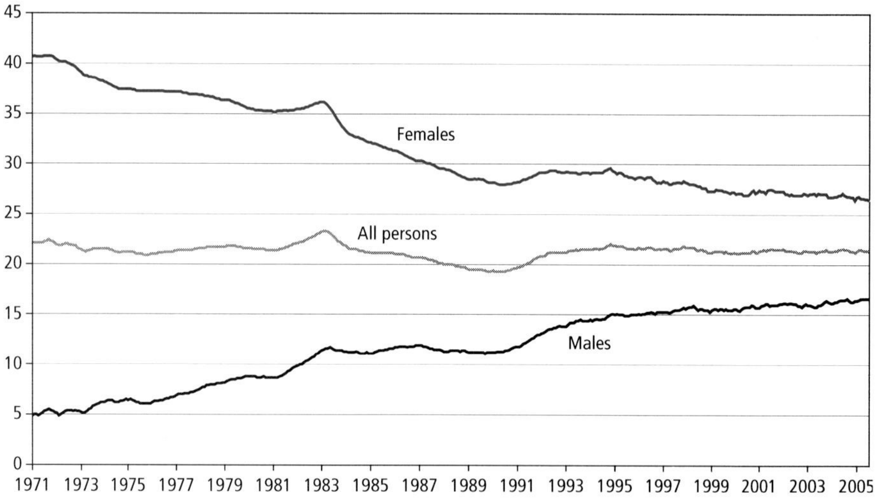

1 Working age

2 Seasonally adjusted.

Source: Labour Force Survey

Despite this stability, there have been some distinctive changes in the composition of the economically inactive group.

The total number of economically inactive people of working age in the UK stood at 7.89 million for the three months to September 2005, a rise of approximately 870,000 since the beginning of 1971. Despite this, the economic inactivity rate has remained stable over this period because the total working-age population has also increased.

The proportion of the working-age population who were economically inactive fluctuated at around 21 and 22 per cent throughout the 1970s (Figure 5.1). Inactivity increased during the recession of the early 1980s, with the rate reaching 23 per cent during the first half of 1983. As the economy improved in the late 1980s, the inactivity rate resumed its downward path, dropping to around 19.3 per cent for the majority of 1990. However, the 1990s recession drove it back up, and it then levelled off. Since the middle of 1992, the inactivity rate has remained relatively flat at 21 to 22 per cent, which is similar to the level experienced in the 1970's. Looking at 2005, the working-age inactivity rate showed signs of increasing at the beginning of the year but then fell back down to a rate of 21.3 per cent in the three months to September 2005.

Characteristics of economically inactive people

The LFS shows that there is considerable variation in rates of economic inactivity among people with different demographic characteristics. In particular inactivity was higher among people from minority ethnic groups, those with low qualifications, those with disabilities and those in lower socio-economic groups.

The relative stability of the economic inactivity rate in the UK in recent years masks the different trends for men and women over time (Figure 5.1). Among men, the inactivity rate has grown from 4.9 per cent in 1971 to 16.6 per cent in

2005. In comparison, the female inactivity rate has declined from 40.6 per cent in 1971 to 26.4 per cent in 2005. This is a result of the increase in the number of women continuing their employment or re-entering the labour market after having children.

Looking at a breakdown by age, there has been an increase in economic inactivity among young people, particularly 16- to 17-year-olds. In summer 1998, the inactivity rate for those aged 16–17 reached a low of 38.7 per cent. This rate has been gradually increasing so that by autumn 2005, the inactivity rate for this age group was 52.1 per cent. In part this reflects the growing number of young people staying on in full-time education until they are 18. Inactivity has also increased among those aged 18–24; the rate for this age group increased from 21.8 per cent in spring 1992, the earliest figures are available for, to 26.3 per cent in autumn 2005.

Information on disability status is available in the LFS back to 1998. It shows that people with a long-term disability were more likely to be economically inactive than those without. In autumn 2005, 45.5 per cent of people with a long-term disability were inactive, a fall of four percentage points from autumn 1998. In comparison 15.6 per cent of people without a long-term disability were inactive in 2005, a growth of 0.6 percentage points on seven years earlier.

People in the non-White ethnic groups were more likely than their White counterparts to be economically inactive (Figure 5.2). In 2004–2005, the Bangladeshi and Pakistani ethnic group had the highest inactivity rate at 50.4 per cent. This was more than double that for the White group, at 20.1 per cent. The Indian group had the second lowest inactivity rate after the whole group of 25.1 per cent in 2004–2005.

Figure 5.2

Economic inactivity rates:[1] by ethnic group, 2004–2005[2]

United Kingdom

Percentages

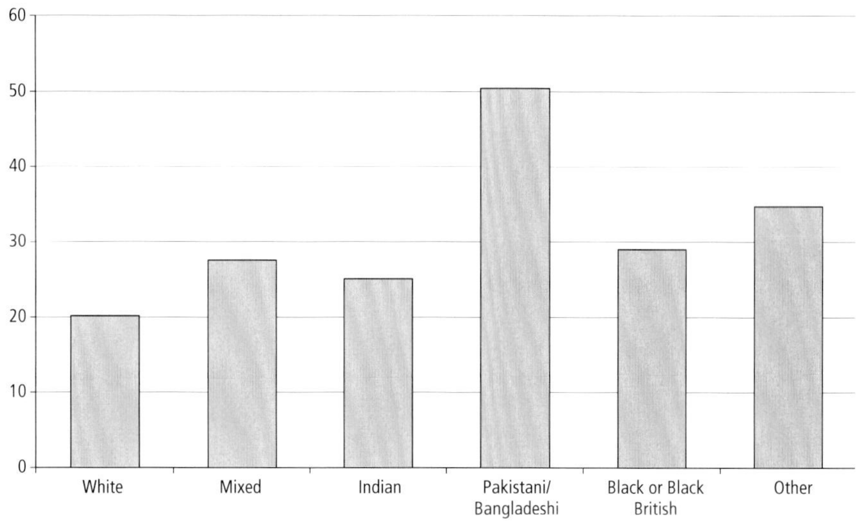

1 Working age.

2 Winter 2004 to autumn 2005. Not seasonally adjusted.

Source: Labour Force Survey

Figure 5.3

Economic inactivity rates:[1] by sex and highest educational qualification, 2003–2004[2]

United Kingdom

Percentages

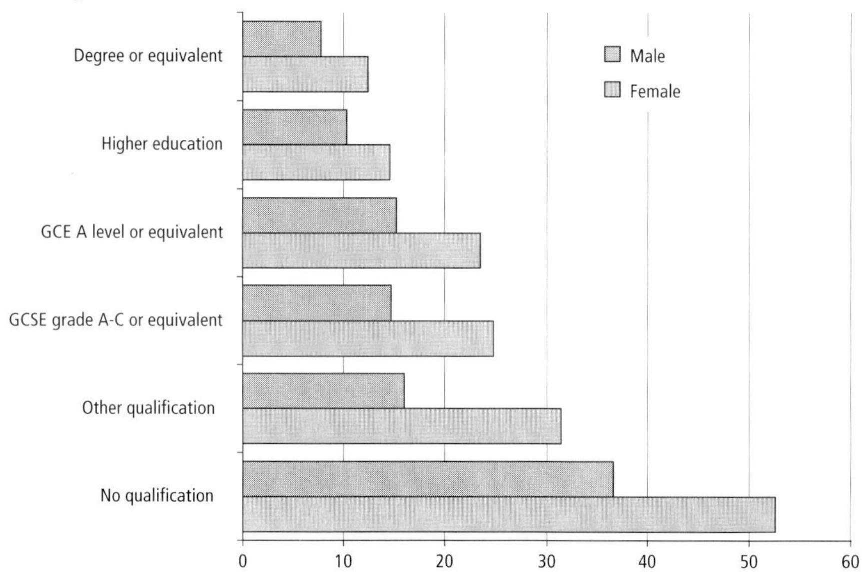

1 Working age.

2 December 2003 to November 2004. Not seasonally adjusted.

Source: Labour Force Survey

Skill level is usually measured using the highest level of qualification held. Economic inactivity rates vary considerably by highest educational qualification. In 2004, 36.6 per cent of males with no qualifications were inactive, compared with only 14.7 per cent of those whose highest qualification was a GCSE or equivalent and 7.8 per cent of those with a degree (Figure 5.3). The same pattern was evident among females, although those with no qualifications were more likely to be inactive than their male counterparts. Among graduates the difference in inactivity rates between males and females was much smaller. For example, there was a gap in the inactivity rate of 16 percentage points between males and females with no qualifications compared with 4.6 percentage points between those with a degree.

Qualifications

Characteristics

Reasons for economic inactivity

The characteristics described above give an indication of the composition of the economically inactive population. These characteristics do not, however, explain why certain people are more likely to be inactive than others. The LFS asks respondents the main reasons why they are inactive, and these can be grouped broadly into long-term sick or disabled, looking after the family or home, students and retired (Figure 5.4).

Reasons for inactivity

Figure 5.4
Reasons for inactivity,[1] 1995 and 2005[2]
United Kingdom

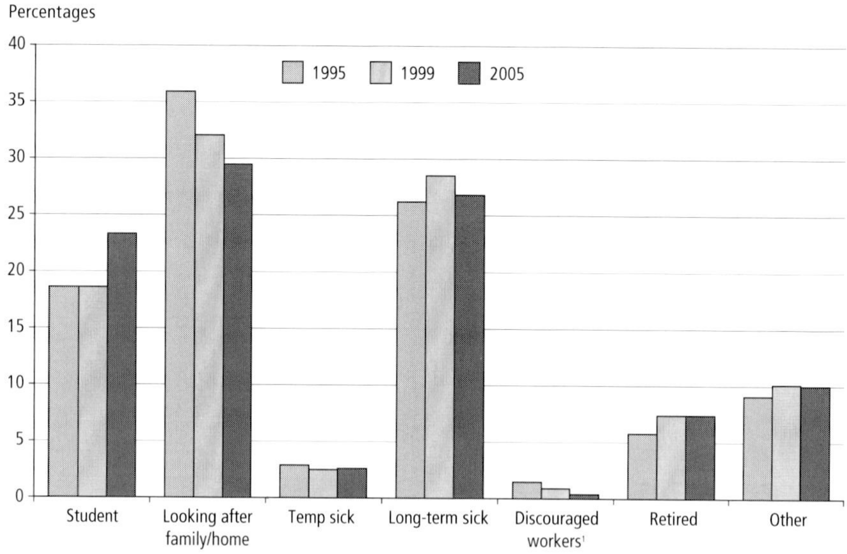

1 Seasonally adjusted.
2 September to November.
Source: Labour Force Survey

The largest group among the economically inactive is those looking after the family or home. The size of this group has, however, declined in recent years as more women, particularly those with children, enter the labour market. In autumn 2005, 29.5 per cent of people reported looking after the family/home as their reason for inactivity. Inactivity among the next largest group, the long-term sick, has remained fairly stable over the last five years. In autumn 2005, 2.1 million people were inactive due to long-term sickness, 26.8 per cent of all those who were inactive.

Between the sexes, the main differences in the reasons for inactivity were related to family responsibilities; 70.8 per cent of females aged 25–34 gave this as their reason for inactivity compared with 11.6 per cent of males of the same age (Table 5.5). Around three-fifths of inactive females aged 35–49 also gave looking after the family or home as their reason for inactivity. This compares with under a fifth of males. One noticeable aspect is that among all men aged over 25 years the main reason for inactivity reported was long-term sickness and disability. For those aged 35–49, over three in five were inactive due to a long-term sickness or disability.

The economically inactive student group has grown during the last decade or so. As a proportion of the working-age, inactive population, inactive students increased from 17.9 per cent in summer 1998, the lowest figures since 1993 when this information was first collected, to 23.3 per cent in autumn 2005, which equates to approximately 493,000 people. Although full-time education is not classified as employment, it does have an impact on future employment prospects. Those with higher educational qualifications are highly likely to participate in the labour market in the future and by investing in 'human capital' they are more likely to have better employment prospects and access to higher earnings later in life.

While growth in the number of full-time students has been a factor in an increased inactivity rate for young people, there has also been an increase in inactivity among young people not in full-time education. This has been particularly marked among those non-students aged 16–17, with the inactivity rate rising from a low of 11.4 per cent in the three months to December 1998 to 28.1 per cent in the three months to September 2005 (Figure 5.6). For those aged 18–24 the rate has remained relatively stable over the last decade or

Table 5.5
Main reasons for economic inactivity:[1] by age and sex, 2005[2]
United Kingdom Percentages

		16–24	25–34	35–49	50–59/64	Total 16–59/64
Males	Long-term sick/disabled	5	37	60	52	38
	Looking after family/home	1	13	16	4	6
	Student	81	23	4	0	28
	Retired	-	-	0	31	13
	Other	12	27	19	12	15
Total		100	100	100	100	100
Females	Long-term sick/disabled	4	10	24	41	21
	Looking after family/home	24	72	59	27	45
	Student	61	8	4	1	18
	Retired	-	-	0	16	4
	Other	11	10	12	16	13
Total		100	100	100	100	100
All persons	Long-term sick/disabled	5	16	34	47	27
	Looking after family/home	13	58	48	15	30
	Student	70	12	4	0	22
	Retired	-	-	0	24	8
	Other	12	14	14	14	13
Total		100	100	100	100	100

1 Not seasonally adjusted.
2 Spring quarter.
Source: Labour Force Survey

Figure 5.6
Economic inactivity rates among young people aged 16–17 and 18–24 years not in full-time education,[1] March–May 1992 to July–September 2005
United Kingdom

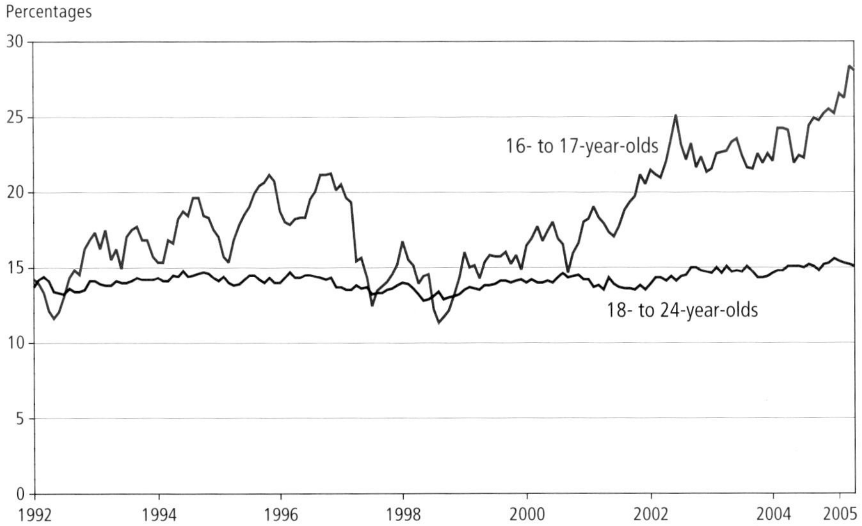

1 Seasonally adjusted.
Source: Labour Force Survey

so and in the three months to September 2005, the inactivity rate for people of this age not in full-time education was 15.1 per cent.

It is possible to look at movements from economic inactivity into employment and unemployment using the longitudinal LFS. This analysis gives some idea of which groups are moving out of inactivity and are an indicator of the characteristics of those moving into employment. Based on a four-quarter average, the number of working-age adults moving from inactivity to employment over a three-month period (one-quarter) increased from 424,000 in 1994 to 511,000 in 2004. The reasons for inactivity differ for males and females. Table 5.7 overleaf shows that in 2004 there was considerable variation in the number of females moving from inactivity to employment by age group and reason for inactivity. Just over half of all females moving from inactivity to employment were aged 16–24 and nearly 80 per cent of these were students. For the 25–34 and 35–44 age groups, over 50 per cent of those moving into employment had been inactive because they were looking after a family or home and this decreased to 38 per cent for the 45–54 age group and 27 per cent for the 55–59 age group. The largest component of the 'other' group consists of those who have not stated a reason for inactivity.

Table 5.7

Percentage of working-age females moving from inactivity into employment: by reason for inactivity, 2004[1]

United Kingdom Percentages

Reason for inactivity	16–24	25–34	35–44	45–54	55–59	All females
Looking after family/home	*7*	*58*	*55*	*38*	*27*	*28*
Student	*79*	*15*	*10*	*3*	*1*	*44*
Other[2]	*15*	*27*	*35*	*59*	*72*	*28*
All females	*100*	*100*	*100*	*100*	*100*	*100*
All females (thousands)	*152*	*55*	*50*	*30*	*16*	*302*

1 Four quarter average.
2 Includes no reason stated, short-term sick, long-term sick/disabled and retired.

Source: Labour Force Survey

Improving economic inactivity questions in the LFS

In order to be classified as economically inactive according to the ILO definitions, respondents in the LFS have to state whether they want work, whether they are seeking work, and whether they are available for work. The answers to these questions determine whether the individual is unemployed or inactive.

Recent research has found that these wanting, seeking, available categories, for people who are economically inactive are not accurate predictors of movement into work in the future. Cognitive research also found that the issues involved in whether people would or would not like work are so complex that they are unlikely to be successfully covered in a single question. For these reasons, ONS decided to develop a more accurate method of measuring future labour supply. These questions were first included in LFS datasets in spring 2005 and involved:

- Extending the list of reasons for inactivity
- Collecting information about people's propensity to work in the future
- Collecting information about when this is likely to be

Initial results show some interesting findings:

- 93 per cent of inactive students said they **definitely will** work in the future
- 66 per cent of those looking after the family or home said they would **definitely or probably** work in the future
- 51 per cent of long term sick or disabled said they **definitely will not** work in the future

Further work is planned to investigate these new questions in more detail.

Working-age benefits

The classification of people's labour market status following internationally agreed guidelines depends upon information about their reported behaviour in relation to work, job seeking and job availability. It does not depend on any knowledge of an individual's benefit status. Its compilation is therefore not affected by changes in the benefit system. The behaviour of people claiming working-age benefits is likely to be influenced by the conditions they must meet in order to qualify for these benefits. The nature of the social security system can therefore have a significant impact on the aspects of behaviour that determine labour market status.

The main benefits available to people of working age are Jobseeker's Allowance, Income Support and Incapacity Benefit.

Working-age benefits

International comparisons of economic inactivity

Comparable international data for economic inactivity is limited. Data for the EU-25 and the Eurozone-12 for 2003 show relatively high inactivity rates at 30.7 per cent and 31.4 per cent respectively. The inactivity rates for France (30.9 per cent) and Germany (27.9 per cent) for the same period were also much higher than for the UK. Data for Canada, Japan and the United States are available for 2004. The inactivity rates in Japan and the United States were 24.6 and 27.6 per cent per cent respectively. Canada had a much lower inactivity rate at 21.8 per cent, similar to the UK. These figures, however, should be compared with caution as there are many underlying reasons for the differences in inactivity rates, not least the variations in the social and political structures in these countries.

Sickness absence

Employers are increasingly becoming aware of the direct and indirect costs of absence to their organisations. The direct costs include statutory sick pay, cost of replacement staff and loss of output. Indirect or hidden costs are harder to quantify. These include low morale among staff who have to carry out additional work to cover for those who are absent, the cost of managing absence, and the impact on training and development, all of which impact on overall levels of output for the organisation.

The LFS collects information from respondents on whether they took days off because of sickness or injury in the reference week. The main characteristics from spring 2004 include:

- Days lost to absence are fairly evenly spread across the week days
- Female employees and younger employees aged 16–34 were more likely than other groups to take at least one day off sick
- Lone mothers had the highest rate of sickness absence, followed by females with no dependent children (4.4 per cent and 3.4 per cent respectively). Males without dependent children had the lowest rates of absence
- The proportion of employees who took at least one day sick was higher in the public sector than in the private sector (3.1 per cent compared with 2.8 per cent).

  For further information see: www.statistics.gov.uk/cci/article.asp?ID=1117

Chapter 6

Labour costs

- In September 2005, the rate of growth of average earnings over the past year (the Average Earnings Index) was 4.1 per cent.
- Public sector earnings showed a growth rate of 4.2 per cent in the year to September 2005 compared with figures for the private sector of 4.0 per cent.
- The median gross weekly pay for full-time employees in the UK grew to £431 in 2005. Median gross hourly earnings of full-time adults grew to £10.79 in 2005, up by 3.2 per cent on 2004.
- Differences still exist in the distribution of earnings by gender. In 2005 females earned on average 87 per cent as much as males, compared with 85.5 per cent in 2004, narrowing the gender pay gap to its lowest levels since comparable estimates began in 1998.
- The 'electricity gas and water supply' industry had the highest median pay in 2005 (£542.60), while the 'hotels and restaurants' industry had the lowest (£271.30).
- The number of jobs paid below the National Minimum Wage in the UK was estimated to be 327,000, representing 1.3 per cent of all jobs in the labour market.

Labour costs and distribution straddle both labour demand and labour supply within the labour market framework (see Figure A in the Introduction). From the demand side, labour is a necessary factor of production: firms need people to make their output, which they will trade with consumers. From the supply side, people choose to trade their time in order to increase their real income. In other words people choose to work so that they are paid. If there is a shortage of people with the required skills to do the work then a firm will have to increase wages to attract workers. Conversely, if there is an increase in the size of the available labour force then wages can be decreased as workers become easier to attract. These are the dynamics of labour supply, labour demand and labour costs, represented at the most simplistic level.

Labour costs

Labour costs are the whole range of costs employers incur when employing workers. They include wages and salaries, national insurance and social contributions, redundancy payments, benefits in kind, overheads and other non-wage components. On the labour demand side, an employer has to consider all these costs in assessing the impact on the business of recruiting and employing staff. Figure 6.1 shows that by far the largest component of labour costs in 2000 was wages and salaries which made up over four-fifths of the total.

On the supply side, the disposable income of an individual is made up of wages and salaries, occupational pensions, investments, non-government sources and government sources (cash benefits), less any direct taxes, national insurance contributions and council tax. All of these sources of income influence an individual's decision to supply their labour.

Figure 6.1
Structure of labour costs, 2000
United Kingdom
Percentages

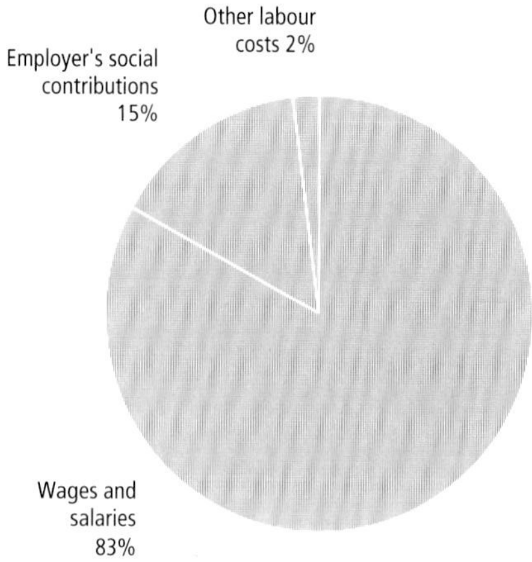

Source: Labour Cost Survey 2000

Analysis of labour costs and distribution is limited by the availability of relevant information. For this reason, ONS focuses on earnings (wages and salaries), the largest and most important component of labour cost and the most collected, in the majority of its analyses.

Labour Costs and Pay

Earnings

The growth in whole economy earnings is measured by the Average Earnings Index (AEI), which uses a fixed distribution of employees to monitor change from one period to the next. The AEI shows an overall picture of steady earnings growth in 2005. The 'including bonus series' shows that earnings rose by 4.1 per cent in the year to September 2005. This was a faster rate of increase than in 2004, 2003 and 2002 when the increases were 3.8, 3.7 and 3.7 per cent respectively, but lower than the 4.6 per cent in September 2001. It was also much slower than the growth observed in the 1970s, 1980s and early 1990s.

AEI

It is worth noting that September falls outside the main bonus season – which runs from December to April. As such, though it is an 'including' bonus figure, the annual growth figure for September will be largely unaffected by growth in bonuses, which as one-off payments paid in a particular month, do not affect basic

Figure 6.2
AEI whole economy growth rate (including bonuses), year on year growth of the RPI (all items) and derived real earnings growth[1] March 1964–September 2005
Great Britain/United Kingdom[1]
Per cent

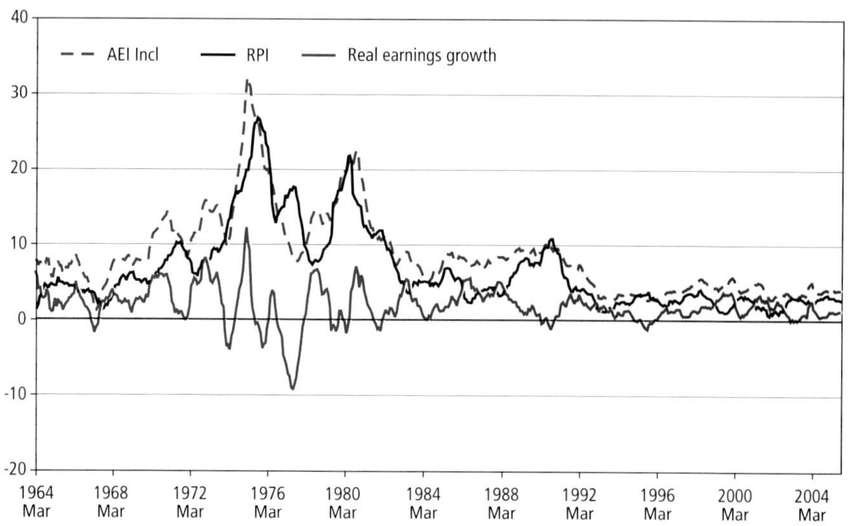

1 *The AEI covers Great Britain and the RPI covers the United Kingdom.*
Source: Average Earnings Index, Retail Price Index

pay for the rest of the year. Compared to September, earnings growth during the bonus season has tended to be higher in recent years, for example, in March 2005 it was 4.5 per cent, and in March 2004 it was 4.7 per cent. ONS also publishes an excluding bonus series which has edged down since the recent peak observed towards the end of 2004, suggesting that wage pressures in the economy are easing. The excluding bonus series increased by 3.7 per cent in the year to September 2005 compared with an increase of 4.2 per cent in the year to September 2004. On either measure the overall picture is of steady earnings growth, exceeding the rate of growth in retail prices.

Growth in average earnings can be compared with growth in the price of goods, to help understand real earnings growth. This is more indicative of the purchasing power of earnings. In other words, it indicates whether the growth in earnings allows people to purchase more or if the cost of goods has also gone up. Figure 6.2 displays the real earnings growth, calculated from AEI earnings growth (including bonuses) *minus* the all-items Retail Price Index (RPI), an indicator of domestic inflation. In September 2005, the annual rate of increase in the all-items RPI was 2.7 per cent which was below earnings growth, implying a real earnings growth of over 1 per cent during 2005. Real earnings growth has been generally positive over time, with the exception of periods in the mid 1970s.

RPI

Earnings and Pay

The Average Weekly Earnings (AWE) is an experimental monthly series that uses the same data source as the AEI, the Monthly Wages and Salaries Survey. It estimates the average weekly wage and can produce a number of analyses that were previously unavailable from other short-term earnings statistics. Figure 6.3 compares earning levels including bonuses and arrears (total pay) and earning levels excluding bonuses and arrears (regular pay). As the figure shows, there has been a steady increase in both total and regular pay since the beginning of 2000, with regular pay reaching its highest point in September 2005 at £373. The figure also highlights the seasonal effect of bonuses on the average weekly earnings which causes the peaks in the winter months.

AWE

Using the AEI and looking at earnings growth by sector in the year to September 2005, the private sector earnings growth (including bonuses) was 4.0 per cent compared with public sector earnings growth of 4.2 per cent (Figure 6.4).

Figure 6.3
Average weekly earnings in the whole economy: 2000–2005
Great Britain

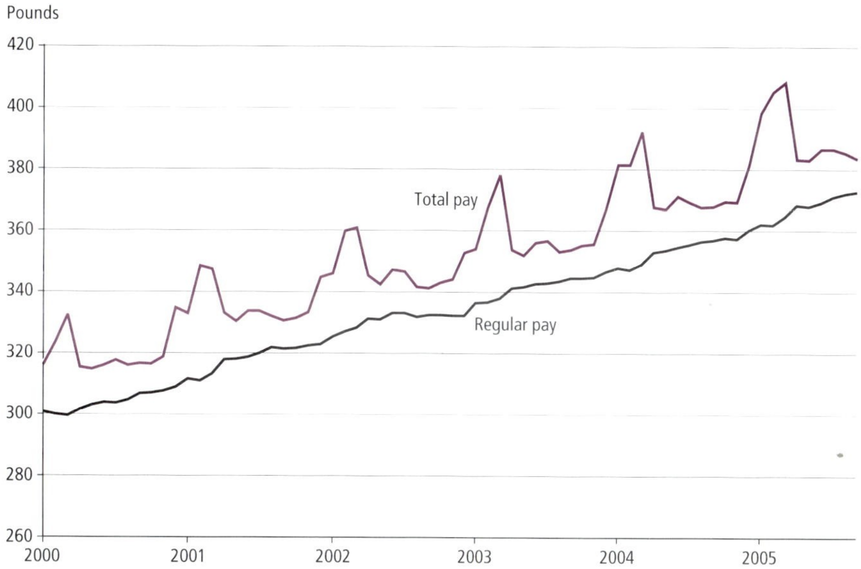

Source: Average Weekly Earnings

Figure 6.4
Year on year growth rates of public and private sector earnings (including bonuses): March 1991–September 2005
Great Britain

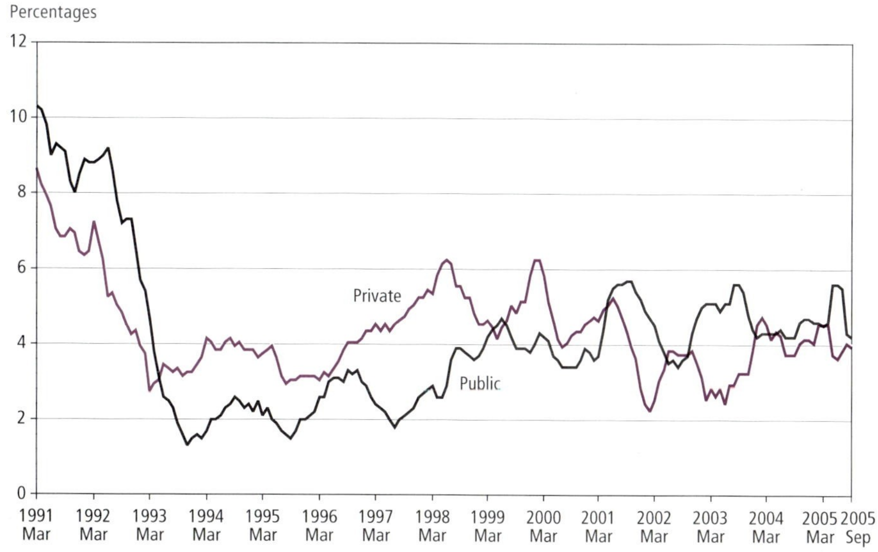

Source: Average Earnings Index

Earnings growth in the public sector has been higher for most of the period since mid 2001, when the previous trend of higher private sector earnings (since 1993) was reversed.

In the year to September 2005, earnings (including bonuses) in the manufacturing sector grew by 4.1 per cent, which represents an increase since a low of 2.6 per cent in June 2005 (Figure 6.5). In 2005, earnings in the services sector also increased by 4.1 per cent, a deceleration since the most recent peak earlier in the year of 5 per cent.

Non-wage costs

The Index of Labour Costs per Hour (ILCH) provides a timely indicator of changes in the cost of labour per hours worked. It reflects the changes in wages and salaries, non-wage costs and the quantity of hours worked over time period. This measure assists in the analysis of inflationary pressures originating from the labour market which result from changes in total labour costs per hour. It can be used alongside other earnings indicators (such as the AEI or the Average Weekly Earnings, both covered earlier) to see how the movement of non-wage costs affect the overall cost of labour. The non-wage costs included in the index are sickness, maternity and paternity costs, pension contributions, benefit in kind and national insurance contributions.

The ILCH is more sensitive to movements in employment patterns throughout the year than other measures of earnings (Figure 6.6). The main difference is in the third quarter of the year where the ILCH has higher growth. Fewer hours are worked in the summer months and wages stay broadly constant and so the relative cost of labour increases. This effect is removed when the index is seasonally adjusted.

Figure 6.5

Year on year earnings growth rates in the manufacturing and services sectors (including bonuses), March 1983–September 2005

Great Britain

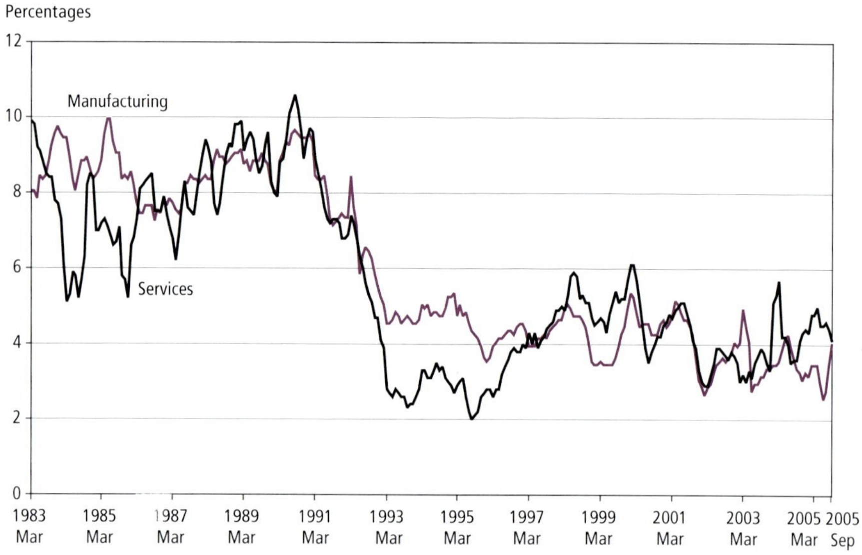

Source: Average Earnings Index

Figure 6.6

Growth rates of total labour costs, total wage costs and total other costs, 2000 Q1–2005 Q1

Great Britain

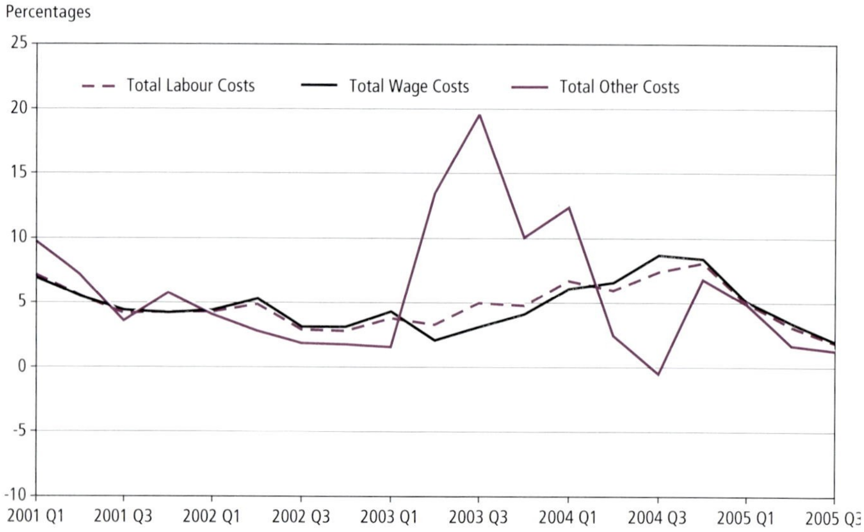

Source: Index of Labour Costs per Hour

Total labour cost increases have generally been in the range 3 to 5 per cent compared with a year earlier. The high growth rate shown from the second quarter of 2003 can be explained by the significant increase in the National Insurance contributions in this quarter. These growth rates decreased from the second quarter of 2004.

Other Labour Costs

Earnings distribution

Information on earnings is available from the Annual Survey of Hours and Earnings (ASHE), along with a number of employee characteristics. The AEI is the preferred measure of growth in earnings but the ASHE provides more detail on the distribution, for example, by sex or industry. According to the ASHE the median gross weekly pay for full-time employees in the UK grew to £431 in 2005. The median is the middle point of a population with exactly the same number of data values above and below. It is a better way of comparing the levels of earnings than the mean as it is less influenced by extreme values at the top end of the pay distribution. The median gross hourly earnings of full-time adults grew to £10.79 in 2005, up by 3.2 per cent on 2004. This is based on adults who worked full time whose pay was unaffected by absence and excludes overtime.

The overall growth in earnings has led to noticeable changes in the rate of growth for the highest and lowest earners in 2005 compared with the previous year (Figure 6.7). Full-time adults in the bottom 10 per cent of earners received £236 a week (including overtime) in 2005, 1.6 percentage points higher than in 2004. Full-time adults in the top 10 per cent earned more than £850 a week (including overtime), 2.7 percentage points higher than in 2004.

Figure 6.8 shows the levels of earnings in 2005 by industry, compared with the UK average. It presents comparisons of the median levels of gross weekly earnings for employees whose pay was not affected by absence. In 2005, the median gross weekly pay for the UK was £431.20. The 'electricity gas and water supply' industry had the highest median pay in 2005 (at £542.60), while the 'hotels and restaurants' industry had the lowest (£271.30).

Figure 6.7
Gross median weekly earnings for the 10th and 90th percentiles of the earnings distribution, 1998–2005
United Kingdom

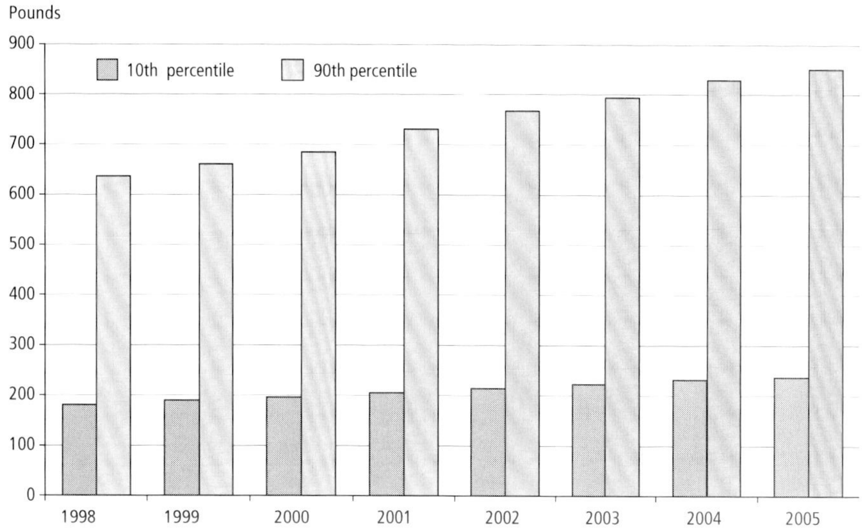

Source: Annual Survey of Hours and Earnings

Figure 6.8
Percentage difference from United Kingdom average gross weekly pay, by industry,[1] 2005
United Kingdom

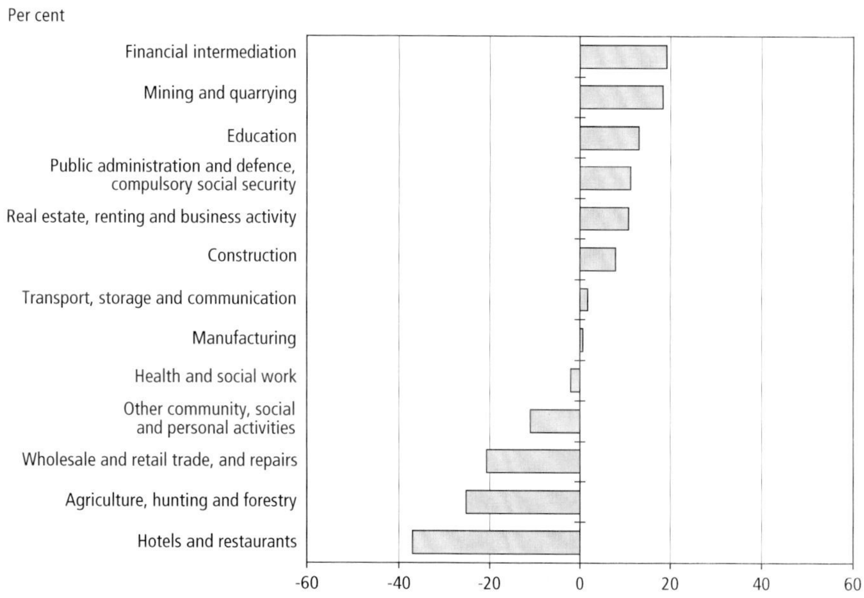

1 The sample size is too small to produce a reliable estimate for fishing.
Source: Annual Survey of Hours and Earnings

National minimum wage

The ASHE estimates for spring 2005 show that there were 327,000 jobs held by people aged 16 and over who were paid below the national minimum wage (NMW). This equates to 1.3 per cent of the number of UK jobs. It is estimated that 57,000 jobs (3.2 per cent of jobs held by these in this age group) are held by people aged 18 to 21 and 249,000 (1.1 per cent) by those aged 22 and over.

Gender pay gap

The gender pay gap (as measured by the median hourly pay of full-time employees, excluding overtime) narrowed between 2004 and 2005 to its lowest value since records began. The gap between women's median hourly pay and men's was 13.0 per cent, compared with the 14.5 per cent recorded in April 2004. The median hourly rate for men went up 3.1 per cent to £11.31, while the rate for women increased by 4.9 per cent to £9.84. This means that females earned on average 87 per cent as much as males compared with 85.5 per cent in 2004.

Gender Pay Gap

Figure 6.9
Ratio of female hourly pay to males, excluding overtime, 1998–2005
United Kingdom

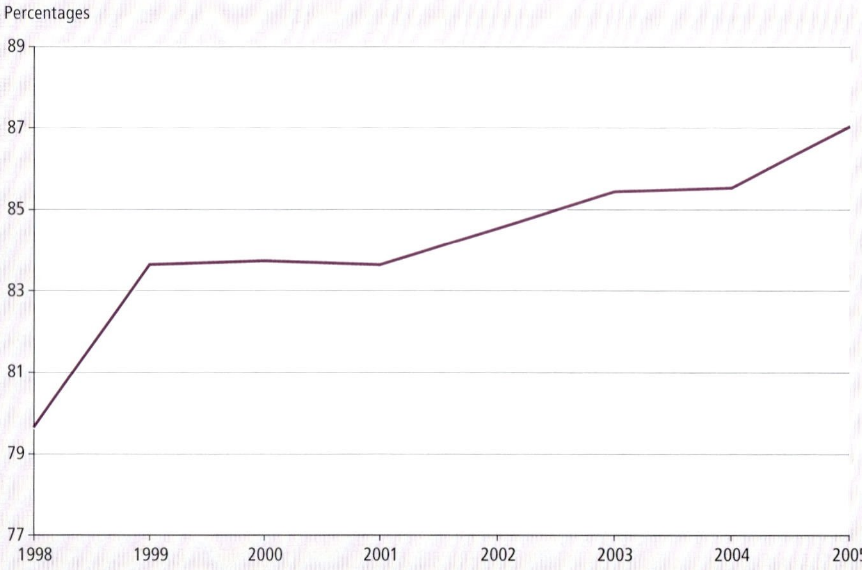

Source: Annual Survey of Hours and Earnings

On the internationally comparable measure based on mean earnings, women's average hourly pay (excluding overtime) was 17.1 per cent less than men's pay, a narrowing compared to the 2004 figure of 17.8 per cent.

Women's weekly earnings, including overtime, were lower than men's, partly because they worked fewer hours per week. However, women's earnings increased faster across the distribution compared with men's. The full-time hourly earnings excluding overtime of the bottom 10 per cent of women grew by 3.8 per cent compared with 3.0 per cent for their male counterparts. In comparison, the hourly earnings of the top 10 per cent grew by 5.5 per cent and 4.5 per cent respectively.

Although median hourly pay provides a useful comparison between the earnings of men and women, it does not necessarily indicate differences in rates of pay for comparable jobs. Pay medians are affected by the different work patterns of men and women, such as the proportions in different occupations and their length of time in jobs.

Table 6.10

Percentage of jobs and level of jobs paid below the national minimum wage, 1998–2004[1,2]

United Kingdom

	Percentage of jobs Percentages			Level of jobs Thousands		
	18–21	22 and over	All jobs	18–21	22 and over	All jobs
1998[2]	7.2	5.4	5.6	111	1,170	1,280
1999	2.4	2.1	2.1	40	460	490
2000	2.2	0.9	1.0	30	190	230
2001	2.1	0.9	1.0	40	210	240
2002	2.7	1.3	1.4	50	290	340
2003	2.9	0.9	1.0	50	200	250
2004	2.4	1.0	1.1	44	235	279
2005	3.2	1.1	1.3	57	249	327

1 *Spring each year. Estimates for 1998 to 2003 are based on a central estimate of the Labour Force Survey and the Annual Survey of Hours and Earnings.*
2 *Figures for spring 1998, before the National Minimum Wage was introduced, are for the number of jobs paid at less than £3.00 per hour (aged 18 to 21) or £3.60 per hour (aged 22 and over).*

Source: Labour Force Survey; Annual Survey of Hours and Earnings

The percentage of jobs below the NMW in 2005 (1.3 per cent) was slightly higher than in 2004 (1.1 per cent), and was driven mainly by an increase of 0.8 per cent among 18- to 21- year-olds. The percentage of those 22 and over paid below NMW was 1.1 per cent. This figure of 1.3 per cent is still lower than when the NMW was introduced in 1999.

A new methodology developed in 2004 using ASHE data improves the coverage of the low end of the pay distribution and estimates the number of jobs paid below the national minimum wage (NMW). This methodology is based on ASHE data only for 2004 and 2005, and a combination of ASHE and LFS data for 1998–2003.

In spring 2005, the NMW was £4.10 for those aged between 18 and 21 and £4.85 for those aged 22 and over. More detail of the pay rates for the NMW is given in Appendix A.

It should be noted that estimates of jobs paid below the NMW do not measure non-compliance with the NMW legislation. This is because the survey data used to provide the estimates do not indicate whether an individual is eligible for the minimum wage. For example, some people, such as apprentices or new trainees, are exempt from the minimum wage or are only entitled to lower rates. Also, if employees receive free accommodation, employers are entitled to offset hourly rates.

Low Pay Estimates

Tables

Labour Force Survey historical time series (1971–2005)

Summary by sex, seasonally adjusted

Note: Population estimates in the LFS

On 20 October 2005 the Government Actuary's Department (GAD) published revised population projections for 2005 and later years based on the ONS population estimates published on 25 August 2005. These revised population estimates have been incorporated into LFS estimates back to July–September 2004.

As the tables and text used in this publication were prepared before these revisions were made, there may be slight differences between the tables and the chapters.

SUMMARY OF NATIONAL LFS DATA

1 Labour Force Survey, summary by sex United Kingdom (thousands) seasonally adjusted

All aged 16 & over

	All aged 16 & over	Total economically active	Total in employment	Unemployed	Economically inactive	Economic Activity rate (%)	Employment rate (%)	Unemployment rate (%)	Economic inactivity rate (%)
	1	2	3	4	5	6	7	8	9
All Persons	MGSL	MGSF	MGRZ	MGSC	MGSI	MGWG	MGSR	MGSX	YBTC
Jan-Mar 1971	40,513	25,593	24,613	980	14,919	63.2	60.8	3.8	36.8
Feb-Apr 1971	40,531	25,573	24,575	998	14,959	63.1	60.6	3.9	36.9
Mar-May 1971	40,550	25,582	24,559	1,023	14,968	63.1	60.6	4.0	36.9
Apr-Jun 1971	40,568	25,600	24,556	1,045	14,968	63.1	60.5	4.1	36.9
May-Jul 1971	40,587	25,603	24,541	1,062	14,984	63.1	60.5	4.1	36.9
Jun-Aug 1971	40,605	25,576	24,508	1,068	15,029	63.0	60.4	4.2	37.0
Jul-Sep 1971	40,618	25,539	24,464	1,076	15,079	62.9	60.2	4.2	37.1
Aug-Oct 1971	40,631	25,515	24,424	1,090	15,117	62.8	60.1	4.3	37.2
Sep-Nov 1971	40,645	25,511	24,398	1,113	15,134	62.8	60.0	4.4	37.2
Oct-Dec 1971	40,658	25,528	24,395	1,133	15,130	62.8	60.0	4.4	37.2
Nov-Jan 1972	40,671	25,560	24,416	1,143	15,111	62.8	60.0	4.5	37.2
Dec-Feb 1972	40,684	25,605	24,455	1,149	15,079	62.9	60.1	4.5	37.1
Jan-Mar 1972	40,697	25,656	24,501	1,155	15,041	63.0	60.2	4.5	37.0
Feb-Apr 1972	40,710	25,690	24,529	1,161	15,020	63.1	60.3	4.5	36.9
Mar-May 1972	40,723	25,694	24,539	1,155	15,029	63.1	60.3	4.5	36.9
Apr-Jun 1972	40,736	25,682	24,542	1,140	15,055	63.0	60.2	4.4	37.0
May-Jul 1972	40,750	25,663	24,541	1,122	15,087	63.0	60.2	4.4	37.0
Jun-Aug 1972	40,763	25,664	24,557	1,107	15,099	63.0	60.2	4.3	37.0
Jul-Sep 1972	40,777	25,685	24,585	1,100	15,092	63.0	60.3	4.3	37.0
Aug-Oct 1972	40,792	25,706	24,614	1,092	15,086	63.0	60.3	4.2	37.0
Sep-Nov 1972	40,807	25,728	24,643	1,085	15,079	63.0	60.4	4.2	37.0
Oct-Dec 1972	40,821	25,758	24,689	1,070	15,063	63.1	60.5	4.2	36.9
Nov-Jan 1973	40,836	25,796	24,748	1,049	15,040	63.2	60.6	4.1	36.8
Dec-Feb 1973	40,851	25,848	24,825	1,024	15,002	63.3	60.8	4.0	36.7
Jan-Mar 1973	40,865	25,904	24,903	1,002	14,961	63.4	60.9	3.9	36.6
Feb-Apr 1973	40,880	25,949	24,962	987	14,931	63.5	61.1	3.8	36.5
Mar-May 1973	40,895	25,963	24,986	977	14,932	63.5	61.1	3.8	36.5
Apr-Jun 1973	40,909	25,954	24,986	968	14,955	63.4	61.1	3.7	36.6
May-Jul 1973	40,924	25,932	24,975	957	14,992	63.4	61.0	3.7	36.6
Jun-Aug 1973	40,939	25,908	24,965	943	15,030	63.3	61.0	3.6	36.7
Jul-Sep 1973	40,952	25,899	24,972	927	15,053	63.2	61.0	3.6	36.8
Aug-Oct 1973	40,965	25,898	24,984	913	15,067	63.2	61.0	3.5	36.8
Sep-Nov 1973	40,978	25,898	24,997	901	15,080	63.2	61.0	3.5	36.8
Oct-Dec 1973	40,991	25,887	24,999	888	15,104	63.2	61.0	3.4	36.8
Nov-Jan 1974	41,004	25,891	25,000	892	15,113	63.1	61.0	3.4	36.9
Dec-Feb 1974	41,018	25,899	24,995	904	15,119	63.1	60.9	3.5	36.9
Jan-Mar 1974	41,031	25,908	24,984	923	15,123	63.1	60.9	3.6	36.9
Feb-Apr 1974	41,044	25,916	24,984	931	15,128	63.1	60.9	3.6	36.9
Mar-May 1974	41,057	25,919	24,985	933	15,138	63.1	60.9	3.6	36.9
Apr-Jun 1974	41,070	25,940	25,002	937	15,131	63.2	60.9	3.6	36.8
May-Jul 1974	41,083	25,961	25,020	941	15,122	63.2	60.9	3.6	36.8
Jun-Aug 1974	41,096	25,995	25,044	951	15,102	63.3	60.9	3.7	36.7
Jul-Sep 1974	41,112	26,024	25,066	958	15,088	63.3	61.0	3.7	36.7
Aug-Oct 1974	41,127	26,042	25,077	965	15,085	63.3	61.0	3.7	36.7
Sep-Nov 1974	41,142	26,044	25,075	969	15,098	63.3	60.9	3.7	36.7
Oct-Dec 1974	41,158	26,041	25,065	976	15,117	63.3	60.9	3.7	36.7
Nov-Jan 1975	41,173	26,033	25,044	989	15,140	63.2	60.8	3.8	36.8
Dec-Feb 1975	41,189	26,025	25,018	1,007	15,164	63.2	60.7	3.9	36.8
Jan-Mar 1975	41,204	26,025	24,996	1,029	15,179	63.2	60.7	4.0	36.8
Feb-Apr 1975	41,219	26,036	24,980	1,055	15,184	63.2	60.6	4.1	36.8
Mar-May 1975	41,235	26,054	24,965	1,089	15,180	63.2	60.5	4.2	36.8
Apr-Jun 1975	41,250	26,081	24,955	1,126	15,169	63.2	60.5	4.3	36.8
May-Jul 1975	41,265	26,107	24,945	1,162	15,158	63.3	60.4	4.5	36.7
Jun-Aug 1975	41,281	26,127	24,934	1,193	15,154	63.3	60.4	4.6	36.7
Jul-Sep 1975	41,300	26,139	24,918	1,221	15,161	63.3	60.3	4.7	36.7
Aug-Oct 1975	41,319	26,149	24,897	1,252	15,170	63.3	60.3	4.8	36.7
Sep-Nov 1975	41,338	26,167	24,880	1,286	15,172	63.3	60.2	4.9	36.7
Oct-Dec 1975	41,358	26,183	24,864	1,319	15,175	63.3	60.1	5.0	36.7

Labour Force Survey, summary by sex United Kingdom (thousands) seasonally adjusted (Continued)

All aged 16 & over

	All aged 16 & over	Total economically active	Total in employment	Unemployed	Economically inactive	Economic Activity rate (%)	Employment rate (%)	Unemployment rate (%)	Economic inactivity rate (%)
	1	2	3	4	5	6	7	8	9
All Persons	MGSL	MGSF	MGRZ	MGSC	MGSI	MGWG	MGSR	MGSX	YBTC
Nov-Jan 1976	41,377	26,190	24,847	1,343	15,187	63.3	60.1	5.1	36.7
Dec-Feb 1976	41,396	26,188	24,825	1,363	15,208	63.3	60.0	5.2	36.7
Jan-Mar 1976	41,415	26,187	24,809	1,379	15,228	63.2	59.9	5.3	36.8
Feb-Apr 1976	41,435	26,185	24,793	1,392	15,250	63.2	59.8	5.3	36.8
Mar-May 1976	41,454	26,193	24,788	1,405	15,261	63.2	59.8	5.4	36.8
Apr-Jun 1976	41,473	26,192	24,779	1,413	15,281	63.2	59.7	5.4	36.8
May-Jul 1976	41,492	26,195	24,776	1,419	15,298	63.1	59.7	5.4	36.9
Jun-Aug 1976	41,512	26,196	24,772	1,425	15,315	63.1	59.7	5.4	36.9
Jul-Sep 1976	41,535	26,198	24,768	1,430	15,336	63.1	59.6	5.5	36.9
Aug-Oct 1976	41,558	26,203	24,771	1,432	15,355	63.1	59.6	5.5	36.9
Sep-Nov 1976	41,581	26,210	24,779	1,431	15,371	63.0	59.6	5.5	37.0
Oct-Dec 1976	41,604	26,220	24,788	1,432	15,384	63.0	59.6	5.5	37.0
Nov-Jan 1977	41,627	26,232	24,797	1,435	15,395	63.0	59.6	5.5	37.0
Dec-Feb 1977	41,650	26,236	24,800	1,436	15,414	63.0	59.5	5.5	37.0
Jan-Mar 1977	41,674	26,239	24,803	1,436	15,434	63.0	59.5	5.5	37.0
Feb-Apr 1977	41,697	26,238	24,801	1,437	15,459	62.9	59.5	5.5	37.1
Mar-May 1977	41,720	26,240	24,799	1,441	15,480	62.9	59.4	5.5	37.1
Apr Jun 1977	41,743	26,254	24,802	1,452	15,489	62.9	59.4	5.5	37.1
May-Jul 1977	41,766	26,267	24,800	1,467	15,499	62.9	59.4	5.6	37.1
Jun-Aug 1977	41,789	26,285	24,804	1,481	15,504	62.9	59.4	5.6	37.1
Jul-Sep 1977	41,813	26,302	24,809	1,493	15,511	62.9	59.3	5.7	37.1
Aug-Oct 1977	41,837	26,312	24,813	1,498	15,526	62.9	59.3	5.7	37.1
Sep-Nov 1977	41,862	26,319	24,818	1,502	15,542	62.9	59.3	5.7	37.1
Oct-Dec 1977	41,886	26,321	24,822	1,499	15,565	62.8	59.3	5.7	37.2
Nov-Jan 1978	41,910	26,326	24,833	1,493	15,584	62.8	59.3	5.7	37.2
Dec-Feb 1978	41,934	26,328	24,844	1,484	15,606	62.8	59.2	5.6	37.2
Jan-Mar 1978	41,958	26,336	24,862	1,474	15,622	62.8	59.3	5.6	37.2
Feb-Apr 1978	41,982	26,343	24,874	1,469	15,639	62.7	59.3	5.6	37.3
Mar-May 1978	42,006	26,352	24,886	1,466	15,654	62.7	59.2	5.6	37.3
Apr-Jun 1978	42,030	26,360	24,897	1,463	15,670	62.7	59.2	5.6	37.3
May-Jul 1978	42,054	26,367	24,908	1,459	15,687	62.7	59.2	5.5	37.3
Jun-Aug 1978	42,079	26,378	24,919	1,459	15,701	62.7	59.2	5.5	37.3
Jul-Sep 1978	42,105	26,396	24,941	1,455	15,709	62.7	59.2	5.5	37.3
Aug-Oct 1978	42,132	26,425	24,975	1,449	15,708	62.7	59.3	5.5	37.3
Sep-Nov 1978	42,159	26,452	25,017	1,435	15,708	62.7	59.3	5.4	37.3
Oct-Dec 1978	42,186	26,480	25,059	1,421	15,706	62.8	59.4	5.4	37.2
Nov-Jan 1979	42,213	26,501	25,087	1,413	15,713	62.8	59.4	5.3	37.2
Dec-Feb 1979	42,240	26,523	25,106	1,417	15,718	62.8	59.4	5.3	37.2
Jan-Mar 1979	42,267	26,533	25,113	1,420	15,734	62.8	59.4	5.4	37.2
Feb-Apr 1979	42,294	26,535	25,121	1,414	15,759	62.7	59.4	5.3	37.3
Mar-May 1979	42,321	26,541	25,136	1,405	15,780	62.7	59.4	5.3	37.3
Apr-Jun 1979	42,348	26,565	25,159	1,405	15,783	62.7	59.4	5.3	37.3
May-Jul 1979	42,375	26,602	25,186	1,415	15,773	62.8	59.4	5.3	37.2
Jun-Aug 1979	42,402	26,633	25,211	1,422	15,769	62.8	59.5	5.3	37.2
Jul-Sep 1979	42,432	26,659	25,229	1,430	15,773	62.8	59.5	5.4	37.2
Aug-Oct 1979	42,462	26,689	25,248	1,441	15,772	62.9	59.5	5.4	37.1
Sep-Nov 1979	42,491	26,718	25,265	1,453	15,773	62.9	59.5	5.4	37.1
Oct-Dec 1979	42,521	26,750	25,280	1,471	15,770	62.9	59.5	5.5	37.1
Nov-Jan 1980	42,551	26,769	25,280	1,490	15,781	62.9	59.4	5.6	37.1
Dec-Feb 1980	42,580	26,791	25,270	1,521	15,789	62.9	59.3	5.7	37.1
Jan-Mar 1980	42,610	26,808	25,250	1,558	15,802	62.9	59.3	5.8	37.1
Feb-Apr 1980	42,639	26,837	25,235	1,603	15,802	62.9	59.2	6.0	37.1
Mar-May 1980	42,669	26,863	25,215	1,648	15,806	63.0	59.1	6.1	37.0
Apr-Jun 1980	42,699	26,890	25,190	1,700	15,809	63.0	59.0	6.3	37.0
May-Jul 1980	42,728	26,916	25,160	1,756	15,812	63.0	58.9	6.5	37.0
Jun-Aug 1980	42,758	26,938	25,110	1,828	15,820	63.0	58.7	6.8	37.0
Jul-Sep 1980	42,784	26,955	25,050	1,905	15,829	63.0	58.5	7.1	37.0
Aug-Oct 1980	42,810	26,974	24,985	1,989	15,836	63.0	58.4	7.4	37.0
Sep-Nov 1980	42,836	26,992	24,915	2,077	15,844	63.0	58.2	7.7	37.0
Oct-Dec 1980	42,862	27,024	24,855	2,169	15,837	63.1	58.0	8.0	36.9

Labour Force Survey, summary by sex United Kingdom (thousands) seasonally adjusted (Continued)

All aged 16 & over

	All aged 16 & over	Total economically active	Total in employment	Unemployed	Economically inactive	Economic Activity rate (%)	Employment rate (%)	Unemployment rate (%)	Economic inactivity rate (%)
	1	2	3	4	5	6	7	8	9
All Persons	MGSL	MGSF	MGRZ	MGSC	MGSI	MGWG	MGSR	MGSX	YBTC
Nov-Jan 1981	42,888	27,040	24,785	2,255	15,847	63.0	57.8	8.3	37.0
Dec-Feb 1981	42,914	27,050	24,720	2,330	15,863	63.0	57.6	8.6	37.0
Jan-Mar 1981	42,940	27,063	24,661	2,403	15,876	63.0	57.4	8.9	37.0
Feb-Apr 1981	42,965	27,082	24,606	2,476	15,883	63.0	57.3	9.1	37.0
Mar-May 1981	42,991	27,093	24,549	2,544	15,898	63.0	57.1	9.4	37.0
Apr-Jun 1981	43,017	27,082	24,495	2,588	15,935	63.0	56.9	9.6	37.0
May-Jul 1981	43,043	27,068	24,444	2,624	15,975	62.9	56.8	9.7	37.1
Jun-Aug 1981	43,069	27,053	24,398	2,654	16,016	62.8	56.6	9.8	37.2
Jul-Sep 1981	43,084	27,039	24,355	2,684	16,045	62.8	56.5	9.9	37.2
Aug-Oct 1981	43,100	27,024	24,311	2,713	16,076	62.7	56.4	10.0	37.3
Sep-Nov 1981	43,115	27,001	24,261	2,740	16,114	62.6	56.3	10.1	37.4
Oct-Dec 1981	43,130	26,970	24,209	2,761	16,160	62.5	56.1	10.2	37.5
Nov-Jan 1982	43,146	26,949	24,169	2,780	16,197	62.5	56.0	10.3	37.5
Dec-Feb 1982	43,161	26,931	24,139	2,792	16,230	62.4	55.9	10.4	37.6
Jan-Mar 1982	43,176	26,923	24,120	2,803	16,254	62.4	55.9	10.4	37.6
Feb-Apr 1982	43,192	26,905	24,092	2,813	16,287	62.3	55.8	10.5	37.7
Mar-May 1982	43,207	26,892	24,067	2,824	16,315	62.2	55.7	10.5	37.8
Apr-Jun 1982	43,222	26,868	24,027	2,841	16,354	62.2	55.6	10.6	37.8
May-Jul 1982	43,238	26,848	23,992	2,857	16,389	62.1	55.5	10.6	37.9
Jun-Aug 1982	43,253	26,826	23,949	2,877	16,427	62.0	55.4	10.7	38.0
Jul-Sep 1982	43,274	26,797	23,901	2,897	16,476	61.9	55.2	10.8	38.1
Aug-Oct 1982	43,295	26,769	23,852	2,917	16,526	61.8	55.1	10.9	38.2
Sep-Nov 1982	43,316	26,741	23,803	2,938	16,575	61.7	55.0	11.0	38.3
Oct-Dec 1982	43,337	26,714	23,755	2,960	16,622	61.6	54.8	11.1	38.4
Nov-Jan 1983	43,357	26,688	23,712	2,976	16,670	61.6	54.7	11.2	38.4
Dec-Feb 1983	43,378	26,663	23,675	2,988	16,715	61.5	54.6	11.2	38.5
Jan-Mar 1983	43,399	26,649	23,651	2,998	16,750	61.4	54.5	11.3	38.6
Feb-Apr 1983	43,420	26,644	23,636	3,008	16,776	61.4	54.4	11.3	38.6
Mar-May 1983	43,441	26,653	23,630	3,023	16,788	61.4	54.4	11.3	38.6
Apr-Jun 1983	43,462	26,696	23,647	3,049	16,765	61.4	54.4	11.4	38.6
May-Jul 1983	43,483	26,762	23,687	3,074	16,721	61.5	54.5	11.5	38.5
Jun-Aug 1983	43,504	26,834	23,741	3,093	16,670	61.7	54.6	11.5	38.3
Jul-Sep 1983	43,527	26,918	23,809	3,109	16,608	61.8	54.7	11.5	38.2
Aug-Oct 1983	43,549	27,004	23,879	3,125	16,545	62.0	54.8	11.6	38.0
Sep-Nov 1983	43,572	27,094	23,947	3,146	16,478	62.2	55.0	11.6	37.8
Oct-Dec 1983	43,595	27,161	23,994	3,167	16,434	62.3	55.0	11.7	37.7
Nov-Jan 1984	43,618	27,234	24,044	3,189	16,384	62.4	55.1	11.7	37.6
Dec-Feb 1984	43,641	27,300	24,085	3,215	16,340	62.6	55.2	11.8	37.4
Jan-Mar 1984	43,664	27,368	24,125	3,243	16,296	62.7	55.3	11.8	37.3
Feb-Apr 1984	43,687	27,428	24,165	3,263	16,258	62.8	55.3	11.9	37.2
Mar-May 1984	43,709	27,485	24,208	3,278	16,224	62.9	55.4	11.9	37.1
Apr-Jun 1984	43,732	27,510	24,245	3,265	16,222	62.9	55.4	11.9	37.1
May-Jul 1984	43,755	27,530	24,275	3,256	16,225	62.9	55.5	11.8	37.1
Jun-Aug 1984	43,778	27,547	24,305	3,242	16,231	62.9	55.5	11.8	37.1
Jul-Sep 1984	43,801	27,573	24,335	3,238	16,228	63.0	55.6	11.7	37.0
Aug-Oct 1984	43,824	27,603	24,370	3,233	16,220	63.0	55.6	11.7	37.0
Sep-Nov 1984	43,846	27,629	24,400	3,229	16,218	63.0	55.6	11.7	37.0
Oct-Dec 1984	43,869	27,652	24,435	3,217	16,217	63.0	55.7	11.6	37.0
Nov-Jan 1985	43,892	27,676	24,470	3,206	16,216	63.1	55.8	11.6	36.9
Dec-Feb 1985	43,915	27,685	24,490	3,195	16,230	63.0	55.8	11.5	37.0
Jan-Mar 1985	43,937	27,695	24,515	3,180	16,243	63.0	55.8	11.5	37.0
Feb-Apr 1985	43,960	27,709	24,540	3,169	16,251	63.0	55.8	11.4	37.0
Mar-May 1985	43,983	27,710	24,554	3,156	16,273	63.0	55.8	11.4	37.0
Apr-Jun 1985	44,006	27,722	24,570	3,152	16,284	63.0	55.8	11.4	37.0
May-Jul 1985	44,029	27,735	24,590	3,145	16,294	63.0	55.8	11.3	37.0
Jun-Aug 1985	44,051	27,749	24,610	3,139	16,302	63.0	55.9	11.3	37.0
Jul-Sep 1985	44,069	27,762	24,625	3,137	16,307	63.0	55.9	11.3	37.0
Aug-Oct 1985	44,087	27,770	24,635	3,135	16,317	63.0	55.9	11.3	37.0
Sep-Nov 1985	44,104	27,783	24,650	3,133	16,321	63.0	55.9	11.3	37.0
Oct-Dec 1985	44,122	27,795	24,660	3,135	16,328	63.0	55.9	11.3	37.0

Labour Force Survey, summary by sex United Kingdom (thousands) seasonally adjusted (Continued)

All aged 16 & over	All aged 16 & over	Total economically active	Total in employment	Unemployed	Economically inactive	Economic Activity rate (%)	Employment rate (%)	Unemployment rate (%)	Economic inactivity rate (%)
	1	2	3	4	5	6	7	8	9
All Persons	MGSL	MGSF	MGRZ	MGSC	MGSI	MGWG	MGSR	MGSX	YBTC
Nov-Jan 1986	44,140	27,798	24,660	3,138	16,342	63.0	55.9	11.3	37.0
Dec-Feb 1986	44,158	27,813	24,670	3,143	16,345	63.0	55.9	11.3	37.0
Jan-Mar 1986	44,175	27,820	24,670	3,150	16,356	63.0	55.8	11.3	37.0
Feb-Apr 1986	44,193	27,826	24,675	3,151	16,367	63.0	55.8	11.3	37.0
Mar-May 1986	44,211	27,837	24,683	3,154	16,373	63.0	55.8	11.3	37.0
Apr-Jun 1986	44,228	27,853	24,695	3,159	16,375	63.0	55.8	11.3	37.0
May-Jul 1986	44,246	27,888	24,720	3,168	16,358	63.0	55.9	11.4	37.0
Jun-Aug 1986	44,264	27,915	24,740	3,175	16,348	63.1	55.9	11.4	36.9
Jul-Sep 1986	44,282	27,947	24,770	3,177	16,335	63.1	55.9	11.4	36.9
Aug-Oct 1986	44,299	27,971	24,800	3,171	16,328	63.1	56.0	11.3	36.9
Sep-Nov 1986	44,317	27,995	24,830	3,165	16,323	63.2	56.0	11.3	36.8
Oct-Dec 1986	44,335	28,006	24,850	3,156	16,330	63.2	56.1	11.3	36.8
Nov-Jan 1987	44,353	28,025	24,875	3,150	16,328	63.2	56.1	11.2	36.8
Dec-Feb 1987	44,371	28,034	24,900	3,134	16,337	63.2	56.1	11.2	36.8
Jan-Mar 1987	44,389	28,038	24,925	3,113	16,351	63.2	56.2	11.1	36.8
Feb-Apr 1987	44,407	28,060	24,970	3,090	16,347	63.2	56.2	11.0	36.8
Mar-May 1987	44,425	28,092	25,031	3,061	16,333	63.2	56.3	10.9	36.8
Apr-Jun 1987	44,443	28,131	25,110	3,021	16,312	63.3	56.5	10.7	36.7
May-Jul 1987	44,461	28,163	25,190	2,973	16,298	63.3	56.7	10.6	36.7
Jun-Aug 1987	44,479	28,199	25,270	2,929	16,279	63.4	56.8	10.4	36.6
Jul-Sep 1987	44,491	28,230	25,345	2,885	16,261	63.5	57.0	10.2	36.5
Aug-Oct 1987	44,504	28,258	25,420	2,838	16,245	63.5	57.1	10.0	36.5
Sep-Nov 1987	44,516	28,283	25,495	2,788	16,233	63.5	57.3	9.9	36.5
Oct-Dec 1987	44,528	28,316	25,575	2,741	16,212	63.6	57.4	9.7	36.4
Nov-Jan 1988	44,541	28,352	25,655	2,697	16,189	63.7	57.6	9.5	36.3
Dec-Feb 1988	44,553	28,387	25,730	2,657	16,166	63.7	57.8	9.4	36.3
Jan-Mar 1988	44,565	28,407	25,795	2,613	16,158	63.7	57.9	9.2	36.3
Feb-Apr 1988	44,578	28,429	25,860	2,569	16,149	63.8	58.0	9.0	36.2
Mar-May 1988	44,590	28,439	25,913	2,526	16,152	63.8	58.1	8.9	36.2
Apr-Jun 1988	44,603	28,460	25,970	2,490	16,143	63.8	58.2	8.7	36.2
May-Jul 1988	44,615	28,482	26,030	2,452	16,133	63.8	58.3	8.6	36.2
Jun-Aug 1988	44,627	28,516	26,100	2,416	16,112	63.9	58.5	8.5	36.1
Jul-Sep 1988	44,640	28,545	26,160	2,385	16,094	63.9	58.6	8.4	36.1
Aug-Oct 1988	44,652	28,591	26,230	2,361	16,061	64.0	58.7	8.3	36.0
Sep-Nov 1988	44,664	28,623	26,290	2,333	16,041	64.1	58.9	8.2	35.9
Oct-Dec 1988	44,676	28,648	26,355	2,293	16,028	64.1	59.0	8.0	35.9
Nov-Jan 1989	44,688	28,683	26,430	2,253	16,005	64.2	59.1	7.9	35.8
Dec-Feb 1989	44,701	28,723	26,510	2,213	15,977	64.3	59.3	7.7	35.7
Jan-Mar 1989	44,713	28,769	26,590	2,179	15,944	64.3	59.5	7.6	35.7
Feb-Apr 1989	44,725	28,800	26,660	2,140	15,925	64.4	59.6	7.4	35.6
Mar-May 1989	44,737	28,815	26,709	2,106	15,922	64.4	59.7	7.3	35.6
Apr-Jun 1989	44,750	28,813	26,730	2,083	15,937	64.4	59.7	7.2	35.6
May-Jul 1989	44,762	28,821	26,750	2,071	15,941	64.4	59.8	7.2	35.6
Jun-Aug 1989	44,774	28,832	26,775	2,057	15,942	64.4	59.8	7.1	35.6
Jul-Sep 1989	44,782	28,840	26,795	2,045	15,942	64.4	59.8	7.1	35.6
Aug-Oct 1989	44,790	28,854	26,820	2,034	15,935	64.4	59.9	7.1	35.6
Sep-Nov 1989	44,798	28,877	26,850	2,027	15,920	64.5	59.9	7.0	35.5
Oct-Dec 1989	44,805	28,901	26,880	2,021	15,905	64.5	60.0	7.0	35.5
Nov-Jan 1990	44,813	28,902	26,890	2,012	15,912	64.5	60.0	7.0	35.5
Dec-Feb 1990	44,821	28,906	26,900	2,006	15,915	64.5	60.0	6.9	35.5
Jan-Mar 1990	44,829	28,904	26,900	2,004	15,925	64.5	60.0	6.9	35.5
Feb-Apr 1990	44,836	28,914	26,910	2,004	15,923	64.5	60.0	6.9	35.5
Mar-May 1990	44,844	28,925	26,922	2,004	15,919	64.5	60.0	6.9	35.5
Apr-Jun 1990	44,852	28,937	26,935	2,002	15,915	64.5	60.1	6.9	35.5
May-Jul 1990	44,860	28,954	26,945	2,009	15,906	64.5	60.1	6.9	35.5
Jun-Aug 1990	44,868	28,954	26,930	2,024	15,913	64.5	60.0	7.0	35.5
Jul-Sep 1990	44,875	28,949	26,900	2,049	15,926	64.5	59.9	7.1	35.5
Aug-Oct 1990	44,883	28,934	26,855	2,079	15,949	64.5	59.8	7.2	35.5
Sep-Nov 1990	44,890	28,920	26,805	2,115	15,970	64.4	59.7	7.3	35.6
Oct-Dec 1990	44,898	28,908	26,750	2,158	15,990	64.4	59.6	7.5	35.6

Labour Force Survey, summary by sex United Kingdom (thousands) seasonally adjusted (Continued)

All aged 16 & over

	All aged 16 & over	Total economically active	Total in employment	Unemployed	Economically inactive	Economic Activity rate (%)	Employment rate (%)	Unemployment rate (%)	Economic inactivity rate (%)
	1	2	3	4	5	6	7	8	9
All Persons	MGSL	MGSF	MGRZ	MGSC	MGSI	MGWG	MGSR	MGSX	YBTC
Nov-Jan 1991	44,905	28,881	26,685	2,196	16,025	64.3	59.4	7.6	35.7
Dec-Feb 1991	44,913	28,859	26,615	2,244	16,053	64.3	59.3	7.8	35.7
Jan-Mar 1991	44,920	28,836	26,530	2,306	16,085	64.2	59.1	8.0	35.8
Feb-Apr 1991	44,928	28,828	26,450	2,378	16,100	64.2	58.9	8.2	35.8
Mar-May 1991	44,935	28,807	26,365	2,442	16,128	64.1	58.7	8.5	35.9
Apr-Jun 1991	44,941	28,767	26,275	2,492	16,174	64.0	58.5	8.7	36.0
May-Jul 1991	44,947	28,730	26,190	2,540	16,217	63.9	58.3	8.8	36.1
Jun-Aug 1991	44,952	28,690	26,105	2,585	16,262	63.8	58.1	9.0	36.2
Jul-Sep 1991	44,958	28,649	26,025	2,624	16,309	63.7	57.9	9.2	36.3
Aug-Oct 1991	44,964	28,607	25,955	2,652	16,357	63.6	57.7	9.3	36.4
Sep-Nov 1991	44,970	28,560	25,885	2,675	16,409	63.5	57.6	9.4	36.5
Oct-Dec 1991	44,975	28,517	25,820	2,697	16,459	63.4	57.4	9.5	36.6
Nov-Jan 1992	44,981	28,489	25,775	2,714	16,492	63.3	57.3	9.5	36.7
Dec-Feb 1992	44,987	28,476	25,740	2,735	16,511	63.3	57.2	9.6	36.7
Jan-Mar 1992	44,992	28,472	25,710	2,762	16,520	63.3	57.1	9.7	36.7
Feb-Apr 1992	44,998	28,467	25,685	2,782	16,531	63.3	57.1	9.8	36.7
Mar-May 1992	44,997	28,428	25,632	2,796	16,569	63.2	57.0	9.8	36.7
Apr-Jun 1992	45,001	28,376	25,597	2,780	16,624	63.1	56.9	9.8	36.8
May-Jul 1992	45,004	28,338	25,532	2,807	16,666	63.0	56.7	9.9	36.9
Jun-Aug 1992	45,008	28,337	25,518	2,819	16,671	63.0	56.7	9.9	37.0
Jul-Sep 1992	45,010	28,320	25,503	2,817	16,689	62.9	56.7	9.9	37.0
Aug-Oct 1992	45,012	28,302	25,449	2,853	16,710	62.9	56.5	10.1	37.1
Sep-Nov 1992	45,014	28,305	25,404	2,901	16,709	62.9	56.4	10.3	37.1
Oct-Dec 1992	45,016	28,267	25,335	2,932	16,749	62.8	56.3	10.4	37.1
Nov-Jan 1993	45,018	28,285	25,299	2,986	16,734	62.8	56.2	10.6	37.2
Dec-Feb 1993	45,020	28,300	25,273	3,027	16,720	62.9	56.1	10.7	37.2
Jan-Mar 1993	45,023	28,286	25,283	3,003	16,736	62.8	56.2	10.6	37.1
Feb-Apr 1993	45,025	28,244	25,256	2,988	16,781	62.7	56.1	10.6	37.2
Mar-May 1993	45,027	28,234	25,281	2,953	16,793	62.7	56.1	10.5	37.3
Apr-Jun 1993	45,029	28,218	25,284	2,934	16,811	62.7	56.2	10.4	37.3
May-Jul 1993	45,031	28,215	25,283	2,932	16,816	62.7	56.1	10.4	37.3
Jun-Aug 1993	45,033	28,177	25,268	2,909	16,856	62.6	56.1	10.3	37.3
Jul-Sep 1993	45,037	28,200	25,308	2,892	16,837	62.6	56.2	10.3	37.4
Aug-Oct 1993	45,042	28,208	25,314	2,894	16,834	62.6	56.2	10.3	37.4
Sep-Nov 1993	45,046	28,202	25,315	2,887	16,844	62.6	56.2	10.2	37.4
Oct-Dec 1993	45,050	28,214	25,325	2,889	16,836	62.6	56.2	10.2	37.4
Nov-Jan 1993	45,054	28,211	25,318	2,893	16,843	62.6	56.2	10.3	37.4
Dec-Feb 1994	45,059	28,208	25,361	2,847	16,851	62.6	56.3	10.1	37.4
Jan-Mar 1994	45,063	28,213	25,408	2,804	16,850	62.6	56.4	9.9	37.4
Feb-Apr 1994	45,067	28,217	25,449	2,768	16,851	62.6	56.5	9.8	37.4
Mar-May 1994	45,072	28,201	25,451	2,750	16,871	62.6	56.5	9.8	37.4
Apr-Jun 1994	45,076	28,181	25,445	2,737	16,895	62.5	56.4	9.7	37.4
May-Jul 1994	45,080	28,215	25,508	2,707	16,865	62.6	56.6	9.6	37.5
Jun-Aug 1994	45,084	28,202	25,511	2,691	16,883	62.6	56.6	9.5	37.4
Jul-Sep 1994	45,096	28,193	25,554	2,639	16,903	62.5	56.7	9.4	37.4
Aug-Oct 1994	45,108	28,164	25,556	2,608	16,944	62.4	56.7	9.3	37.5
Sep-Nov 1994	45,119	28,146	25,590	2,557	16,973	62.4	56.7	9.1	37.6
Oct-Dec 1994	45,131	28,117	25,598	2,520	17,014	62.3	56.7	9.0	37.6
Nov-Jan 1994	45,143	28,078	25,580	2,498	17,064	62.2	56.7	8.9	37.7
Dec-Feb 1995	45,154	28,131	25,635	2,497	17,023	62.3	56.8	8.9	37.8
Jan-Mar 1995	45,166	28,166	25,671	2,495	17,000	62.4	56.8	8.9	37.7
Feb-Apr 1995	45,178	28,191	25,703	2,487	16,987	62.4	56.9	8.8	37.6
Mar-May 1995	45,189	28,202	25,731	2,470	16,988	62.4	56.9	8.8	37.6
Apr-Jun 1995	45,201	28,208	25,767	2,441	16,993	62.4	57.0	8.7	37.6
May-Jul 1995	45,212	28,232	25,787	2,445	16,981	62.4	57.0	8.7	37.6
Jun-Aug 1995	45,224	28,269	25,835	2,433	16,955	62.5	57.1	8.6	37.6
Jul-Sep 1995	45,237	28,292	25,848	2,444	16,945	62.5	57.1	8.6	37.5
Aug-Oct 1995	45,250	28,300	25,864	2,436	16,950	62.5	57.2	8.6	37.5
Sep-Nov 1995	45,263	28,307	25,886	2,421	16,956	62.5	57.2	8.6	37.5
Oct-Dec 1995	45,276	28,331	25,979	2,352	16,946	62.6	57.4	8.3	37.4

Labour Force Survey, summary by sex United Kingdom (thousands) seasonally adjusted (Continued)

All aged 16 & over	All aged 16 & over	Total economically active	Total in employment	Unemployed	Economically inactive	Economic Activity rate (%)	Employment rate (%)	Unemployment rate (%)	Economic inactivity rate (%)
	1	2	3	4	5	6	7	8	9
All Persons	MGSL	MGSF	MGRZ	MGSC	MGSI	MGWG	MGSR	MGSX	YBTC
Nov-Jan 1996	45,289	28,362	25,984	2,378	16,927	62.6	57.4	8.4	37.4
Dec-Feb 1996	45,302	28,339	25,981	2,358	16,964	62.6	57.3	8.3	37.4
Jan-Mar 1996	45,316	28,300	25,971	2,329	17,016	62.5	57.3	8.2	37.5
Feb-Apr 1996	45,329	28,324	25,977	2,347	17,004	62.5	57.3	8.3	37.5
Mar-May 1996	45,342	28,345	26,000	2,344	16,997	62.5	57.3	8.3	37.5
Apr-Jun 1996	45,355	28,345	26,009	2,336	17,010	62.5	57.3	8.2	37.5
May-Jul 1996	45,368	28,314	26,004	2,311	17,054	62.4	57.3	8.2	37.6
Jun-Aug 1996	45,381	28,343	26,064	2,279	17,038	62.5	57.4	8.0	37.5
Jul-Sep 1996	45,394	28,342	26,062	2,280	17,052	62.4	57.4	8.0	37.6
Aug-Oct 1996	45,407	28,402	26,118	2,284	17,004	62.6	57.5	8.0	37.4
Sep-Nov 1996	45,419	28,434	26,174	2,261	16,985	62.6	57.6	8.0	37.4
Oct-Dec 1996	45,432	28,424	26,197	2,227	17,008	62.6	57.7	7.8	37.4
Nov-Jan 1997	45,445	28,438	26,257	2,181	17,007	62.6	57.8	7.7	37.4
Dec-Feb 1997	45,458	28,459	26,328	2,131	16,999	62.6	57.9	7.5	37.4
Jan-Mar 1997	45,471	28,463	26,380	2,082	17,008	62.6	58.0	7.3	37.4
Feb-Apr 1997	45,484	28,477	26,427	2,050	17,007	62.6	58.1	7.2	37.4
Mar-May 1997	45,497	28,492	26,448	2,045	17,004	62.6	58.1	7.2	37.4
Apr-Jun 1997	45,509	28,561	26,513	2,048	16,949	62.8	58.3	7.2	37.2
May-Jul 1997	45,522	28,572	26,492	2,080	16,950	62.8	58.2	7.3	37.2
Jun-Aug 1997	45,535	28,527	26,512	2,015	17,008	62.6	58.2	7.1	37.4
Jul-Sep 1997	45,549	28,519	26,572	1,947	17,030	62.6	58.3	6.8	37.4
Aug-Oct 1997	45,563	28,509	26,603	1,906	17,054	62.6	58.4	6.7	37.4
Sep-Nov 1997	45,577	28,506	26,622	1,884	17,071	62.5	58.4	6.6	37.5
Oct-Dec 1997	45,591	28,497	26,636	1,860	17,094	62.5	58.4	6.5	37.5
Nov-Jan 1998	45,605	28,453	26,634	1,819	17,152	62.4	58.4	6.4	37.6
Dec-Feb 1998	45,619	28,485	26,671	1,814	17,134	62.4	58.5	6.4	37.6
Jan-Mar 1998	45,633	28,492	26,682	1,810	17,141	62.4	58.5	6.4	37.6
Feb-Apr 1998	45,647	28,509	26,713	1,796	17,138	62.5	58.5	6.3	37.5
Mar-May 1998	45,661	28,497	26,713	1,783	17,164	62.4	58.5	6.3	37.6
Apr-Jun 1998	45,675	28,509	26,721	1,788	17,166	62.4	58.5	6.3	37.6
May-Jul 1998	45,689	28,572	26,776	1,796	17,117	62.5	58.6	6.3	37.5
Jun-Aug 1998	45,703	28,629	26,829	1,800	17,074	62.6	58.7	6.3	37.4
Jul-Sep 1998	45,721	28,615	26,832	1,783	17,106	62.6	58.7	6.2	37.4
Aug-Oct 1998	45,738	28,655	26,874	1,781	17,083	62.7	58.8	6.2	37.3
Sep-Nov 1998	45,756	28,699	26,931	1,767	17,057	62.7	58.9	6.2	37.3
Oct-Dec 1998	45,774	28,709	26,946	1,763	17,065	62.7	58.9	6.1	37.3
Nov-Jan 1999	45,791	28,785	26,996	1,789	17,007	62.9	59.0	6.2	37.1
Dec-Feb 1999	45,809	28,821	27,029	1,792	16,988	62.9	59.0	6.2	37.1
Jan-Mar 1999	45,827	28,811	27,035	1,775	17,016	62.9	59.0	6.2	37.1
Feb-Apr 1999	45,845	28,810	27,039	1,771	17,035	62.8	59.0	6.1	37.2
Mar-May 1999	45,862	28,811	27,052	1,759	17,051	62.8	59.0	6.1	37.2
Apr-Jun 1999	45,880	28,833	27,090	1,743	17,047	62.8	59.0	6.0	37.2
May-Jul 1999	45,898	28,829	27,108	1,722	17,068	62.8	59.1	6.0	37.2
Jun-Aug 1999	45,916	28,863	27,162	1,701	17,053	62.9	59.2	5.9	37.1
Jul-Sep 1999	45,937	28,907	27,206	1,702	17,030	62.9	59.2	5.9	37.1
Aug-Oct 1999	45,958	28,887	27,201	1,686	17,071	62.9	59.2	5.8	37.1
Sep-Nov 1999	45,979	28,947	27,255	1,692	17,032	63.0	59.3	5.8	37.0
Oct-Dec 1999	46,001	28,987	27,302	1,684	17,014	63.0	59.4	5.8	37.0
Nov-Jan 2000	46,022	28,999	27,300	1,700	17,022	63.0	59.3	5.9	37.0
Dec-Feb 2000	46,043	29,004	27,322	1,682	17,039	63.0	59.3	5.8	37.0
Jan-Mar 2000	46,064	29,038	27,363	1,675	17,026	63.0	59.4	5.8	37.0
Feb-Apr 2000	46,085	29,052	27,401	1,651	17,034	63.0	59.5	5.7	37.0
Mar-May 2000	46,107	29,071	27,434	1,638	17,035	63.1	59.5	5.6	36.9
Apr-Jun 2000	46,128	29,061	27,461	1,599	17,067	63.0	59.5	5.5	37.0
May-Jul 2000	46,149	29,069	27,521	1,548	17,080	63.0	59.6	5.3	37.0
Jun-Aug 2000	46,170	29,080	27,557	1,523	17,090	63.0	59.7	5.2	37.0
Jul-Sep 2000	46,197	29,087	27,542	1,545	17,110	63.0	59.6	5.3	37.0
Aug-Oct 2000	46,224	29,085	27,517	1,568	17,139	62.9	59.5	5.4	37.1
Sep-Nov 2000	46,251	29,039	27,502	1,537	17,213	62.8	59.5	5.3	37.2
Oct-Dec 2000	46,278	29,045	27,524	1,521	17,233	62.8	59.5	5.2	37.2

Labour Force Survey, summary by sex United Kingdom (thousands) seasonally adjusted (Continued)

All aged 16 & over

	All aged 16 & over	Total economically active	Total in employment	Unemployed	Economically inactive	Economic Activity rate (%)	Employment rate (%)	Unemployment rate (%)	Economic inactivity rate (%)
	1	2	3	4	5	6	7	8	9
All Persons	MGSL	MGSF	MGRZ	MGSC	MGSI	MGWG	MGSR	MGSX	YBTC
Nov-Jan 2001	46,305	29,135	27,634	1,501	17,171	62.9	59.7	5.2	37.1
Dec-Feb 2001	46,332	29,147	27,636	1,511	17,185	62.9	59.6	5.2	37.1
Jan-Mar 2001	46,359	29,105	27,634	1,472	17,254	62.8	59.6	5.1	37.2
Feb-Apr 2001	46,386	29,116	27,660	1,456	17,270	62.8	59.6	5.0	37.2
Mar-May 2001	46,413	29,122	27,691	1,431	17,292	62.7	59.7	4.9	37.3
Apr-Jun 2001	46,440	29,167	27,694	1,472	17,274	62.8	59.6	5.0	37.2
May-Jul 2001	46,467	29,159	27,690	1,470	17,308	62.8	59.6	5.0	37.2
Jun-Aug 2001	46,494	29,191	27,714	1,477	17,303	62.8	59.6	5.1	37.2
Jul-Sep 2001	46,518	29,188	27,705	1,483	17,330	62.7	59.6	5.1	37.3
Aug-Oct 2001	46,541	29,210	27,725	1,485	17,331	62.8	59.6	5.1	37.2
Sep-Nov 2001	46,564	29,264	27,770	1,493	17,300	62.8	59.6	5.1	37.2
Oct-Dec 2001	46,587	29,297	27,774	1,523	17,290	62.9	59.6	5.2	37.1
Nov-Jan 2002	46,611	29,282	27,769	1,513	17,328	62.8	59.6	5.2	37.2
Dec-Feb 2002	46,634	29,302	27,802	1,500	17,332	62.8	59.6	5.1	37.2
Jan-Mar 2002	46,657	29,288	27,777	1,511	17,369	62.8	59.5	5.2	37.2
Feb-Apr 2002	46,680	29,354	27,836	1,517	17,326	62.9	59.6	5.2	37.1
Mar-May 2002	46,704	29,399	27,866	1,533	17,305	62.9	59.7	5.2	37.1
Apr-Jun 2002	46,727	29,420	27,905	1,515	17,306	63.0	59.7	5.2	37.0
May-Jul 2002	46,750	29,406	27,884	1,522	17,344	62.9	59.6	5.2	37.1
Jun-Aug 2002	46,773	29,453	27,921	1,532	17,320	63.0	59.7	5.2	37.0
Jul-Sep 2002	46,798	29,473	27,912	1,561	17,325	63.0	59.6	5.3	37.0
Aug-Oct 2002	46,823	29,544	28,001	1,543	17,279	63.1	59.8	5.2	36.9
Sep-Nov 2002	46,847	29,558	28,029	1,529	17,290	63.1	59.8	5.2	36.9
Oct-Dec 2002	46,872	29,588	28,074	1,514	17,284	63.1	59.9	5.1	36.9
Nov-Jan 2003	46,897	29,521	28,045	1,476	17,376	62.9	59.8	5.0	37.1
Dec-Feb 2003	46,921	29,536	28,025	1,511	17,386	62.9	59.7	5.1	37.1
Jan-Mar 2003	46,946	29,588	28,065	1,524	17,358	63.0	59.8	5.1	37.0
Feb-Apr 2003	46,971	29,620	28,110	1,510	17,351	63.1	59.8	5.1	36.9
Mar-May 2003	46,995	29,643	28,167	1,476	17,353	63.1	59.9	5.0	36.9
Apr-Jun 2003	47,020	29,654	28,191	1,463	17,366	63.1	60.0	4.9	36.9
May-Jul 2003	47,045	29,705	28,205	1,500	17,340	63.1	60.0	5.0	36.9
Jun-Aug 2003	47,069	29,684	28,186	1,498	17,386	63.1	59.9	5.0	36.9
Jul-Sep 2003	47,098	29,721	28,222	1,499	17,377	63.1	59.9	5.0	36.9
Aug-Oct 2003	47,126	29,724	28,249	1,476	17,402	63.1	59.9	5.0	36.9
Sep-Nov 2003	47,154	29,709	28,245	1,464	17,445	63.0	59.9	4.9	37.0
Oct-Dec 2003	47,183	29,712	28,254	1,458	17,470	63.0	59.9	4.9	37.0
Nov-Jan 2004	47,211	29,784	28,344	1,441	17,427	63.1	60.0	4.8	36.9
Dec-Feb 2004	47,239	29,814	28,380	1,434	17,425	63.1	60.1	4.8	36.9
Jan-Mar 2004	47,268	29,830	28,398	1,432	17,438	63.1	60.1	4.8	36.9
Feb-Apr 2004	47,296	29,825	28,391	1,434	17,471	63.1	60.0	4.8	36.9
Mar-May 2004	47,324	29,835	28,409	1,426	17,489	63.0	60.0	4.8	37.0
Apr-Jun 2004	47,352	29,844	28,410	1,434	17,509	63.0	60.0	4.8	37.0
May-Jul 2004	47,381	29,830	28,416	1,414	17,551	63.0	60.0	4.7	37.0
Jun-Aug 2004	47,409	29,810	28,414	1,396	17,599	62.9	59.9	4.7	37.1
Jul-Sep 2004	47,444	29,859	28,467	1,392	17,585	62.9	60.0	4.7	37.1
Aug-Oct 2004	47,480	29,881	28,487	1,394	17,598	62.9	60.0	4.7	37.1
Sep-Nov 2004	47,515	29,950	28,542	1,408	17,565	63.0	60.1	4.7	37.0
Oct-Dec 2004	47,550	30,004	28,586	1,418	17,546	63.1	60.1	4.7	36.9
Nov-Jan 2005	47,585	30,047	28,628	1,419	17,539	63.1	60.2	4.7	36.9
Dec-Feb 2005	47,621	30,132	28,693	1,439	17,488	63.3	60.3	4.8	36.7
Jan-Mar 2005	47,656	30,087	28,679	1,409	17,569	63.1	60.2	4.7	36.9
Feb-Apr 2005	47,691	30,071	28,665	1,407	17,620	63.1	60.1	4.7	36.9
Mar-May 2005	47,727	30,101	28,676	1,425	17,626	63.1	60.1	4.7	36.9
Apr-Jun 2005	47,762	30,132	28,698	1,435	17,629	63.1	60.1	4.8	36.9
May-Jul 2005	47,797	30,173	28,755	1,419	17,624	63.1	60.2	4.7	36.9
Jun-Aug 2005	47,832	30,203	28,786	1,418	17,629	63.1	60.2	4.7	36.9
Jul-Sep 2005	47,863	30,259	28,825	1,434	17,605	63.2	60.2	4.7	36.8
Aug-Oct 2005	47,895	30,304	28,813	1,491	17,591	63.3	60.2	4.9	36.7
Sep-Nov 2005	**47,926**	**30,292**	**28,764**	**1,528**	**17,634**	**63.2**	**60.0**	**5.0**	**36.8**

Labour Force Survey, summary by sex United Kingdom (thousands) seasonally adjusted (Continued)

All aged 16 & over

	All aged 16 & over	Total economically active	Total in employment	Unemployed	Economically inactive	Economic Activity rate (%)	Employment rate (%)	Unemployment rate (%)	Economic inactivity rate (%)
	1	2	3	4	5	6	7	8	9
Male	MGSM	MGSG	MGSA	MGSD	MGSJ	MGWH	MGSS	MGSY	YBTD
Jan-Mar 1971	19,265	16,103	15,591	512	3,161	83.6	80.9	3.2	16.4
Feb-Apr 1971	19,275	16,088	15,561	527	3,187	83.5	80.7	3.3	16.5
Mar-May 1971	19,285	16,097	15,549	549	3,188	83.5	80.6	3.4	16.5
Apr-Jun 1971	19,294	16,108	15,540	568	3,186	83.5	80.5	3.5	16.5
May-Jul 1971	19,304	16,105	15,522	583	3,199	83.4	80.4	3.6	16.6
Jun-Aug 1971	19,314	16,088	15,499	589	3,226	83.3	80.2	3.7	16.7
Jul-Sep 1971	19,322	16,057	15,461	596	3,265	83.1	80.0	3.7	16.9
Aug-Oct 1971	19,330	16,039	15,431	607	3,291	83.0	79.8	3.8	17.0
Sep-Nov 1971	19,337	16,035	15,410	625	3,303	82.9	79.7	3.9	17.1
Oct-Dec 1971	19,345	16,042	15,401	641	3,303	82.9	79.6	4.0	17.1
Nov-Jan 1972	19,353	16,061	15,410	651	3,292	83.0	79.6	4.1	17.0
Dec-Feb 1972	19,360	16,087	15,431	656	3,274	83.1	79.7	4.1	16.9
Jan-Mar 1972	19,368	16,114	15,453	661	3,254	83.2	79.8	4.1	16.8
Feb-Apr 1972	19,376	16,129	15,464	665	3,247	83.2	79.8	4.1	16.8
Mar-May 1972	19,383	16,121	15,463	658	3,262	83.2	79.8	4.1	16.8
Apr-Jun 1972	19,391	16,105	15,462	644	3,285	83.1	79.7	4.0	16.9
May-Jul 1972	19,399	16,080	15,452	628	3,319	82.9	79.7	3.9	17.1
Jun-Aug 1972	19,406	16,070	15,454	616	3,336	82.8	79.6	3.8	17.2
Jul-Sep 1972	19,414	16,075	15,465	610	3,339	82.8	79.7	3.8	17.2
Aug-Oct 1972	19,423	16,079	15,476	603	3,344	82.8	79.7	3.7	17.2
Sep-Nov 1972	19,431	16,081	15,486	595	3,350	82.8	79.7	3.7	17.2
Oct-Dec 1972	19,440	16,088	15,508	580	3,351	82.8	79.8	3.6	17.2
Nov-Jan 1973	19,448	16,100	15,538	562	3,348	82.8	79.9	3.5	17.2
Dec-Feb 1973	19,456	16,120	15,580	540	3,337	82.9	80.1	3.3	17.1
Jan-Mar 1973	19,465	16,142	15,621	521	3,323	82.9	80.3	3.2	17.1
Feb-Apr 1973	19,473	16,158	15,651	507	3,315	83.0	80.4	3.1	17.0
Mar-May 1973	19,481	16,152	15,654	498	3,329	82.9	80.4	3.1	17.1
Apr-Jun 1973	19,490	16,135	15,644	491	3,355	82.8	80.3	3.0	17.2
May-Jul 1973	19,498	16,107	15,624	483	3,391	82.6	80.1	3.0	17.4
Jun-Aug 1973	19,506	16,076	15,604	472	3,430	82.4	80.0	2.9	17.6
Jul-Sep 1973	19,514	16,054	15,596	459	3,460	82.3	79.9	2.9	17.7
Aug-Oct 1973	19,522	16,043	15,594	448	3,479	82.2	79.9	2.8	17.8
Sep-Nov 1973	19,529	16,026	15,588	438	3,503	82.1	79.8	2.7	17.9
Oct-Dec 1973	19,537	16,005	15,577	428	3,532	81.9	79.7	2.7	18.1
Nov-Jan 1974	19,545	15,997	15,567	431	3,547	81.9	79.6	2.7	18.1
Dec-Feb 1974	19,553	15,990	15,549	441	3,562	81.8	79.5	2.8	18.2
Jan-Mar 1974	19,560	15,988	15,529	459	3,572	81.7	79.4	2.9	18.3
Feb-Apr 1974	19,568	15,984	15,519	465	3,584	81.7	79.3	2.9	18.3
Mar-May 1974	19,576	15,974	15,509	466	3,601	81.6	79.2	2.9	18.4
Apr-Jun 1974	19,583	15,978	15,510	468	3,606	81.6	79.2	2.9	18.4
May-Jul 1974	19,591	15,982	15,511	471	3,609	81.6	79.2	2.9	18.4
Jun-Aug 1974	19,599	16,000	15,519	480	3,599	81.6	79.2	3.0	18.4
Jul-Sep 1974	19,608	16,010	15,523	487	3,598	81.6	79.2	3.0	18.4
Aug-Oct 1974	19,617	16,017	15,523	494	3,600	81.6	79.1	3.1	18.4
Sep-Nov 1974	19,626	16,012	15,514	498	3,615	81.6	79.0	3.1	18.4
Oct-Dec 1974	19,636	16,007	15,504	504	3,628	81.5	79.0	3.1	18.5
Nov-Jan 1975	19,645	15,998	15,484	514	3,647	81.4	78.8	3.2	18.6
Dec-Feb 1975	19,654	15,990	15,462	528	3,664	81.4	78.7	3.3	18.6
Jan-Mar 1975	19,663	15,987	15,443	544	3,676	81.3	78.5	3.4	18.7
Feb-Apr 1975	19,672	15,995	15,431	564	3,677	81.3	78.4	3.5	18.7
Mar-May 1975	19,682	16,004	15,414	590	3,678	81.3	78.3	3.7	18.7
Apr-Jun 1975	19,691	16,022	15,404	619	3,668	81.4	78.2	3.9	18.6
May-Jul 1975	19,700	16,042	15,394	648	3,658	81.4	78.1	4.0	18.6
Jun-Aug 1975	19,709	16,057	15,384	673	3,653	81.5	78.1	4.2	18.5
Jul-Sep 1975	19,719	16,067	15,372	695	3,652	81.5	78.0	4.3	18.5
Aug-Oct 1975	19,730	16,071	15,353	718	3,659	81.5	77.8	4.5	18.5
Sep-Nov 1975	19,740	16,084	15,341	742	3,656	81.5	77.7	4.6	18.5
Oct-Dec 1975	19,750	16,090	15,324	766	3,660	81.5	77.6	4.8	18.5

Labour Force Survey, summary by sex United Kingdom (thousands) seasonally adjusted (Continued)

All aged 16 & over	All aged 16 & over	Total economically active	Total in employment	Unemployed	Economically inactive	Economic Activity rate (%)	Employment rate (%)	Unemployment rate (%)	Economic inactivity rate (%)
	1	2	3	4	5	6	7	8	9
Male	MGSM	MGSG	MGSA	MGSD	MGSJ	MGWH	MGSS	MGSY	YBTD
Nov-Jan 1976	19,760	16,096	15,313	783	3,664	81.5	77.5	4.9	18.5
Dec-Feb 1976	19,771	16,090	15,294	796	3,681	81.4	77.4	4.9	18.6
Jan-Mar 1976	19,781	16,088	15,282	806	3,693	81.3	77.3	5.0	18.7
Feb-Apr 1976	19,791	16,083	15,270	813	3,708	81.3	77.2	5.1	18.7
Mar-May 1976	19,801	16,084	15,262	821	3,718	81.2	77.1	5.1	18.8
Apr-Jun 1976	19,812	16,078	15,252	826	3,733	81.2	77.0	5.1	18.8
May-Jul 1976	19,822	16,072	15,244	829	3,750	81.1	76.9	5.2	18.9
Jun-Aug 1976	19,832	16,070	15,241	829	3,762	81.0	76.8	5.2	19.0
Jul-Sep 1976	19,844	16,062	15,232	830	3,781	80.9	76.8	5.2	19.1
Aug-Oct 1976	19,855	16,059	15,231	828	3,796	80.9	76.7	5.2	19.1
Sep-Nov 1976	19,867	16,057	15,232	825	3,810	80.8	76.7	5.1	19.2
Oct-Dec 1976	19,878	16,056	15,232	824	3,822	80.8	76.6	5.1	19.2
Nov-Jan 1977	19,890	16,057	15,233	824	3,833	80.7	76.6	5.1	19.3
Dec-Feb 1977	19,902	16,049	15,226	823	3,853	80.6	76.5	5.1	19.4
Jan-Mar 1977	19,913	16,046	15,225	821	3,868	80.6	76.5	5.1	19.4
Feb-Apr 1977	19,925	16,037	15,216	821	3,888	80.5	76.4	5.1	19.5
Mar-May 1977	19,936	16,030	15,207	823	3,906	80.4	76.3	5.1	19.6
Apr-Jun 1977	19,948	16,036	15,205	831	3,912	80.4	76.2	5.2	19.6
May-Jul 1977	19,960	16,035	15,196	839	3,925	80.3	76.1	5.2	19.7
Jun-Aug 1977	19,971	16,042	15,194	847	3,929	80.3	76.1	5.3	19.7
Jul-Sep 1977	19,983	16,041	15,187	854	3,942	80.3	76.0	5.3	19.7
Aug-Oct 1977	19,995	16,041	15,185	856	3,954	80.2	75.9	5.3	19.8
Sep-Nov 1977	20,006	16,034	15,177	856	3,972	80.1	75.9	5.3	19.9
Oct-Dec 1977	20,018	16,022	15,170	852	3,996	80.0	75.8	5.3	20.0
Nov-Jan 1978	20,029	16,017	15,170	847	4,013	80.0	75.7	5.3	20.0
Dec-Feb 1978	20,041	16,008	15,169	839	4,033	79.9	75.7	5.2	20.1
Jan-Mar 1978	20,053	16,002	15,170	832	4,051	79.8	75.7	5.2	20.2
Feb-Apr 1978	20,064	15,994	15,169	826	4,070	79.7	75.6	5.2	20.3
Mar-May 1978	20,076	15,984	15,163	822	4,092	79.6	75.5	5.1	20.4
Apr-Jun 1978	20,087	15,979	15,162	817	4,108	79.5	75.5	5.1	20.5
May-Jul 1978	20,099	15,974	15,162	812	4,125	79.5	75.4	5.1	20.5
Jun-Aug 1978	20,111	15,971	15,161	810	4,139	79.4	75.4	5.1	20.6
Jul-Sep 1978	20,125	15,971	15,165	806	4,155	79.4	75.4	5.0	20.6
Aug-Oct 1978	20,140	15,983	15,183	800	4,158	79.4	75.4	5.0	20.6
Sep-Nov 1978	20,155	15,985	15,197	788	4,170	79.3	75.4	4.9	20.7
Oct-Dec 1978	20,170	15,993	15,216	777	4,176	79.3	75.4	4.9	20.7
Nov-Jan 1979	20,184	15,998	15,227	771	4,187	79.3	75.4	4.8	20.7
Dec-Feb 1979	20,199	16,011	15,237	774	4,188	79.3	75.4	4.8	20.7
Jan-Mar 1979	20,214	16,015	15,239	776	4,199	79.2	75.4	4.8	20.8
Feb-Apr 1979	20,229	16,009	15,240	770	4,219	79.1	75.3	4.8	20.9
Mar-May 1979	20,244	16,000	15,241	759	4,244	79.0	75.3	4.7	21.0
Apr-Jun 1979	20,258	15,997	15,240	757	4,261	79.0	75.2	4.7	21.0
May-Jul 1979	20,273	16,003	15,242	761	4,270	78.9	75.2	4.8	21.1
Jun-Aug 1979	20,288	16,008	15,244	764	4,279	78.9	75.1	4.8	21.1
Jul-Sep 1979	20,303	16,014	15,245	769	4,289	78.9	75.1	4.8	21.1
Aug-Oct 1979	20,318	16,023	15,245	778	4,295	78.9	75.0	4.9	21.1
Sep-Nov 1979	20,333	16,029	15,242	786	4,304	78.8	75.0	4.9	21.2
Oct-Dec 1979	20,348	16,033	15,235	798	4,315	78.8	74.9	5.0	21.2
Nov-Jan 1980	20,363	16,035	15,225	810	4,328	78.7	74.8	5.1	21.3
Dec-Feb 1980	20,378	16,036	15,205	832	4,342	78.7	74.6	5.2	21.3
Jan-Mar 1980	20,393	16,041	15,185	857	4,352	78.7	74.5	5.3	21.3
Feb-Apr 1980	20,408	16,056	15,167	889	4,352	78.7	74.3	5.5	21.3
Mar-May 1980	20,423	16,070	15,147	923	4,354	78.7	74.2	5.7	21.3
Apr-Jun 1980	20,438	16,086	15,125	961	4,352	78.7	74.0	6.0	21.3
May-Jul 1980	20,453	16,098	15,095	1,003	4,355	78.7	73.8	6.2	21.3
Jun-Aug 1980	20,468	16,101	15,045	1,056	4,367	78.7	73.5	6.6	21.3
Jul-Sep 1980	20,481	16,110	14,995	1,115	4,371	78.7	73.2	6.9	21.3
Aug-Oct 1980	20,493	16,121	14,942	1,179	4,372	78.7	72.9	7.3	21.3
Sep-Nov 1980	20,506	16,128	14,882	1,246	4,377	78.7	72.6	7.7	21.3
Oct-Dec 1980	20,518	16,148	14,832	1,316	4,370	78.7	72.3	8.2	21.3

Labour Force Survey, summary by sex United Kingdom (thousands) seasonally adjusted (Continued)

All aged 16 & over

	All aged 16 & over	Total economically active	Total in employment	Unemployed	Economically inactive	Economic Activity rate (%)	Employment rate (%)	Unemployment rate (%)	Economic inactivity rate (%)
	1	2	3	4	5	6	7	8	9
Male	MGSM	MGSG	MGSA	MGSD	MGSJ	MGWH	MGSS	MGSY	YBTD
Nov-Jan 1981	20,531	16,154	14,772	1,381	4,377	78.7	72.0	8.6	21.3
Dec-Feb 1981	20,543	16,157	14,720	1,437	4,386	78.7	71.7	8.9	21.3
Jan-Mar 1981	20,556	16,163	14,670	1,493	4,393	78.6	71.4	9.2	21.4
Feb-Apr 1981	20,568	16,171	14,622	1,550	4,397	78.6	71.1	9.6	21.4
Mar-May 1981	20,581	16,180	14,576	1,604	4,401	78.6	70.8	9.9	21.4
Apr-Jun 1981	20,593	16,174	14,538	1,637	4,419	78.5	70.6	10.1	21.5
May-Jul 1981	20,606	16,163	14,498	1,664	4,443	78.4	70.4	10.3	21.6
Jun-Aug 1981	20,618	16,146	14,461	1,686	4,472	78.3	70.1	10.4	21.7
Jul-Sep 1981	20,626	16,135	14,428	1,707	4,491	78.2	70.0	10.6	21.8
Aug-Oct 1981	20,633	16,116	14,390	1,726	4,517	78.1	69.7	10.7	21.9
Sep-Nov 1981	20,641	16,094	14,350	1,744	4,547	78.0	69.5	10.8	22.0
Oct-Dec 1981	20,648	16,069	14,310	1,759	4,579	77.8	69.3	10.9	22.2
Nov-Jan 1982	20,656	16,054	14,280	1,774	4,601	77.7	69.1	11.0	22.3
Dec-Feb 1982	20,663	16,044	14,260	1,784	4,619	77.6	69.0	11.1	22.4
Jan-Mar 1982	20,671	16,041	14,250	1,791	4,630	77.6	68.9	11.2	22.4
Feb-Apr 1982	20,678	16,026	14,229	1,797	4,652	77.5	68.8	11.2	22.5
Mar-May 1982	20,686	16,015	14,211	1,804	4,670	77.4	68.7	11.3	22.6
Apr-Jun 1982	20,693	15,998	14,181	1,816	4,696	77.3	68.5	11.4	22.7
May-Jul 1982	20,701	15,988	14,159	1,828	4,713	77.2	68.4	11.4	22.8
Jun-Aug 1982	20,708	15,974	14,130	1,844	4,734	77.1	68.2	11.5	22.9
Jul-Sep 1982	20,719	15,957	14,100	1,857	4,762	77.0	68.1	11.6	23.0
Aug-Oct 1982	20,730	15,940	14,069	1,871	4,790	76.9	67.9	11.7	23.1
Sep-Nov 1982	20,741	15,923	14,039	1,884	4,818	76.8	67.7	11.8	23.2
Oct-Dec 1982	20,752	15,907	14,008	1,899	4,845	76.7	67.5	11.9	23.3
Nov-Jan 1983	20,764	15,889	13,979	1,910	4,875	76.5	67.3	12.0	23.5
Dec-Feb 1983	20,775	15,873	13,958	1,916	4,901	76.4	67.2	12.1	23.6
Jan-Mar 1983	20,786	15,859	13,940	1,920	4,926	76.3	67.1	12.1	23.7
Feb-Apr 1983	20,797	15,852	13,927	1,924	4,945	76.2	67.0	12.1	23.8
Mar-May 1983	20,808	15,839	13,909	1,930	4,969	76.1	66.8	12.2	23.9
Apr-Jun 1983	20,819	15,838	13,901	1,936	4,981	76.1	66.8	12.2	23.9
May-Jul 1983	20,830	15,851	13,911	1,940	4,979	76.1	66.8	12.2	23.9
Jun-Aug 1983	20,841	15,869	13,930	1,939	4,973	76.1	66.8	12.2	23.9
Jul-Sep 1983	20,854	15,894	13,960	1,934	4,960	76.2	66.9	12.2	23.8
Aug-Oct 1983	20,866	15,920	13,990	1,929	4,946	76.3	67.0	12.1	23.7
Sep-Nov 1983	20,879	15,947	14,021	1,926	4,931	76.4	67.2	12.1	23.6
Oct-Dec 1983	20,891	15,956	14,033	1,923	4,935	76.4	67.2	12.1	23.6
Nov-Jan 1984	20,903	15,975	14,053	1,922	4,929	76.4	67.2	12.0	23.6
Dec-Feb 1984	20,916	15,998	14,072	1,925	4,918	76.5	67.3	12.0	23.5
Jan-Mar 1984	20,928	16,020	14,092	1,928	4,908	76.5	67.3	12.0	23.5
Feb-Apr 1984	20,941	16,042	14,112	1,929	4,899	76.6	67.4	12.0	23.4
Mar-May 1984	20,953	16,061	14,132	1,928	4,893	76.6	67.4	12.0	23.4
Apr-Jun 1984	20,966	16,067	14,148	1,919	4,899	76.6	67.5	11.9	23.4
May-Jul 1984	20,978	16,077	14,162	1,915	4,901	76.6	67.5	11.9	23.4
Jun-Aug 1984	20,990	16,081	14,172	1,909	4,909	76.6	67.5	11.9	23.4
Jul-Sep 1984	21,002	16,098	14,188	1,910	4,905	76.6	67.6	11.9	23.4
Aug-Oct 1984	21,014	16,111	14,200	1,911	4,903	76.7	67.6	11.9	23.3
Sep-Nov 1984	21,026	16,121	14,210	1,911	4,905	76.7	67.6	11.9	23.3
Oct-Dec 1984	21,037	16,124	14,218	1,907	4,913	76.6	67.6	11.8	23.4
Nov-Jan 1985	21,049	16,133	14,230	1,903	4,916	76.6	67.6	11.8	23.4
Dec-Feb 1985	21,061	16,130	14,230	1,900	4,931	76.6	67.6	11.8	23.4
Jan-Mar 1985	21,072	16,136	14,242	1,894	4,936	76.6	67.6	11.7	23.4
Feb-Apr 1985	21,084	16,140	14,250	1,890	4,944	76.6	67.6	11.7	23.4
Mar-May 1985	21,096	16,129	14,246	1,882	4,967	76.5	67.5	11.7	23.5
Apr-Jun 1985	21,107	16,119	14,240	1,879	4,989	76.4	67.5	11.7	23.6
May-Jul 1985	21,119	16,113	14,240	1,873	5,006	76.3	67.4	11.6	23.7
Jun-Aug 1985	21,131	16,109	14,240	1,869	5,021	76.2	67.4	11.6	23.8
Jul-Sep 1985	21,139	16,104	14,238	1,866	5,035	76.2	67.4	11.6	23.8
Aug-Oct 1985	21,147	16,097	14,232	1,865	5,051	76.1	67.3	11.6	23.9
Sep-Nov 1985	21,156	16,093	14,230	1,863	5,063	76.1	67.3	11.6	23.9
Oct-Dec 1985	21,164	16,084	14,220	1,864	5,080	76.0	67.2	11.6	24.0

Labour Force Survey, summary by sex United Kingdom (thousands) seasonally adjusted (Continued)

All aged 16 & over	All aged 16 & over	Total economically active	Total in employment	Unemployed	Economically inactive	Economic Activity rate (%)	Employment rate (%)	Unemployment rate (%)	Economic inactivity rate (%)
	1	2	3	4	5	6	7	8	9
Male	MGSM	MGSG	MGSA	MGSD	MGSJ	MGWH	MGSS	MGSY	YBTD
Nov-Jan 1986	21,173	16,076	14,210	1,866	5,096	75.9	67.1	11.6	24.1
Dec-Feb 1986	21,181	16,079	14,210	1,869	5,102	75.9	67.1	11.6	24.1
Jan-Mar 1986	21,190	16,075	14,200	1,875	5,114	75.9	67.0	11.7	24.1
Feb-Apr 1986	21,198	16,063	14,188	1,875	5,135	75.8	66.9	11.7	24.2
Mar-May 1986	21,206	16,056	14,179	1,876	5,150	75.7	66.9	11.7	24.3
Apr-Jun 1986	21,215	16,048	14,172	1,876	5,167	75.6	66.8	11.7	24.4
May-Jul 1986	21,223	16,059	14,180	1,879	5,164	75.7	66.8	11.7	24.3
Jun-Aug 1986	21,232	16,061	14,180	1,881	5,171	75.6	66.8	11.7	24.4
Jul-Sep 1986	21,241	16,069	14,190	1,879	5,172	75.7	66.8	11.7	24.3
Aug-Oct 1986	21,250	16,074	14,200	1,874	5,177	75.6	66.8	11.7	24.4
Sep-Nov 1986	21,259	16,070	14,200	1,870	5,190	75.6	66.8	11.6	24.4
Oct-Dec 1986	21,269	16,065	14,200	1,865	5,204	75.5	66.8	11.6	24.5
Nov-Jan 1987	21,278	16,065	14,202	1,863	5,213	75.5	66.7	11.6	24.5
Dec-Feb 1987	21,287	16,065	14,210	1,855	5,222	75.5	66.8	11.5	24.5
Jan-Mar 1987	21,296	16,072	14,228	1,844	5,225	75.5	66.8	11.5	24.5
Feb-Apr 1987	21,306	16,081	14,250	1,831	5,225	75.5	66.9	11.4	24.5
Mar-May 1987	21,315	16,095	14,281	1,814	5,220	75.5	67.0	11.3	24.5
Apr-Jun 1987	21,324	16,110	14,320	1,790	5,214	75.5	67.2	11.1	24.5
May-Jul 1987	21,333	16,121	14,360	1,761	5,212	75.6	67.3	10.9	24.4
Jun-Aug 1987	21,343	16,143	14,410	1,733	5,199	75.6	67.5	10.7	24.4
Jul-Sep 1987	21,349	16,160	14,452	1,707	5,190	75.7	67.7	10.6	24.3
Aug-Oct 1987	21,356	16,168	14,490	1,678	5,188	75.7	67.9	10.4	24.3
Sep-Nov 1987	21,362	16,179	14,532	1,647	5,183	75.7	68.0	10.2	24.3
Oct-Dec 1987	21,369	16,189	14,572	1,617	5,180	75.8	68.2	10.0	24.2
Nov-Jan 1988	21,375	16,199	14,612	1,587	5,176	75.8	68.4	9.8	24.2
Dec-Feb 1988	21,382	16,219	14,660	1,559	5,163	75.9	68.6	9.6	24.1
Jan-Mar 1988	21,389	16,232	14,702	1,530	5,156	75.9	68.7	9.4	24.1
Feb-Apr 1988	21,395	16,242	14,740	1,502	5,153	75.9	68.9	9.2	24.1
Mar-May 1988	21,402	16,242	14,767	1,475	5,160	75.9	69.0	9.1	24.1
Apr-Jun 1988	21,408	16,243	14,790	1,453	5,166	75.9	69.1	8.9	24.1
May-Jul 1988	21,415	16,238	14,810	1,428	5,177	75.8	69.2	8.8	24.2
Jun-Aug 1988	21,421	16,245	14,840	1,405	5,176	75.8	69.3	8.7	24.2
Jul-Sep 1988	21,428	16,246	14,860	1,386	5,181	75.8	69.3	8.5	24.2
Aug-Oct 1988	21,435	16,263	14,890	1,373	5,172	75.9	69.5	8.4	24.1
Sep-Nov 1988	21,441	16,275	14,920	1,355	5,166	75.9	69.6	8.3	24.1
Oct-Dec 1988	21,448	16,272	14,942	1,329	5,176	75.9	69.7	8.2	24.1
Nov-Jan 1989	21,454	16,282	14,980	1,302	5,172	75.9	69.8	8.0	24.1
Dec-Feb 1989	21,461	16,296	15,020	1,276	5,165	75.9	70.0	7.8	24.1
Jan-Mar 1989	21,467	16,315	15,060	1,255	5,152	76.0	70.2	7.7	24.0
Feb-Apr 1989	21,474	16,333	15,100	1,233	5,141	76.1	70.3	7.5	23.9
Mar-May 1989	21,481	16,340	15,126	1,213	5,141	76.1	70.4	7.4	23.9
Apr-Jun 1989	21,487	16,341	15,140	1,201	5,146	76.0	70.5	7.3	24.0
May-Jul 1989	21,494	16,345	15,150	1,195	5,149	76.0	70.5	7.3	24.0
Jun-Aug 1989	21,500	16,355	15,168	1,187	5,146	76.1	70.5	7.3	23.9
Jul-Sep 1989	21,506	16,357	15,178	1,179	5,149	76.1	70.6	7.2	23.9
Aug-Oct 1989	21,511	16,363	15,190	1,173	5,147	76.1	70.6	7.2	23.9
Sep-Nov 1989	21,516	16,359	15,190	1,169	5,157	76.0	70.6	7.1	24.0
Oct-Dec 1989	21,521	16,367	15,200	1,167	5,155	76.0	70.6	7.1	24.0
Nov-Jan 1990	21,526	16,362	15,200	1,162	5,165	76.0	70.6	7.1	24.0
Dec-Feb 1990	21,532	16,360	15,200	1,160	5,172	76.0	70.6	7.1	24.0
Jan-Mar 1990	21,537	16,360	15,200	1,160	5,177	76.0	70.6	7.1	24.0
Feb-Apr 1990	21,542	16,361	15,200	1,161	5,181	76.0	70.6	7.1	24.0
Mar-May 1990	21,547	16,357	15,194	1,162	5,191	75.9	70.5	7.1	24.1
Apr-Jun 1990	21,553	16,354	15,192	1,161	5,199	75.9	70.5	7.1	24.1
May-Jul 1990	21,558	16,351	15,182	1,168	5,207	75.8	70.4	7.1	24.2
Jun-Aug 1990	21,563	16,352	15,170	1,182	5,211	75.8	70.4	7.2	24.2
Jul-Sep 1990	21,566	16,353	15,150	1,203	5,214	75.8	70.2	7.4	24.2
Aug-Oct 1990	21,570	16,340	15,112	1,227	5,230	75.8	70.1	7.5	24.2
Sep-Nov 1990	21,573	16,328	15,072	1,256	5,245	75.7	69.9	7.7	24.3
Oct-Dec 1990	21,577	16,315	15,025	1,290	5,262	75.6	69.6	7.9	24.4

Labour Force Survey, summary by sex United Kingdom (thousands) seasonally adjusted (Continued)

All aged 16 & over

	All aged 16 & over	Total economically active	Total in employment	Unemployed	Economically inactive	Economic Activity rate (%)	Employment rate (%)	Unemployment rate (%)	Economic inactivity rate (%)
	1	2	3	4	5	6	7	8	9
Male	MGSM	MGSG	MGSA	MGSD	MGSJ	MGWH	MGSS	MGSY	YBTD
Nov-Jan 1991	21,580	16,291	14,972	1,319	5,289	75.5	69.4	8.1	24.5
Dec-Feb 1991	21,584	16,279	14,922	1,357	5,305	75.4	69.1	8.3	24.6
Jan-Mar 1991	21,587	16,268	14,865	1,404	5,319	75.4	68.9	8.6	24.6
Feb-Apr 1991	21,591	16,268	14,810	1,458	5,322	75.3	68.6	9.0	24.7
Mar-May 1991	21,594	16,251	14,744	1,508	5,343	75.3	68.3	9.3	24.7
Apr-Jun 1991	21,597	16,218	14,668	1,550	5,380	75.1	67.9	9.6	24.9
May-Jul 1991	21,601	16,189	14,595	1,594	5,412	74.9	67.6	9.8	25.1
Jun-Aug 1991	21,604	16,163	14,528	1,635	5,441	74.8	67.2	10.1	25.2
Jul-Sep 1991	21,607	16,138	14,468	1,670	5,469	74.7	67.0	10.3	25.3
Aug-Oct 1991	21,610	16,116	14,418	1,698	5,494	74.6	66.7	10.5	25.4
Sep-Nov 1991	21,613	16,090	14,368	1,723	5,523	74.4	66.5	10.7	25.6
Oct-Dec 1991	21,616	16,066	14,320	1,746	5,550	74.3	66.2	10.9	25.7
Nov-Jan 1992	21,619	16,044	14,278	1,766	5,575	74.2	66.0	11.0	25.8
Dec-Feb 1992	21,622	16,034	14,245	1,789	5,588	74.2	65.9	11.2	25.8
Jan-Mar 1992	21,626	16,032	14,215	1,817	5,593	74.1	65.7	11.3	25.9
Feb-Apr 1992	21,629	16,027	14,187	1,840	5,602	74.1	65.6	11.5	25.9
Mar-May 1992	21,623	15,987	14,131	1,855	5,636	73.9	65.4	11.6	26.1
Apr-Jun 1992	21,624	15,958	14,120	1,838	5,666	73.8	65.3	11.5	26.2
May-Jul 1992	21,625	15,936	14,080	1,856	5,689	73.7	65.1	11.6	26.3
Jun-Aug 1992	21,626	15,925	14,057	1,867	5,701	73.6	65.0	11.7	26.4
Jul-Sep 1992	21,627	15,907	14,033	1,874	5,720	73.6	64.9	11.8	26.4
Aug-Oct 1992	21,628	15,892	13,988	1,904	5,735	73.5	64.7	12.0	26.5
Sep-Nov 1992	21,628	15,870	13,932	1,939	5,758	73.4	64.4	12.2	26.6
Oct-Dec 1992	21,629	15,837	13,879	1,959	5,792	73.2	64.2	12.4	26.8
Nov-Jan 1993	21,630	15,847	13,861	1,987	5,782	73.3	64.1	12.5	26.7
Dec-Feb 1993	21,630	15,860	13,847	2,012	5,771	73.3	64.0	12.7	26.7
Jan-Mar 1993	21,631	15,857	13,845	2,012	5,774	73.3	64.0	12.7	26.7
Feb-Apr 1993	21,632	15,800	13,800	2,000	5,832	73.0	63.8	12.7	27.0
Mar-May 1993	21,632	15,774	13,804	1,970	5,858	72.9	63.8	12.5	27.1
Apr-Jun 1993	21,633	15,757	13,822	1,935	5,876	72.8	63.9	12.3	27.2
May-Jul 1993	21,634	15,747	13,810	1,937	5,887	72.8	63.8	12.3	27.2
Jun-Aug 1993	21,634	15,720	13,805	1,915	5,915	72.7	63.8	12.2	27.3
Jul-Sep 1993	21,636	15,724	13,806	1,919	5,911	72.7	63.8	12.2	27.3
Aug-Oct 1993	21,637	15,712	13,814	1,897	5,925	72.6	63.8	12.1	27.4
Sep-Nov 1993	21,638	15,722	13,826	1,895	5,916	72.7	63.9	12.1	27.3
Oct-Dec 1993	21,640	15,726	13,826	1,899	5,914	72.7	63.9	12.1	27.3
Nov-Jan 1993	21,641	15,728	13,822	1,906	5,913	72.7	63.9	12.1	27.3
Dec-Feb 1994	21,642	15,722	13,865	1,858	5,920	72.6	64.1	11.8	27.4
Jan-Mar 1994	21,644	15,711	13,881	1,830	5,932	72.6	64.1	11.6	27.4
Feb-Apr 1994	21,645	15,719	13,909	1,810	5,926	72.6	64.3	11.5	27.4
Mar-May 1994	21,646	15,709	13,903	1,806	5,938	72.6	64.2	11.5	27.4
Apr-Jun 1994	21,648	15,692	13,887	1,805	5,955	72.5	64.1	11.5	27.5
May-Jul 1994	21,649	15,718	13,928	1,790	5,931	72.6	64.3	11.4	27.4
Jun-Aug 1994	21,650	15,719	13,941	1,778	5,932	72.6	64.4	11.3	27.4
Jul-Sep 1994	21,657	15,710	13,980	1,730	5,947	72.5	64.5	11.0	27.5
Aug-Oct 1994	21,664	15,705	13,998	1,706	5,959	72.5	64.6	10.9	27.5
Sep-Nov 1994	21,670	15,695	14,021	1,674	5,975	72.4	64.7	10.7	27.6
Oct-Dec 1994	21,677	15,683	14,033	1,650	5,994	72.4	64.7	10.5	27.6
Nov-Jan 1994	21,684	15,655	14,022	1,633	6,028	72.2	64.7	10.4	27.8
Dec-Feb 1995	21,690	15,659	14,033	1,626	6,031	72.2	64.7	10.4	27.8
Jan-Mar 1995	21,697	15,663	14,045	1,617	6,034	72.2	64.7	10.3	27.8
Feb-Apr 1995	21,703	15,660	14,061	1,599	6,044	72.2	64.8	10.2	27.8
Mar-May 1995	21,710	15,682	14,091	1,591	6,028	72.2	64.9	10.1	27.8
Apr-Jun 1995	21,717	15,682	14,101	1,581	6,035	72.2	64.9	10.1	27.8
May-Jul 1995	21,723	15,680	14,101	1,579	6,043	72.2	64.9	10.1	27.8
Jun-Aug 1995	21,730	15,686	14,115	1,571	6,044	72.2	65.0	10.0	27.8
Jul-Sep 1995	21,737	15,695	14,120	1,575	6,043	72.2	65.0	10.0	27.8
Aug-Oct 1995	21,744	15,688	14,108	1,579	6,057	72.1	64.9	10.1	27.9
Sep-Nov 1995	21,752	15,682	14,128	1,553	6,070	72.1	65.0	9.9	27.9
Oct-Dec 1995	21,759	15,685	14,173	1,512	6,074	72.1	65.1	9.6	27.9

Labour Force Survey, summary by sex United Kingdom (thousands) seasonally adjusted (Continued)

All aged 16 & over

	All aged 16 & over	Total economically active	Total in employment	Unemployed	Economically inactive	Economic Activity rate (%)	Employment rate (%)	Unemployment rate (%)	Economic inactivity rate (%)
	1	2	3	4	5	6	7	8	9
Male	MGSM	MGSG	MGSA	MGSD	MGSJ	MGWH	MGSS	MGSY	YBTD
Nov-Jan 1996	21,766	15,690	14,142	1,549	6,076	72.1	65.0	9.9	27.9
Dec-Feb 1996	21,773	15,685	14,140	1,545	6,088	72.0	64.9	9.8	28.0
Jan-Mar 1996	21,780	15,679	14,140	1,539	6,101	72.0	64.9	9.8	28.0
Feb-Apr 1996	21,787	15,689	14,151	1,539	6,098	72.0	64.9	9.8	28.0
Mar-May 1996	21,794	15,686	14,163	1,524	6,108	72.0	65.0	9.7	28.0
Apr-Jun 1996	21,801	15,682	14,166	1,517	6,119	71.9	65.0	9.7	28.1
May-Jul 1996	21,809	15,670	14,176	1,494	6,138	71.9	65.0	9.5	28.1
Jun-Aug 1996	21,816	15,681	14,209	1,473	6,135	71.9	65.1	9.4	28.1
Jul-Sep 1996	21,822	15,673	14,202	1,471	6,150	71.8	65.1	9.4	28.2
Aug-Oct 1996	21,829	15,691	14,218	1,472	6,139	71.9	65.1	9.4	28.1
Sep-Nov 1996	21,836	15,703	14,263	1,440	6,132	71.9	65.3	9.2	28.1
Oct-Dec 1996	21,843	15,668	14,268	1,400	6,175	71.7	65.3	8.9	28.3
Nov-Jan 1997	21,849	15,674	14,310	1,364	6,176	71.7	65.5	8.7	28.3
Dec-Feb 1997	21,856	15,679	14,348	1,331	6,177	71.7	65.6	8.5	28.3
Jan-Mar 1997	21,863	15,690	14,393	1,297	6,173	71.8	65.8	8.3	28.2
Feb-Apr 1997	21,869	15,688	14,421	1,267	6,181	71.7	65.9	8.1	28.3
Mar-May 1997	21,876	15,687	14,405	1,283	6,189	71.7	65.8	8.2	28.3
Apr-Jun 1997	21,883	15,707	14,442	1,265	6,175	71.8	66.0	8.1	28.2
May-Jul 1997	21,889	15,715	14,426	1,289	6,175	71.8	65.9	8.2	28.2
Jun-Aug 1997	21,896	15,698	14,460	1,238	6,198	71.7	66.0	7.9	28.3
Jul-Sep 1997	21,903	15,685	14,488	1,197	6,218	71.6	66.1	7.6	28.4
Aug-Oct 1997	21,911	15,695	14,524	1,171	6,216	71.6	66.3	7.5	28.4
Sep-Nov 1997	21,918	15,686	14,530	1,156	6,231	71.6	66.3	7.4	28.4
Oct-Dec 1997	21,925	15,678	14,537	1,141	6,246	71.5	66.3	7.3	28.5
Nov-Jan 1998	21,932	15,662	14,555	1,106	6,271	71.4	66.4	7.1	28.6
Dec-Feb 1998	21,939	15,678	14,581	1,096	6,262	71.5	66.5	7.0	28.5
Jan-Mar 1998	21,946	15,661	14,560	1,101	6,286	71.4	66.3	7.0	28.6
Feb-Apr 1998	21,954	15,653	14,560	1,092	6,301	71.3	66.3	7.0	28.7
Mar-May 1998	21,961	15,647	14,571	1,076	6,314	71.2	66.3	6.9	28.8
Apr-Jun 1998	21,968	15,650	14,576	1,074	6,318	71.2	66.4	6.9	28.8
May-Jul 1998	21,975	15,682	14,603	1,079	6,293	71.4	66.5	6.9	28.6
Jun-Aug 1998	21,982	15,712	14,625	1,087	6,270	71.5	66.5	6.9	28.5
Jul-Sep 1998	21,992	15,699	14,607	1,092	6,294	71.4	66.4	7.0	28.6
Aug-Oct 1998	22,002	15,693	14,599	1,093	6,310	71.3	66.4	7.0	28.7
Sep-Nov 1998	22,012	15,719	14,636	1,083	6,293	71.4	66.5	6.9	28.6
Oct-Dec 1998	22,022	15,729	14,651	1,079	6,293	71.4	66.5	6.9	28.6
Nov-Jan 1999	22,032	15,750	14,650	1,100	6,282	71.5	66.5	7.0	28.5
Dec-Feb 1999	22,042	15,789	14,693	1,096	6,253	71.6	66.7	6.9	28.4
Jan-Mar 1999	22,051	15,770	14,690	1,080	6,282	71.5	66.6	6.8	28.5
Feb-Apr 1999	22,061	15,764	14,688	1,075	6,298	71.5	66.6	6.8	28.5
Mar-May 1999	22,071	15,774	14,704	1,070	6,297	71.5	66.6	6.8	28.5
Apr-Jun 1999	22,081	15,790	14,731	1,059	6,291	71.5	66.7	6.7	28.5
May-Jul 1999	22,091	15,788	14,750	1,038	6,303	71.5	66.8	6.6	28.5
Jun-Aug 1999	22,101	15,802	14,779	1,023	6,299	71.5	66.9	6.5	28.5
Jul-Sep 1999	22,112	15,818	14,792	1,026	6,294	71.5	66.9	6.5	28.5
Aug-Oct 1999	22,123	15,800	14,797	1,003	6,323	71.4	66.9	6.3	28.6
Sep-Nov 1999	22,134	15,835	14,823	1,012	6,300	71.5	67.0	6.4	28.5
Oct-Dec 1999	22,146	15,839	14,837	1,002	6,307	71.5	67.0	6.3	28.5
Nov-Jan 2000	22,157	15,851	14,835	1,016	6,306	71.5	67.0	6.4	28.5
Dec-Feb 2000	22,168	15,832	14,837	994	6,336	71.4	66.9	6.3	28.6
Jan-Mar 2000	22,179	15,848	14,864	984	6,331	71.5	67.0	6.2	28.5
Feb-Apr 2000	22,190	15,875	14,899	976	6,316	71.5	67.1	6.1	28.5
Mar-May 2000	22,202	15,882	14,908	974	6,320	71.5	67.1	6.1	28.5
Apr-Jun 2000	22,213	15,854	14,897	957	6,359	71.4	67.1	6.0	28.6
May-Jul 2000	22,224	15,836	14,924	913	6,388	71.3	67.2	5.8	28.7
Jun-Aug 2000	22,235	15,827	14,924	903	6,408	71.2	67.1	5.7	28.8
Jul-Sep 2000	22,251	15,830	14,919	910	6,421	71.1	67.1	5.8	28.9
Aug-Oct 2000	22,267	15,842	14,920	922	6,425	71.1	67.0	5.8	28.9
Sep-Nov 2000	22,283	15,832	14,916	916	6,450	71.1	66.9	5.8	28.9
Oct-Dec 2000	22,298	15,849	14,937	912	6,449	71.1	67.0	5.8	28.9

Labour Force Survey, summary by sex United Kingdom (thousands) seasonally adjusted (Continued)

All aged 16 & over

	All aged 16 & over	Total economically active	Total in employment	Unemployed	Economically inactive	Economic Activity rate (%)	Employment rate (%)	Unemployment rate (%)	Economic inactivity rate (%)
	1	2	3	4	5	6	7	8	9
Male	MGSM	MGSG	MGSA	MGSD	MGSJ	MGWH	MGSS	MGSY	YBTD
Nov-Jan 2001	22,314	15,883	14,980	903	6,432	71.2	67.1	5.7	28.8
Dec-Feb 2001	22,330	15,910	14,991	919	6,420	71.2	67.1	5.8	28.8
Jan-Mar 2001	22,346	15,896	15,011	885	6,449	71.1	67.2	5.6	28.9
Feb-Apr 2001	22,361	15,878	15,009	869	6,484	71.0	67.1	5.5	29.0
Mar-May 2001	22,377	15,867	15,020	847	6,510	70.9	67.1	5.3	29.1
Apr-Jun 2001	22,393	15,875	14,994	882	6,518	70.9	67.0	5.6	29.1
May-Jul 2001	22,409	15,890	15,002	888	6,519	70.9	66.9	5.6	29.1
Jun-Aug 2001	22,424	15,927	15,031	896	6,497	71.0	67.0	5.6	29.0
Jul-Sep 2001	22,438	15,930	15,033	897	6,508	71.0	67.0	5.6	29.0
Aug-Oct 2001	22,452	15,931	15,029	902	6,521	71.0	66.9	5.7	29.0
Sep-Nov 2001	22,466	15,946	15,045	901	6,520	71.0	67.0	5.7	29.0
Oct-Dec 2001	22,480	15,959	15,045	914	6,521	71.0	66.9	5.7	29.0
Nov-Jan 2002	22,494	15,944	15,031	913	6,550	70.9	66.8	5.7	29.1
Dec-Feb 2002	22,508	15,957	15,050	907	6,551	70.9	66.9	5.7	29.1
Jan-Mar 2002	22,522	15,935	15,016	919	6,587	70.8	66.7	5.8	29.2
Feb-Apr 2002	22,536	15,953	15,036	917	6,583	70.8	66.7	5.7	29.2
Mar-May 2002	22,550	15,971	15,052	919	6,579	70.8	66.7	5.8	29.2
Apr-Jun 2002	22,564	15,978	15,068	910	6,586	70.8	66.8	5.7	29.2
May-Jul 2002	22,578	15,983	15,067	916	6,595	70.8	66.7	5.7	29.2
Jun-Aug 2002	22,592	16,000	15,083	918	6,591	70.8	66.8	5.7	29.2
Jul-Sep 2002	22,606	16,015	15,070	945	6,591	70.8	66.7	5.9	29.2
Aug-Oct 2002	22,621	16,076	15,153	923	6,544	71.1	67.0	5.7	28.9
Sep-Nov 2002	22,635	16,084	15,173	912	6,551	71.1	67.0	5.7	28.9
Oct-Dec 2002	22,650	16,117	15,226	891	6,533	71.2	67.2	5.5	28.8
Nov-Jan 2003	22,665	16,076	15,206	870	6,588	70.9	67.1	5.4	29.1
Dec-Feb 2003	22,679	16,078	15,165	913	6,601	70.9	66.9	5.7	29.1
Jan-Mar 2003	22,694	16,107	15,181	926	6,586	71.0	66.9	5.8	29.0
Feb-Apr 2003	22,708	16,133	15,218	915	6,575	71.0	67.0	5.7	29.0
Mar-May 2003	22,723	16,162	15,259	903	6,561	71.1	67.2	5.6	28.9
Apr-Jun 2003	22,738	16,177	15,291	886	6,560	71.1	67.3	5.5	28.9
May-Jul 2003	22,752	16,193	15,290	903	6,559	71.2	67.2	5.6	28.8
Jun-Aug 2003	22,767	16,174	15,275	899	6,592	71.0	67.1	5.6	29.0
Jul-Sep 2003	22,783	16,180	15,285	896	6,602	71.0	67.1	5.5	29.0
Aug-Oct 2003	22,798	16,165	15,276	889	6,633	70.9	67.0	5.5	29.1
Sep-Nov 2003	22,814	16,144	15,266	878	6,671	70.8	66.9	5.4	29.2
Oct-Dec 2003	22,830	16,140	15,261	879	6,691	70.7	66.8	5.4	29.3
Nov-Jan 2004	22,846	16,162	15,302	860	6,684	70.7	67.0	5.3	29.3
Dec-Feb 2004	22,862	16,181	15,332	849	6,681	70.8	67.1	5.2	29.2
Jan-Mar 2004	22,878	16,190	15,348	841	6,688	70.8	67.1	5.2	29.2
Feb-Apr 2004	22,894	16,185	15,342	843	6,708	70.7	67.0	5.2	29.3
Mar-May 2004	22,910	16,192	15,363	829	6,718	70.7	67.1	5.1	29.3
Apr-Jun 2004	22,926	16,195	15,353	841	6,731	70.6	67.0	5.2	29.4
May-Jul 2004	22,942	16,195	15,366	829	6,746	70.6	67.0	5.1	29.4
Jun-Aug 2004	22,957	16,198	15,374	823	6,759	70.6	67.0	5.1	29.4
Jul-Sep 2004	22,977	16,208	15,393	815	6,769	70.5	67.0	5.0	29.5
Aug-Oct 2004	22,997	16,207	15,401	806	6,790	70.5	67.0	5.0	29.5
Sep-Nov 2004	23,017	16,264	15,433	832	6,752	70.7	67.0	5.1	29.3
Oct-Dec 2004	23,037	16,284	15,450	834	6,753	70.7	67.1	5.1	29.3
Nov-Jan 2005	23,056	16,303	15,469	834	6,753	70.7	67.1	5.1	29.3
Dec-Feb 2005	23,076	16,314	15,477	836	6,763	70.7	67.1	5.1	29.3
Jan-Mar 2005	23,096	16,318	15,488	830	6,778	70.7	67.1	5.1	29.3
Feb-Apr 2005	23,116	16,309	15,481	828	6,807	70.6	67.0	5.1	29.4
Mar-May 2005	23,136	16,301	15,460	841	6,835	70.5	66.8	5.2	29.5
Apr-Jun 2005	23,155	16,316	15,481	834	6,839	70.5	66.9	5.1	29.5
May-Jul 2005	23,175	16,331	15,495	837	6,844	70.5	66.9	5.1	29.5
Jun-Aug 2005	23,195	16,349	15,507	843	6,846	70.5	66.9	5.2	29.5
Jul-Sep 2005	23,213	16,376	15,526	849	6,837	70.5	66.9	5.2	29.5
Aug-Oct 2005	23,230	16,419	15,535	884	6,811	70.7	66.9	5.4	29.3
Sep-Nov 2005	**23,248**	**16,430**	**15,530**	**900**	**6,818**	**70.7**	**66.8**	**5.5**	**29.3**

Labour Force Survey, summary by sex United Kingdom (thousands) seasonally adjusted (Continued)

All aged 16 & over

	All aged 16 & over	Total economically active	Total in employment	Unemployed	Economically inactive	Economic Activity rate (%)	Employment rate (%)	Unemployment rate (%)	Economic inactivity rate (%)
	1	2	3	4	5	6	7	8	9
Female	MGSN	MGSH	MGSB	MGSE	MGSK	MGWI	MGST	MGSZ	YBTE
Jan-Mar 1971	21,248	9,490	9,022	468	11,758	44.7	42.5	4.9	55.3
Feb-Apr 1971	21,257	9,485	9,014	471	11,772	44.6	42.4	5.0	55.4
Mar-May 1971	21,265	9,485	9,011	474	11,781	44.6	42.4	5.0	55.4
Apr-Jun 1971	21,274	9,492	9,016	476	11,782	44.6	42.4	5.0	55.4
May-Jul 1971	21,282	9,498	9,019	479	11,785	44.6	42.4	5.0	55.4
Jun-Aug 1971	21,291	9,488	9,009	478	11,803	44.6	42.3	5.0	55.4
Jul-Sep 1971	21,296	9,482	9,002	480	11,814	44.5	42.3	5.1	55.5
Aug-Oct 1971	21,302	9,476	8,993	483	11,826	44.5	42.2	5.1	55.5
Sep-Nov 1971	21,307	9,476	8,988	488	11,831	44.5	42.2	5.1	55.5
Oct-Dec 1971	21,313	9,485	8,994	491	11,828	44.5	42.2	5.2	55.5
Nov-Jan 1972	21,318	9,499	9,006	493	11,819	44.6	42.2	5.2	55.4
Dec-Feb 1972	21,324	9,518	9,025	493	11,806	44.6	42.3	5.2	55.4
Jan-Mar 1972	21,329	9,542	9,048	494	11,787	44.7	42.4	5.2	55.3
Feb-Apr 1972	21,335	9,561	9,065	496	11,773	44.8	42.5	5.2	55.2
Mar-May 1972	21,340	9,573	9,076	497	11,768	44.9	42.5	5.2	55.1
Apr-Jun 1972	21,346	9,576	9,080	496	11,769	44.9	42.5	5.2	55.1
May-Jul 1972	21,351	9,583	9,089	494	11,768	44.9	42.6	5.2	55.1
Jun-Aug 1972	21,357	9,594	9,103	491	11,762	44.9	42.6	5.1	55.1
Jul-Sep 1972	21,363	9,610	9,120	490	11,753	45.0	42.7	5.1	55.0
Aug-Oct 1972	21,369	9,627	9,138	489	11,742	45.1	42.8	5.1	54.9
Sep-Nov 1972	21,376	9,647	9,157	490	11,729	45.1	42.8	5.1	54.9
Oct-Dec 1972	21,382	9,670	9,180	489	11,712	45.2	42.9	5.1	54.8
Nov-Jan 1973	21,388	9,696	9,209	487	11,692	45.3	43.1	5.0	54.7
Dec-Feb 1973	21,395	9,729	9,245	484	11,666	45.5	43.2	5.0	54.5
Jan-Mar 1973	21,401	9,763	9,282	481	11,638	45.6	43.4	4.9	54.4
Feb-Apr 1973	21,407	9,791	9,311	480	11,617	45.7	43.5	4.9	54.3
Mar-May 1973	21,414	9,811	9,332	478	11,603	45.8	43.6	4.9	54.2
Apr-Jun 1973	21,420	9,819	9,342	477	11,600	45.8	43.6	4.9	54.2
May-Jul 1973	21,426	9,826	9,351	475	11,601	45.9	43.6	4.8	54.1
Jun-Aug 1973	21,432	9,833	9,361	472	11,600	45.9	43.7	4.8	54.1
Jul-Sep 1973	21,438	9,845	9,376	468	11,593	45.9	43.7	4.8	54.1
Aug-Oct 1973	21,443	9,855	9,390	465	11,588	46.0	43.8	4.7	54.0
Sep-Nov 1973	21,449	9,872	9,409	463	11,577	46.0	43.9	4.7	54.0
Oct-Dec 1973	21,454	9,882	9,422	460	11,572	46.1	43.9	4.7	53.9
Nov-Jan 1974	21,460	9,894	9,433	461	11,566	46.1	44.0	4.7	53.9
Dec-Feb 1974	21,465	9,908	9,446	462	11,557	46.2	44.0	4.7	53.8
Jan-Mar 1974	21,470	9,920	9,455	465	11,550	46.2	44.0	4.7	53.8
Feb-Apr 1974	21,476	9,932	9,465	467	11,544	46.2	44.1	4.7	53.8
Mar-May 1974	21,481	9,944	9,477	468	11,537	46.3	44.1	4.7	53.7
Apr-Jun 1974	21,487	9,962	9,492	470	11,525	46.4	44.2	4.7	53.6
May-Jul 1974	21,492	9,979	9,509	470	11,513	46.4	44.2	4.7	53.6
Jun-Aug 1974	21,497	9,995	9,524	471	11,502	46.5	44.3	4.7	53.5
Jul-Sep 1974	21,504	10,014	9,543	471	11,490	46.6	44.4	4.7	53.4
Aug-Oct 1974	21,510	10,025	9,554	471	11,484	46.6	44.4	4.7	53.4
Sep-Nov 1974	21,516	10,032	9,561	471	11,484	46.6	44.4	4.7	53.4
Oct-Dec 1974	21,522	10,034	9,562	472	11,488	46.6	44.4	4.7	53.4
Nov-Jan 1975	21,528	10,035	9,560	475	11,493	46.6	44.4	4.7	53.4
Dec-Feb 1975	21,534	10,035	9,555	479	11,500	46.6	44.4	4.8	53.4
Jan-Mar 1975	21,541	10,038	9,553	485	11,503	46.6	44.3	4.8	53.4
Feb-Apr 1975	21,547	10,040	9,549	491	11,507	46.6	44.3	4.9	53.4
Mar-May 1975	21,553	10,051	9,552	499	11,502	46.6	44.3	5.0	53.4
Apr-Jun 1975	21,559	10,058	9,552	507	11,501	46.7	44.3	5.0	53.3
May-Jul 1975	21,565	10,065	9,551	514	11,500	46.7	44.3	5.1	53.3
Jun-Aug 1975	21,571	10,070	9,550	520	11,501	46.7	44.3	5.2	53.3
Jul-Sep 1975	21,580	10,071	9,545	526	11,509	46.7	44.2	5.2	53.3
Aug-Oct 1975	21,590	10,078	9,544	534	11,511	46.7	44.2	5.3	53.3
Sep-Nov 1975	21,599	10,083	9,539	544	11,516	46.7	44.2	5.4	53.3
Oct-Dec 1975	21,608	10,093	9,539	553	11,515	46.7	44.1	5.5	53.3

Labour Force Survey, summary by sex United Kingdom (thousands) seasonally adjusted (Continued)

All aged 16 & over

	All aged 16 & over	Total economically active	Total in employment	Unemployed	Economically inactive	Economic Activity rate (%)	Employment rate (%)	Unemployment rate (%)	Economic inactivity rate (%)
	1	2	3	4	5	6	7	8	9
Female	MGSN	MGSH	MGSB	MGSE	MGSK	MGWI	MGST	MGSZ	YBTE
Nov-Jan 1976	21,617	10,094	9,535	560	11,522	46.7	44.1	5.5	53.3
Dec-Feb 1976	21,626	10,098	9,532	566	11,528	46.7	44.1	5.6	53.3
Jan-Mar 1976	21,635	10,100	9,527	573	11,535	46.7	44.0	5.7	53.3
Feb-Apr 1976	21,644	10,102	9,523	578	11,542	46.7	44.0	5.7	53.3
Mar-May 1976	21,653	10,109	9,526	583	11,544	46.7	44.0	5.8	53.3
Apr-Jun 1976	21,662	10,114	9,527	587	11,548	46.7	44.0	5.8	53.3
May-Jul 1976	21,671	10,122	9,532	590	11,548	46.7	44.0	5.8	53.3
Jun-Aug 1976	21,680	10,126	9,531	595	11,553	46.7	44.0	5.9	53.3
Jul-Sep 1976	21,691	10,136	9,536	600	11,555	46.7	44.0	5.9	53.3
Aug-Oct 1976	21,703	10,144	9,540	604	11,559	46.7	44.0	6.0	53.3
Sep-Nov 1976	21,714	10,153	9,547	606	11,561	46.8	44.0	6.0	53.2
Oct-Dec 1976	21,726	10,164	9,556	608	11,562	46.8	44.0	6.0	53.2
Nov-Jan 1977	21,737	10,175	9,564	611	11,562	46.8	44.0	6.0	53.2
Dec-Feb 1977	21,749	10,187	9,574	613	11,561	46.8	44.0	6.0	53.2
Jan-Mar 1977	21,760	10,193	9,578	615	11,567	46.8	44.0	6.0	53.2
Feb-Apr 1977	21,772	10,201	9,585	616	11,571	46.9	44.0	6.0	53.1
Mar-May 1977	21,783	10,210	9,592	618	11,574	46.9	44.0	6.1	53.1
Apr-Jun 1977	21,795	10,218	9,596	622	11,577	46.9	44.0	6.1	53.1
May-Jul 1977	21,806	10,232	9,604	628	11,575	46.9	44.0	6.1	53.1
Jun-Aug 1977	21,818	10,244	9,610	634	11,574	47.0	44.0	6.2	53.0
Jul-Sep 1977	21,830	10,261	9,622	640	11,569	47.0	44.1	6.2	53.0
Aug-Oct 1977	21,843	10,271	9,628	642	11,572	47.0	44.1	6.3	53.0
Sep-Nov 1977	21,855	10,285	9,640	645	11,570	47.1	44.1	6.3	52.9
Oct-Dec 1977	21,868	10,299	9,653	646	11,569	47.1	44.1	6.3	52.9
Nov-Jan 1978	21,880	10,309	9,663	646	11,571	47.1	44.2	6.3	52.9
Dec-Feb 1978	21,893	10,320	9,676	644	11,573	47.1	44.2	6.2	52.9
Jan-Mar 1978	21,905	10,334	9,692	643	11,571	47.2	44.2	6.2	52.8
Feb-Apr 1978	21,918	10,349	9,706	643	11,569	47.2	44.3	6.2	52.8
Mar-May 1978	21,930	10,368	9,724	644	11,562	47.3	44.3	6.2	52.7
Apr-Jun 1978	21,943	10,381	9,735	646	11,562	47.3	44.4	6.2	52.7
May-Jul 1978	21,955	10,393	9,747	647	11,562	47.3	44.4	6.2	52.7
Jun-Aug 1978	21,968	10,407	9,757	649	11,561	47.4	44.4	6.2	52.6
Jul-Sep 1978	21,980	10,425	9,776	650	11,555	47.4	44.5	6.2	52.6
Aug-Oct 1978	21,992	10,442	9,792	650	11,550	47.5	44.5	6.2	52.5
Sep-Nov 1978	22,004	10,466	9,820	647	11,538	47.6	44.6	6.2	52.4
Oct-Dec 1978	22,017	10,487	9,843	644	11,530	47.6	44.7	6.1	52.4
Nov-Jan 1979	22,029	10,503	9,860	642	11,526	47.7	44.8	6.1	52.3
Dec-Feb 1979	22,041	10,512	9,869	643	11,529	47.7	44.8	6.1	52.3
Jan-Mar 1979	22,053	10,518	9,874	644	11,535	47.7	44.8	6.1	52.3
Feb-Apr 1979	22,066	10,525	9,881	645	11,540	47.7	44.8	6.1	52.3
Mar-May 1979	22,078	10,541	9,895	646	11,536	47.7	44.8	6.1	52.3
Apr-Jun 1979	22,090	10,568	9,919	649	11,522	47.8	44.9	6.1	52.2
May-Jul 1979	22,102	10,599	9,945	654	11,503	48.0	45.0	6.2	52.0
Jun-Aug 1979	22,114	10,625	9,967	658	11,490	48.0	45.1	6.2	52.0
Jul-Sep 1979	22,129	10,645	9,984	660	11,484	48.1	45.1	6.2	51.9
Aug-Oct 1979	22,144	10,666	10,003	663	11,477	48.2	45.2	6.2	51.8
Sep-Nov 1979	22,158	10,689	10,023	667	11,469	48.2	45.2	6.2	51.8
Oct-Dec 1979	22,173	10,718	10,045	673	11,455	48.3	45.3	6.3	51.7
Nov-Jan 1980	22,187	10,735	10,055	679	11,453	48.4	45.3	6.3	51.6
Dec-Feb 1980	22,202	10,755	10,065	690	11,447	48.4	45.3	6.4	51.6
Jan-Mar 1980	22,217	10,766	10,065	701	11,450	48.5	45.3	6.5	51.5
Feb-Apr 1980	22,231	10,781	10,068	713	11,450	48.5	45.3	6.6	51.5
Mar-May 1980	22,246	10,794	10,068	726	11,452	48.5	45.3	6.7	51.5
Apr-Jun 1980	22,260	10,804	10,065	739	11,456	48.5	45.2	6.8	51.5
May-Jul 1980	22,275	10,818	10,065	753	11,457	48.6	45.2	7.0	51.4
Jun-Aug 1980	22,290	10,837	10,065	771	11,453	48.6	45.2	7.1	51.4
Jul-Sep 1980	22,303	10,845	10,055	790	11,458	48.6	45.1	7.3	51.4
Aug-Oct 1980	22,317	10,853	10,043	810	11,463	48.6	45.0	7.5	51.4
Sep-Nov 1980	22,330	10,863	10,033	831	11,467	48.6	44.9	7.6	51.4
Oct-Dec 1980	22,343	10,876	10,023	853	11,468	48.7	44.9	7.8	51.3

Labour Force Survey, summary by sex United Kingdom (thousands) seasonally adjusted (Continued)

All aged 16 & over

	All aged 16 & over	Total economically active	Total in employment	Unemployed	Economically inactive	Economic Activity rate (%)	Employment rate (%)	Unemployment rate (%)	Economic inactivity rate (%)
	1	2	3	4	5	6	7	8	9
Female	MGSN	MGSH	MGSB	MGSE	MGSK	MGWI	MGST	MGSZ	YBTE
Nov-Jan 1981	22,357	10,887	10,013	874	11,470	48.7	44.8	8.0	51.3
Dec-Feb 1981	22,370	10,893	10,000	893	11,478	48.7	44.7	8.2	51.3
Jan-Mar 1981	22,384	10,900	9,991	910	11,483	48.7	44.6	8.3	51.3
Feb-Apr 1981	22,397	10,911	9,985	926	11,486	48.7	44.6	8.5	51.3
Mar-May 1981	22,411	10,913	9,973	940	11,497	48.7	44.5	8.6	51.3
Apr-Jun 1981	22,424	10,908	9,957	951	11,516	48.6	44.4	8.7	51.4
May-Jul 1981	22,438	10,905	9,945	960	11,532	48.6	44.3	8.8	51.4
Jun-Aug 1981	22,451	10,906	9,938	969	11,545	48.6	44.3	8.9	51.4
Jul-Sep 1981	22,459	10,905	9,927	978	11,554	48.6	44.2	9.0	51.4
Aug-Oct 1981	22,467	10,907	9,921	987	11,559	48.5	44.2	9.0	51.5
Sep-Nov 1981	22,474	10,907	9,911	996	11,568	48.5	44.1	9.1	51.5
Oct-Dec 1981	22,482	10,901	9,899	1,002	11,581	48.5	44.0	9.2	51.5
Nov-Jan 1982	22,490	10,894	9,889	1,006	11,596	48.4	44.0	9.2	51.6
Dec-Feb 1982	22,498	10,887	9,879	1,009	11,611	48.4	43.9	9.3	51.6
Jan-Mar 1982	22,506	10,882	9,870	1,012	11,624	48.4	43.9	9.3	51.6
Feb-Apr 1982	22,514	10,879	9,862	1,017	11,635	48.3	43.8	9.3	51.7
Mar-May 1982	22,521	10,877	9,856	1,020	11,645	48.3	43.8	9.4	51.7
Apr-Jun 1982	22,529	10,871	9,846	1,024	11,658	48.3	43.7	9.4	51.7
May-Jul 1982	22,537	10,861	9,832	1,028	11,676	48.2	43.6	9.5	51.8
Jun-Aug 1982	22,545	10,852	9,819	1,034	11,693	48.1	43.6	9.5	51.9
Jul-Sep 1982	22,555	10,840	9,801	1,039	11,714	48.1	43.5	9.6	51.9
Aug-Oct 1982	22,564	10,829	9,782	1,047	11,736	48.0	43.4	9.7	52.0
Sep-Nov 1982	22,574	10,818	9,764	1,053	11,756	47.9	43.3	9.7	52.1
Oct-Dec 1982	22,584	10,807	9,747	1,060	11,777	47.9	43.2	9.8	52.1
Nov-Jan 1983	22,594	10,799	9,732	1,067	11,795	47.8	43.1	9.9	52.2
Dec-Feb 1983	22,604	10,790	9,717	1,073	11,814	47.7	43.0	9.9	52.3
Jan-Mar 1983	22,613	10,790	9,711	1,079	11,823	47.7	42.9	10.0	52.3
Feb-Apr 1983	22,623	10,792	9,708	1,084	11,831	47.7	42.9	10.0	52.3
Mar-May 1983	22,633	10,814	9,721	1,093	11,819	47.8	42.9	10.1	52.2
Apr-Jun 1983	22,643	10,859	9,745	1,113	11,784	48.0	43.0	10.3	52.0
May-Jul 1983	22,653	10,911	9,776	1,135	11,742	48.2	43.2	10.4	51.8
Jun-Aug 1983	22,663	10,965	9,811	1,155	11,697	48.4	43.3	10.5	51.6
Jul-Sep 1983	22,673	11,025	9,849	1,175	11,648	48.6	43.4	10.7	51.4
Aug-Oct 1983	22,683	11,085	9,889	1,196	11,599	48.9	43.6	10.8	51.1
Sep-Nov 1983	22,694	11,147	9,926	1,220	11,547	49.1	43.7	10.9	50.9
Oct-Dec 1983	22,704	11,205	9,962	1,243	11,499	49.4	43.9	11.1	50.6
Nov-Jan 1984	22,715	11,259	9,992	1,267	11,456	49.6	44.0	11.3	50.4
Dec-Feb 1984	22,725	11,303	10,013	1,290	11,422	49.7	44.1	11.4	50.3
Jan-Mar 1984	22,735	11,348	10,033	1,315	11,388	49.9	44.1	11.6	50.1
Feb-Apr 1984	22,746	11,387	10,052	1,334	11,359	50.1	44.2	11.7	49.9
Mar-May 1984	22,756	11,425	10,075	1,349	11,331	50.2	44.3	11.8	49.8
Apr-Jun 1984	22,767	11,444	10,098	1,346	11,323	50.3	44.4	11.8	49.7
May-Jul 1984	22,777	11,453	10,113	1,341	11,324	50.3	44.4	11.7	49.7
Jun-Aug 1984	22,787	11,466	10,133	1,333	11,322	50.3	44.5	11.6	49.7
Jul-Sep 1984	22,799	11,475	10,147	1,328	11,323	50.3	44.5	11.6	49.7
Aug-Oct 1984	22,810	11,493	10,170	1,323	11,317	50.4	44.6	11.5	49.6
Sep-Nov 1984	22,821	11,508	10,190	1,318	11,313	50.4	44.7	11.5	49.6
Oct-Dec 1984	22,832	11,528	10,217	1,311	11,304	50.5	44.8	11.4	49.5
Nov-Jan 1985	22,843	11,543	10,240	1,303	11,300	50.5	44.8	11.3	49.5
Dec-Feb 1985	22,854	11,555	10,260	1,295	11,299	50.6	44.9	11.2	49.4
Jan-Mar 1985	22,865	11,559	10,273	1,286	11,307	50.6	44.9	11.1	49.4
Feb-Apr 1985	22,876	11,569	10,290	1,279	11,307	50.6	45.0	11.1	49.4
Mar-May 1985	22,887	11,581	10,308	1,273	11,307	50.6	45.0	11.0	49.4
Apr-Jun 1985	22,899	11,603	10,330	1,273	11,296	50.7	45.1	11.0	49.3
May-Jul 1985	22,910	11,622	10,350	1,272	11,288	50.7	45.2	10.9	49.3
Jun-Aug 1985	22,921	11,640	10,370	1,270	11,281	50.8	45.2	10.9	49.2
Jul-Sep 1985	22,930	11,658	10,387	1,271	11,272	50.8	45.3	10.9	49.2
Aug-Oct 1985	22,939	11,673	10,403	1,271	11,266	50.9	45.3	10.9	49.1
Sep-Nov 1985	22,949	11,691	10,420	1,271	11,258	50.9	45.4	10.9	49.1
Oct-Dec 1985	22,958	11,710	10,440	1,270	11,247	51.0	45.5	10.8	49.0

Labour Force Survey, summary by sex United Kingdom (thousands) seasonally adjusted (Continued)

All aged 16 & over

	All aged 16 & over	Total economically active	Total in employment	Unemployed	Economically inactive	Economic Activity rate (%)	Employment rate (%)	Unemployment rate (%)	Economic inactivity rate (%)
	1	2	3	4	5	6	7	8	9
Female	MGSN	MGSH	MGSB	MGSE	MGSK	MGWI	MGST	MGSZ	YBTE
Nov-Jan 1986	22,967	11,721	10,450	1,271	11,246	51.0	45.5	10.8	49.0
Dec-Feb 1986	22,976	11,733	10,460	1,273	11,243	51.1	45.5	10.9	48.9
Jan-Mar 1986	22,986	11,744	10,470	1,274	11,241	51.1	45.6	10.9	48.9
Feb-Apr 1986	22,995	11,763	10,488	1,276	11,232	51.2	45.6	10.8	48.8
Mar-May 1986	23,004	11,781	10,504	1,277	11,223	51.2	45.7	10.8	48.8
Apr-Jun 1986	23,013	11,805	10,522	1,283	11,208	51.3	45.7	10.9	48.7
May-Jul 1986	23,023	11,829	10,540	1,289	11,194	51.4	45.8	10.9	48.6
Jun-Aug 1986	23,032	11,854	10,560	1,294	11,178	51.5	45.8	10.9	48.5
Jul-Sep 1986	23,041	11,877	10,580	1,297	11,163	51.5	45.9	10.9	48.5
Aug-Oct 1986	23,049	11,898	10,600	1,298	11,152	51.6	46.0	10.9	48.4
Sep-Nov 1986	23,058	11,925	10,630	1,295	11,133	51.7	46.1	10.9	48.3
Oct-Dec 1986	23,067	11,941	10,650	1,291	11,126	51.8	46.2	10.8	48.2
Nov-Jan 1987	23,075	11,960	10,673	1,287	11,116	51.8	46.3	10.8	48.2
Dec-Feb 1987	23,084	11,969	10,690	1,279	11,115	51.8	46.3	10.7	48.2
Jan-Mar 1987	23,093	11,966	10,697	1,269	11,126	51.8	46.3	10.6	48.2
Feb-Apr 1987	23,101	11,979	10,720	1,259	11,122	51.9	46.4	10.5	48.1
Mar-May 1987	23,110	11,996	10,750	1,247	11,114	51.9	46.5	10.4	48.1
Apr-Jun 1987	23,119	12,021	10,790	1,231	11,098	52.0	46.7	10.2	48.0
May-Jul 1987	23,127	12,042	10,830	1,212	11,085	52.1	46.8	10.1	47.9
Jun-Aug 1987	23,136	12,056	10,860	1,196	11,080	52.1	46.9	9.9	47.9
Jul-Sep 1987	23,142	12,071	10,893	1,178	11,071	52.2	47.1	9.8	47.8
Aug-Oct 1987	23,148	12,090	10,930	1,160	11,058	52.2	47.2	9.6	47.8
Sep-Nov 1987	23,154	12,104	10,963	1,141	11,050	52.3	47.3	9.4	47.7
Oct-Dec 1987	23,159	12,127	11,003	1,124	11,033	52.4	47.5	9.3	47.6
Nov-Jan 1988	23,165	12,153	11,043	1,110	11,013	52.5	47.7	9.1	47.5
Dec-Feb 1988	23,171	12,168	11,070	1,098	11,003	52.5	47.8	9.0	47.5
Jan-Mar 1988	23,177	12,175	11,093	1,083	11,002	52.5	47.9	8.9	47.5
Feb-Apr 1988	23,183	12,187	11,120	1,067	10,996	52.6	48.0	8.8	47.4
Mar-May 1988	23,188	12,197	11,146	1,051	10,992	52.6	48.1	8.6	47.4
Apr-Jun 1988	23,194	12,217	11,180	1,037	10,977	52.7	48.2	8.5	47.3
May-Jul 1988	23,200	12,244	11,220	1,024	10,956	52.8	48.4	8.4	47.2
Jun-Aug 1988	23,206	12,270	11,260	1,010	10,936	52.9	48.5	8.2	47.1
Jul-Sep 1988	23,212	12,299	11,300	999	10,913	53.0	48.7	8.1	47.0
Aug-Oct 1988	23,217	12,328	11,340	988	10,889	53.1	48.8	8.0	46.9
Sep-Nov 1988	23,223	12,348	11,370	978	10,875	53.2	49.0	7.9	46.8
Oct-Dec 1988	23,229	12,376	11,413	964	10,852	53.3	49.1	7.8	46.7
Nov-Jan 1989	23,234	12,401	11,450	951	10,833	53.4	49.3	7.7	46.6
Dec-Feb 1989	23,240	12,427	11,490	937	10,813	53.5	49.4	7.5	46.5
Jan-Mar 1989	23,246	12,454	11,530	924	10,792	53.6	49.6	7.4	46.4
Feb-Apr 1989	23,251	12,467	11,560	907	10,784	53.6	49.7	7.3	46.4
Mar-May 1989	23,257	12,475	11,582	893	10,782	53.6	49.8	7.2	46.4
Apr-Jun 1989	23,262	12,472	11,590	882	10,790	53.6	49.8	7.1	46.4
May-Jul 1989	23,268	12,476	11,600	876	10,792	53.6	49.9	7.0	46.4
Jun-Aug 1989	23,274	12,478	11,607	870	10,796	53.6	49.9	7.0	46.4
Jul-Sep 1989	23,276	12,484	11,617	866	10,793	53.6	49.9	6.9	46.4
Aug-Oct 1989	23,279	12,491	11,630	861	10,788	53.7	50.0	6.9	46.3
Sep-Nov 1989	23,282	12,518	11,660	858	10,764	53.8	50.1	6.9	46.2
Oct-Dec 1989	23,284	12,534	11,680	854	10,750	53.8	50.2	6.8	46.2
Nov-Jan 1990	23,287	12,540	11,690	850	10,747	53.9	50.2	6.8	46.1
Dec-Feb 1990	23,289	12,546	11,700	846	10,743	53.9	50.2	6.7	46.1
Jan-Mar 1990	23,292	12,544	11,700	844	10,748	53.9	50.2	6.7	46.1
Feb-Apr 1990	23,294	12,552	11,710	842	10,742	53.9	50.3	6.7	46.1
Mar-May 1990	23,297	12,569	11,727	841	10,728	54.0	50.3	6.7	46.0
Apr-Jun 1990	23,299	12,583	11,742	841	10,716	54.0	50.4	6.7	46.0
May-Jul 1990	23,302	12,603	11,763	841	10,699	54.1	50.5	6.7	45.9
Jun-Aug 1990	23,305	12,603	11,760	843	10,702	54.1	50.5	6.7	45.9
Jul-Sep 1990	23,309	12,596	11,750	846	10,712	54.0	50.4	6.7	46.0
Aug-Oct 1990	23,313	12,594	11,743	852	10,719	54.0	50.4	6.8	46.0
Sep-Nov 1990	23,317	12,591	11,733	859	10,725	54.0	50.3	6.8	46.0
Oct-Dec 1990	23,321	12,593	11,725	868	10,728	54.0	50.3	6.9	46.0

Labour Force Survey, summary by sex United Kingdom (thousands) seasonally adjusted (Continued)

All aged 16 & over

	All aged 16 & over	Total economically active	Total in employment	Unemployed	Economically inactive	Economic Activity rate (%)	Employment rate (%)	Unemployment rate (%)	Economic inactivity rate (%)
	1	2	3	4	5	6	7	8	9
Female	MGSN	MGSH	MGSB	MGSE	MGSK	MGWI	MGST	MGSZ	YBTE
Nov-Jan 1991	23,325	12,589	11,713	877	10,735	54.0	50.2	7.0	46.0
Dec-Feb 1991	23,329	12,580	11,693	888	10,749	53.9	50.1	7.1	46.1
Jan-Mar 1991	23,333	12,567	11,665	902	10,766	53.9	50.0	7.2	46.1
Feb-Apr 1991	23,337	12,560	11,640	920	10,777	53.8	49.9	7.3	46.2
Mar-May 1991	23,341	12,556	11,621	935	10,785	53.8	49.8	7.4	46.2
Apr-Jun 1991	23,344	12,550	11,608	942	10,794	53.8	49.7	7.5	46.2
May-Jul 1991	23,346	12,541	11,595	946	10,805	53.7	49.7	7.5	46.3
Jun-Aug 1991	23,349	12,527	11,577	950	10,821	53.7	49.6	7.6	46.3
Jul-Sep 1991	23,351	12,511	11,557	954	10,840	53.6	49.5	7.6	46.4
Aug-Oct 1991	23,354	12,491	11,537	954	10,863	53.5	49.4	7.6	46.5
Sep-Nov 1991	23,357	12,470	11,517	952	10,887	53.4	49.3	7.6	46.6
Oct-Dec 1991	23,359	12,450	11,500	950	10,909	53.3	49.2	7.6	46.7
Nov-Jan 1992	23,362	12,445	11,497	948	10,916	53.3	49.2	7.6	46.7
Dec-Feb 1992	23,364	12,442	11,495	947	10,923	53.3	49.2	7.6	46.7
Jan-Mar 1992	23,367	12,440	11,495	945	10,927	53.2	49.2	7.6	46.8
Feb-Apr 1992	23,369	12,440	11,498	942	10,930	53.2	49.2	7.6	46.8
Mar-May 1992	23,374	12,441	11,500	940	10,934	53.2	49.2	7.6	46.8
Apr-Jun 1992	23,377	12,419	11,477	942	10,958	53.1	49.1	7.6	46.9
May-Jul 1992	23,379	12,402	11,451	951	10,977	53.0	49.0	7.7	47.0
Jun-Aug 1992	23,382	12,412	11,460	952	10,969	53.1	49.0	7.7	46.9
Jul-Sep 1992	23,383	12,414	11,471	943	10,969	53.1	49.1	7.6	46.9
Aug-Oct 1992	23,384	12,410	11,461	949	10,975	53.1	49.0	7.6	46.9
Sep-Nov 1992	23,386	12,435	11,472	963	10,951	53.2	49.1	7.7	46.8
Oct-Dec 1992	23,387	12,430	11,456	974	10,957	53.1	49.0	7.8	46.9
Nov-Jan 1993	23,389	12,438	11,438	1,000	10,951	53.2	48.9	8.0	46.8
Dec-Feb 1993	23,390	12,440	11,426	1,014	10,950	53.2	48.9	8.2	46.8
Jan-Mar 1993	23,392	12,429	11,438	991	10,962	53.1	48.9	8.0	46.9
Feb-Apr 1993	23,393	12,444	11,455	989	10,949	53.2	49.0	7.9	46.8
Mar-May 1993	23,394	12,460	11,477	983	10,935	53.3	49.1	7.9	46.7
Apr-Jun 1993	23,396	12,461	11,462	999	10,935	53.3	49.0	8.0	46.7
May-Jul 1993	23,397	12,468	11,473	994	10,930	53.3	49.0	8.0	46.7
Jun-Aug 1993	23,399	12,457	11,464	994	10,941	53.2	49.0	8.0	46.8
Jul-Sep 1993	23,402	12,476	11,502	974	10,926	53.3	49.2	7.8	46.7
Aug-Oct 1993	23,405	12,496	11,500	996	10,908	53.4	49.1	8.0	46.6
Sep-Nov 1993	23,408	12,480	11,489	992	10,927	53.3	49.1	7.9	46.7
Oct-Dec 1993	23,411	12,488	11,499	989	10,922	53.3	49.1	7.9	46.7
Nov-Jan 1993	23,413	12,483	11,496	987	10,930	53.3	49.1	7.9	46.7
Dec-Feb 1994	23,416	12,486	11,496	990	10,931	53.3	49.1	7.9	46.7
Jan-Mar 1994	23,419	12,501	11,527	974	10,918	53.4	49.2	7.8	46.6
Feb-Apr 1994	23,422	12,497	11,540	958	10,925	53.4	49.3	7.7	46.6
Mar-May 1994	23,425	12,492	11,548	944	10,933	53.3	49.3	7.6	46.7
Apr-Jun 1994	23,428	12,489	11,558	931	10,939	53.3	49.3	7.5	46.7
May-Jul 1994	23,431	12,497	11,580	917	10,934	53.3	49.4	7.3	46.7
Jun-Aug 1994	23,434	12,483	11,570	913	10,951	53.3	49.4	7.3	46.7
Jul-Sep 1994	23,439	12,484	11,575	909	10,956	53.3	49.4	7.3	46.7
Aug-Oct 1994	23,444	12,459	11,557	902	10,985	53.1	49.3	7.2	46.9
Sep-Nov 1994	23,449	12,451	11,569	882	10,998	53.1	49.3	7.1	46.9
Oct-Dec 1994	23,454	12,434	11,564	870	11,020	53.0	49.3	7.0	47.0
Nov-Jan 1994	23,459	12,423	11,558	865	11,036	53.0	49.3	7.0	47.0
Dec-Feb 1995	23,464	12,472	11,602	870	10,992	53.2	49.4	7.0	46.8
Jan-Mar 1995	23,469	12,503	11,626	877	10,966	53.3	49.5	7.0	46.7
Feb-Apr 1995	23,474	12,531	11,642	888	10,943	53.4	49.6	7.1	46.6
Mar-May 1995	23,479	12,520	11,640	879	10,959	53.3	49.6	7.0	46.7
Apr-Jun 1995	23,484	12,527	11,666	861	10,957	53.3	49.7	6.9	46.7
May-Jul 1995	23,489	12,551	11,685	866	10,938	53.4	49.7	6.9	46.6
Jun-Aug 1995	23,494	12,583	11,720	863	10,911	53.6	49.9	6.9	46.4
Jul-Sep 1995	23,500	12,597	11,728	869	10,903	53.6	49.9	6.9	46.4
Aug-Oct 1995	23,506	12,613	11,756	857	10,893	53.7	50.0	6.8	46.3
Sep-Nov 1995	23,512	12,625	11,758	868	10,886	53.7	50.0	6.9	46.3
Oct-Dec 1995	23,518	12,646	11,806	840	10,872	53.8	50.2	6.6	46.2

Labour Force Survey, summary by sex United Kingdom (thousands) seasonally adjusted (Continued)

All aged 16 & over	All aged 16 & over	Total economically active	Total in employment	Unemployed	Economically inactive	Economic Activity rate (%)	Employment rate (%)	Unemployment rate (%)	Economic inactivity rate (%)
	1	2	3	4	5	6	7	8	9
Female	MGSN	MGSH	MGSB	MGSE	MGSK	MGWI	MGST	MGSZ	YBTE
Nov-Jan 1996	23,524	12,672	11,842	829	10,852	53.9	50.3	6.5	46.1
Dec-Feb 1996	23,530	12,654	11,840	814	10,876	53.8	50.3	6.4	46.2
Jan-Mar 1996	23,535	12,621	11,831	790	10,914	53.6	50.3	6.3	46.4
Feb-Apr 1996	23,541	12,635	11,826	809	10,906	53.7	50.2	6.4	46.3
Mar-May 1996	23,547	12,658	11,838	820	10,889	53.8	50.3	6.5	46.2
Apr-Jun 1996	23,553	12,663	11,843	820	10,890	53.8	50.3	6.5	46.2
May-Jul 1996	23,559	12,644	11,828	816	10,915	53.7	50.2	6.5	46.3
Jun-Aug 1996	23,565	12,662	11,855	807	10,903	53.7	50.3	6.4	46.3
Jul-Sep 1996	23,571	12,669	11,860	809	10,902	53.7	50.3	6.4	46.3
Aug-Oct 1996	23,577	12,711	11,900	812	10,866	53.9	50.5	6.4	46.1
Sep-Nov 1996	23,584	12,731	11,911	820	10,853	54.0	50.5	6.4	46.0
Oct-Dec 1996	23,590	12,756	11,929	827	10,833	54.1	50.6	6.5	45.9
Nov-Jan 1997	23,596	12,765	11,948	817	10,831	54.1	50.6	6.4	45.9
Dec-Feb 1997	23,602	12,780	11,980	800	10,822	54.1	50.8	6.3	45.9
Jan-Mar 1997	23,608	12,773	11,988	785	10,835	54.1	50.8	6.1	45.9
Feb-Apr 1997	23,614	12,789	12,007	783	10,825	54.2	50.8	6.1	45.8
Mar-May 1997	23,621	12,805	12,043	762	10,815	54.2	51.0	6.0	45.8
Apr-Jun 1997	23,627	12,853	12,071	783	10,773	54.4	51.1	6.1	45.6
May-Jul 1997	23,633	12,857	12,066	791	10,776	54.4	51.1	6.2	45.6
Jun-Aug 1997	23,639	12,829	12,052	777	10,810	54.3	51.0	6.1	45.7
Jul-Sep 1997	23,646	12,834	12,084	750	10,812	54.3	51.1	5.8	45.7
Aug-Oct 1997	23,653	12,814	12,079	735	10,839	54.2	51.1	5.7	45.8
Sep-Nov 1997	23,659	12,820	12,092	728	10,839	54.2	51.1	5.7	45.8
Oct-Dec 1997	23,666	12,818	12,099	719	10,848	54.2	51.1	5.6	45.8
Nov-Jan 1998	23,673	12,792	12,079	713	10,881	54.0	51.0	5.6	46.0
Dec-Feb 1998	23,680	12,807	12,089	718	10,873	54.1	51.1	5.6	45.9
Jan-Mar 1998	23,686	12,831	12,122	709	10,855	54.2	51.2	5.5	45.8
Feb-Apr 1998	23,693	12,856	12,153	704	10,837	54.3	51.3	5.5	45.7
Mar-May 1998	23,700	12,850	12,143	707	10,850	54.2	51.2	5.5	45.8
Apr-Jun 1998	23,707	12,859	12,144	715	10,847	54.2	51.2	5.6	45.8
May-Jul 1998	23,714	12,890	12,173	717	10,823	54.4	51.3	5.6	45.6
Jun-Aug 1998	23,720	12,917	12,204	713	10,803	54.5	51.5	5.5	45.5
Jul-Sep 1998	23,728	12,916	12,224	692	10,812	54.4	51.5	5.4	45.6
Aug-Oct 1998	23,736	12,963	12,275	688	10,773	54.6	51.7	5.3	45.4
Sep-Nov 1998	23,744	12,980	12,296	684	10,764	54.7	51.8	5.3	45.3
Oct-Dec 1998	23,752	12,979	12,295	684	10,773	54.6	51.8	5.3	45.4
Nov-Jan 1999	23,760	13,035	12,346	688	10,725	54.9	52.0	5.3	45.1
Dec-Feb 1999	23,768	13,032	12,337	695	10,735	54.8	51.9	5.3	45.2
Jan-Mar 1999	23,776	13,041	12,346	695	10,735	54.9	51.9	5.3	45.1
Feb-Apr 1999	23,783	13,046	12,351	695	10,737	54.9	51.9	5.3	45.1
Mar-May 1999	23,791	13,037	12,348	689	10,754	54.8	51.9	5.3	45.2
Apr-Jun 1999	23,799	13,043	12,359	684	10,756	54.8	51.9	5.2	45.2
May-Jul 1999	23,807	13,041	12,358	684	10,766	54.8	51.9	5.2	45.2
Jun-Aug 1999	23,815	13,061	12,383	678	10,754	54.8	52.0	5.2	45.2
Jul-Sep 1999	23,825	13,089	12,413	676	10,736	54.9	52.1	5.2	45.1
Aug-Oct 1999	23,835	13,088	12,405	683	10,747	54.9	52.0	5.2	45.1
Sep-Nov 1999	23,845	13,113	12,432	681	10,732	55.0	52.1	5.2	45.0
Oct-Dec 1999	23,855	13,148	12,466	682	10,707	55.1	52.3	5.2	44.9
Nov-Jan 2000	23,865	13,149	12,465	684	10,716	55.1	52.2	5.2	44.9
Dec-Feb 2000	23,875	13,172	12,485	688	10,703	55.2	52.3	5.2	44.8
Jan-Mar 2000	23,885	13,190	12,499	691	10,695	55.2	52.3	5.2	44.8
Feb-Apr 2000	23,895	13,177	12,502	675	10,718	55.1	52.3	5.1	44.9
Mar-May 2000	23,905	13,189	12,526	663	10,716	55.2	52.4	5.0	44.8
Apr-Jun 2000	23,915	13,207	12,565	642	10,708	55.2	52.5	4.9	44.8
May-Jul 2000	23,925	13,233	12,598	635	10,692	55.3	52.7	4.8	44.7
Jun-Aug 2000	23,935	13,253	12,634	619	10,682	55.4	52.8	4.7	44.6
Jul-Sep 2000	23,946	13,257	12,623	635	10,689	55.4	52.7	4.8	44.6
Aug-Oct 2000	23,958	13,243	12,596	646	10,715	55.3	52.6	4.9	44.7
Sep-Nov 2000	23,969	13,207	12,585	621	10,762	55.1	52.5	4.7	44.9
Oct-Dec 2000	23,980	13,196	12,587	609	10,784	55.0	52.5	4.6	45.0

Labour Force Survey, summary by sex United Kingdom (thousands) seasonally adjusted (Continued)

All aged 16 & over

	All aged 16 & over	Total economically active	Total in employment	Unemployed	Economically inactive	Economic Activity rate (%)	Employment rate (%)	Unemployment rate (%)	Economic inactivity rate (%)
	1	2	3	4	5	6	7	8	9
Female	MGSN	MGSH	MGSB	MGSE	MGSK	MGWI	MGST	MGSZ	YBTE
Nov-Jan 2001	23,991	13,252	12,654	598	10,739	55.2	52.7	4.5	44.8
Dec-Feb 2001	24,003	13,237	12,645	592	10,765	55.1	52.7	4.5	44.9
Jan-Mar 2001	24,014	13,209	12,623	586	10,805	55.0	52.6	4.4	45.0
Feb-Apr 2001	24,025	13,238	12,651	588	10,787	55.1	52.7	4.4	44.9
Mar-May 2001	24,036	13,255	12,672	583	10,781	55.1	52.7	4.4	44.9
Apr-Jun 2001	24,047	13,291	12,701	591	10,756	55.3	52.8	4.4	44.7
May-Jul 2001	24,059	13,269	12,688	582	10,789	55.2	52.7	4.4	44.8
Jun-Aug 2001	24,070	13,264	12,683	581	10,806	55.1	52.7	4.4	44.9
Jul-Sep 2001	24,079	13,257	12,671	586	10,822	55.1	52.6	4.4	44.9
Aug-Oct 2001	24,089	13,279	12,695	583	10,810	55.1	52.7	4.4	44.9
Sep-Nov 2001	24,098	13,318	12,726	592	10,780	55.3	52.8	4.4	44.7
Oct-Dec 2001	24,107	13,338	12,729	609	10,769	55.3	52.8	4.6	44.7
Nov-Jan 2002	24,116	13,339	12,739	600	10,778	55.3	52.8	4.5	44.7
Dec-Feb 2002	24,126	13,346	12,752	593	10,780	55.3	52.9	4.4	44.7
Jan-Mar 2002	24,135	13,353	12,760	593	10,782	55.3	52.9	4.4	44.7
Feb-Apr 2002	24,144	13,401	12,800	600	10,744	55.5	53.0	4.5	44.5
Mar-May 2002	24,154	13,428	12,815	614	10,726	55.6	53.1	4.6	44.4
Apr-Jun 2002	24,163	13,443	12,837	606	10,720	55.6	53.1	4.5	44.4
May-Jul 2002	24,172	13,423	12,817	606	10,750	55.5	53.0	4.5	44.5
Jun-Aug 2002	24,182	13,453	12,838	615	10,729	55.6	53.1	4.6	44.4
Jul-Sep 2002	24,192	13,458	12,843	615	10,734	55.6	53.1	4.6	44.4
Aug-Oct 2002	24,202	13,468	12,848	620	10,734	55.6	53.1	4.6	44.4
Sep-Nov 2002	24,212	13,474	12,856	617	10,738	55.6	53.1	4.6	44.4
Oct-Dec 2002	24,222	13,471	12,848	623	10,751	55.6	53.0	4.6	44.4
Nov-Jan 2003	24,232	13,445	12,839	606	10,787	55.5	53.0	4.5	44.5
Dec-Feb 2003	24,242	13,457	12,860	597	10,785	55.5	53.0	4.4	44.5
Jan-Mar 2003	24,252	13,481	12,883	598	10,771	55.6	53.1	4.4	44.4
Feb-Apr 2003	24,262	13,487	12,893	594	10,775	55.6	53.1	4.4	44.4
Mar-May 2003	24,272	13,481	12,908	573	10,792	55.5	53.2	4.3	44.5
Apr-Jun 2003	24,283	13,477	12,900	578	10,805	55.5	53.1	4.3	44.5
May-Jul 2003	24,293	13,512	12,915	597	10,781	55.6	53.2	4.4	44.4
Jun-Aug 2003	24,303	13,509	12,910	599	10,793	55.6	53.1	4.4	44.4
Jul-Sep 2003	24,315	13,541	12,937	603	10,775	55.7	53.2	4.5	44.3
Aug-Oct 2003	24,328	13,559	12,973	586	10,768	55.7	53.3	4.3	44.3
Sep-Nov 2003	24,340	13,566	12,979	587	10,774	55.7	53.3	4.3	44.3
Oct-Dec 2003	24,352	13,572	12,993	579	10,780	55.7	53.4	4.3	44.3
Nov-Jan 2004	24,365	13,622	13,042	580	10,743	55.9	53.5	4.3	44.1
Dec-Feb 2004	24,377	13,633	13,048	585	10,744	55.9	53.5	4.3	44.1
Jan-Mar 2004	24,390	13,640	13,049	591	10,749	55.9	53.5	4.3	44.1
Feb-Apr 2004	24,402	13,639	13,048	591	10,763	55.9	53.5	4.3	44.1
Mar-May 2004	24,414	13,643	13,046	598	10,771	55.9	53.4	4.4	44.1
Apr-Jun 2004	24,427	13,649	13,057	592	10,778	55.9	53.5	4.3	44.1
May-Jul 2004	24,439	13,635	13,049	586	10,804	55.8	53.4	4.3	44.2
Jun-Aug 2004	24,452	13,612	13,039	573	10,840	55.7	53.3	4.2	44.3
Jul-Sep 2004	24,467	13,651	13,074	577	10,816	55.8	53.4	4.2	44.2
Aug-Oct 2004	24,483	13,674	13,086	588	10,809	55.9	53.5	4.3	44.1
Sep-Nov 2004	24,498	13,686	13,110	576	10,812	55.9	53.5	4.2	44.1
Oct-Dec 2004	24,514	13,721	13,136	584	10,793	56.0	53.6	4.3	44.0
Nov-Jan 2005	24,529	13,743	13,158	585	10,786	56.0	53.6	4.3	44.0
Dec-Feb 2005	24,545	13,819	13,216	603	10,726	56.3	53.8	4.4	43.7
Jan-Mar 2005	24,560	13,769	13,191	579	10,791	56.1	53.7	4.2	43.9
Feb-Apr 2005	24,576	13,762	13,184	578	10,813	56.0	53.6	4.2	44.0
Mar-May 2005	24,591	13,800	13,216	584	10,791	56.1	53.7	4.2	43.9
Apr-Jun 2005	24,606	13,817	13,216	600	10,790	56.2	53.7	4.3	43.8
May-Jul 2005	24,622	13,842	13,260	582	10,780	56.2	53.9	4.2	43.8
Jun-Aug 2005	24,638	13,854	13,279	575	10,783	56.2	53.9	4.2	43.8
Jul-Sep 2005	24,651	13,883	13,299	584	10,768	56.3	53.9	4.2	43.7
Aug-Oct 2005	24,664	13,885	13,278	607	10,779	56.3	53.8	4.4	43.7
Sep-Nov 2005	**24,678**	**13,862**	**13,234**	**628**	**10,816**	**56.2**	**53.6**	**4.5**	**43.8**

2 Labour Force Survey, summary by sex United Kingdom (thousands) seasonally adjusted

All aged 16 to 59/64

	All aged 16 to 59/64	Total economically active	Total in employment	Unemployed	Economically inactive	Economic Activity rate (%)	Employment rate (%)	Unemployment rate (%)	Economic inactivity rate (%)
	10	11	12	13	14	15	16	17	18
All Persons	YBTF	YBSK	YBSE	YBSH	YBSN	MGSO	MGSU	YBTI	YBTL
Jan-Mar 1971	31,844	24,821	23,863	958	7,023	77.9	74.9	3.9	22.1
Feb-Apr 1971	31,850	24,806	23,831	976	7,043	77.9	74.8	3.9	22.1
Mar-May 1971	31,855	24,815	23,815	1,000	7,040	77.9	74.8	4.0	22.1
Apr-Jun 1971	31,861	24,834	23,812	1,022	7,027	77.9	74.7	4.1	22.1
May-Jul 1971	31,866	24,836	23,796	1,040	7,030	77.9	74.7	4.2	22.1
Jun-Aug 1971	31,871	24,815	23,769	1,046	7,057	77.9	74.6	4.2	22.1
Jul-Sep 1971	31,874	24,783	23,730	1,054	7,091	77.8	74.4	4.3	22.2
Aug-Oct 1971	31,877	24,758	23,691	1,068	7,119	77.7	74.3	4.3	22.3
Sep-Nov 1971	31,880	24,750	23,659	1,091	7,131	77.6	74.2	4.4	22.4
Oct-Dec 1971	31,883	24,772	23,661	1,111	7,112	77.7	74.2	4.5	22.3
Nov-Jan 1972	31,886	24,798	23,677	1,121	7,089	77.8	74.3	4.5	22.2
Dec-Feb 1972	31,889	24,842	23,715	1,127	7,047	77.9	74.4	4.5	22.1
Jan-Mar 1972	31,892	24,892	23,760	1,133	7,000	78.1	74.5	4.6	21.9
Feb-Apr 1972	31,895	24,931	23,793	1,139	6,964	78.2	74.6	4.6	21.8
Mar-May 1972	31,898	24,935	23,803	1,133	6,963	78.2	74.6	4.5	21.8
Apr-Jun 1972	31,901	24,917	23,800	1,117	6,984	78.1	74.6	4.5	21.9
May-Jul 1972	31,904	24,898	23,799	1,099	7,007	78.0	74.6	4.4	22.0
Jun-Aug 1972	31,907	24,894	23,810	1,085	7,013	78.0	74.6	4.4	22.0
Jul-Sep 1972	31,912	24,915	23,837	1,078	6,997	78.1	74.7	4.3	21.9
Aug-Oct 1972	31,916	24,935	23,865	1,070	6,981	78.1	74.8	4.3	21.9
Sep-Nov 1972	31,920	24,961	23,899	1,063	6,959	78.2	74.9	4.3	21.8
Oct-Dec 1972	31,925	24,981	23,933	1,047	6,944	78.2	75.0	4.2	21.8
Nov-Jan 1973	31,929	25,017	23,991	1,026	6,911	78.4	75.1	4.1	21.6
Dec-Feb 1973	31,933	25,058	24,057	1,001	6,875	78.5	75.3	4.0	21.5
Jan-Mar 1973	31,937	25,113	24,134	980	6,824	78.6	75.6	3.9	21.4
Feb-Apr 1973	31,942	25,152	24,187	964	6,790	78.7	75.7	3.8	21.3
Mar-May 1973	31,946	25,165	24,211	954	6,781	78.8	75.8	3.8	21.2
Apr-Jun 1973	31,950	25,156	24,210	946	6,794	78.7	75.8	3.8	21.3
May-Jul 1973	31,955	25,133	24,198	935	6,821	78.7	75.7	3.7	21.3
Jun-Aug 1973	31,959	25,115	24,194	921	6,844	78.6	75.7	3.7	21.4
Jul-Sep 1973	31,962	25,105	24,200	905	6,857	78.5	75.7	3.6	21.5
Aug-Oct 1973	31,964	25,098	24,207	891	6,866	78.5	75.7	3.6	21.5
Sep-Nov 1973	31,967	25,098	24,220	879	6,869	78.5	75.8	3.5	21.5
Oct-Dec 1973	31,969	25,092	24,226	866	6,877	78.5	75.8	3.5	21.5
Nov-Jan 1974	31,972	25,091	24,221	869	6,881	78.5	75.8	3.5	21.5
Dec-Feb 1974	31,975	25,098	24,216	882	6,877	78.5	75.7	3.5	21.5
Jan-Mar 1974	31,977	25,111	24,210	901	6,866	78.5	75.7	3.6	21.5
Feb-Apr 1974	31,980	25,118	24,209	909	6,862	78.5	75.7	3.6	21.5
Mar-May 1974	31,982	25,121	24,210	911	6,861	78.5	75.7	3.6	21.5
Apr-Jun 1974	31,985	25,137	24,222	915	6,848	78.6	75.7	3.6	21.4
May-Jul 1974	31,988	25,158	24,239	919	6,830	78.6	75.8	3.7	21.4
Jun-Aug 1974	31,990	25,195	24,267	928	6,795	78.8	75.9	3.7	21.2
Jul-Sep 1974	31,996	25,219	24,283	935	6,778	78.8	75.9	3.7	21.2
Aug-Oct 1974	32,002	25,237	24,294	943	6,765	78.9	75.9	3.7	21.1
Sep-Nov 1974	32,008	25,238	24,291	947	6,770	78.9	75.9	3.8	21.1
Oct-Dec 1974	32,014	25,235	24,282	954	6,778	78.8	75.8	3.8	21.2
Nov-Jan 1975	32,020	25,228	24,261	967	6,792	78.8	75.8	3.8	21.2
Dec-Feb 1975	32,026	25,224	24,240	984	6,802	78.8	75.7	3.9	21.2
Jan-Mar 1975	32,031	25,230	24,223	1,007	6,801	78.8	75.6	4.0	21.2
Feb-Apr 1975	32,037	25,235	24,202	1,033	6,802	78.8	75.5	4.1	21.2
Mar-May 1975	32,043	25,259	24,192	1,067	6,784	78.8	75.5	4.2	21.2
Apr-Jun 1975	32,049	25,285	24,182	1,103	6,764	78.9	75.5	4.4	21.1
May-Jul 1975	32,055	25,312	24,172	1,140	6,743	79.0	75.4	4.5	21.0
Jun-Aug 1975	32,061	25,331	24,161	1,170	6,729	79.0	75.4	4.6	21.0
Jul-Sep 1975	32,074	25,344	24,146	1,198	6,730	79.0	75.3	4.7	21.0
Aug-Oct 1975	32,087	25,363	24,134	1,229	6,724	79.0	75.2	4.8	21.0
Sep-Nov 1975	32,100	25,376	24,113	1,263	6,724	79.1	75.1	5.0	20.9
Oct-Dec 1975	32,113	25,393	24,097	1,296	6,721	79.1	75.0	5.1	20.9

Labour Force Survey, summary by sex United Kingdom (thousands) seasonally adjusted (Continued)

All aged 16 to 59/64

	All aged 16 to 59/64	Total economically active	Total in employment	Unemployed	Economically inactive	Economic Activity rate (%)	Employment rate (%)	Unemployment rate (%)	Economic inactivity rate (%)
	10	11	12	13	14	15	16	17	18
All Persons	YBTF	YBSK	YBSE	YBSH	YBSN	MGSO	MGSU	YBTI	YBTL
Nov-Jan 1976	32,126	25,400	24,080	1,320	6,727	79.1	75.0	5.2	20.9
Dec-Feb 1976	32,140	25,403	24,063	1,339	6,737	79.0	74.9	5.3	21.0
Jan-Mar 1976	32,153	25,403	24,047	1,356	6,750	79.0	74.8	5.3	21.0
Feb-Apr 1976	32,166	25,399	24,031	1,369	6,766	79.0	74.7	5.4	21.0
Mar-May 1976	32,179	25,408	24,027	1,381	6,771	79.0	74.7	5.4	21.0
Apr-Jun 1976	32,192	25,407	24,018	1,390	6,785	78.9	74.6	5.5	21.1
May-Jul 1976	32,205	25,409	24,013	1,396	6,796	78.9	74.6	5.5	21.1
Jun-Aug 1976	32,219	25,415	24,014	1,401	6,803	78.9	74.5	5.5	21.1
Jul-Sep 1976	32,236	25,418	24,011	1,407	6,819	78.8	74.5	5.5	21.2
Aug-Oct 1976	32,254	25,422	24,013	1,409	6,832	78.8	74.5	5.5	21.2
Sep-Nov 1976	32,272	25,424	24,016	1,408	6,848	78.8	74.4	5.5	21.2
Oct-Dec 1976	32,290	25,433	24,025	1,408	6,857	78.8	74.4	5.5	21.2
Nov-Jan 1977	32,307	25,445	24,033	1,412	6,862	78.8	74.4	5.5	21.2
Dec-Feb 1977	32,325	25,455	24,042	1,413	6,871	78.7	74.4	5.6	21.3
Jan-Mar 1977	32,343	25,451	24,039	1,412	6,892	78.7	74.3	5.5	21.3
Feb-Apr 1977	32,361	25,451	24,037	1,414	6,910	78.6	74.3	5.6	21.4
Mar-May 1977	32,379	25,456	24,039	1,417	6,922	78.6	74.2	5.6	21.4
Apr-Jun 1977	32,396	25,466	24,037	1,429	6,930	78.6	74.2	5.6	21.4
May-Jul 1977	32,414	25,479	24,035	1,443	6,936	78.6	74.2	5.7	21.4
Jun-Aug 1977	32,432	25,496	24,039	1,457	6,936	78.6	74.1	5.7	21.4
Jul-Sep 1977	32,453	25,517	24,048	1,469	6,936	78.6	74.1	5.8	21.4
Aug-Oct 1977	32,474	25,522	24,047	1,474	6,952	78.6	74.1	5.8	21.4
Sep-Nov 1977	32,495	25,530	24,051	1,478	6,966	78.6	74.0	5.8	21.4
Oct-Dec 1977	32,517	25,531	24,056	1,475	6,985	78.5	74.0	5.8	21.5
Nov-Jan 1978	32,538	25,536	24,066	1,469	7,002	78.5	74.0	5.8	21.5
Dec-Feb 1978	32,559	25,542	24,082	1,460	7,017	78.4	74.0	5.7	21.6
Jan-Mar 1978	32,580	25,545	24,094	1,451	7,035	78.4	74.0	5.7	21.6
Feb-Apr 1978	32,601	25,551	24,106	1,445	7,050	78.4	73.9	5.7	21.6
Mar-May 1978	32,622	25,560	24,118	1,442	7,062	78.4	73.9	5.6	21.6
Apr-Jun 1978	32,643	25,563	24,124	1,439	7,080	78.3	73.9	5.6	21.7
May-Jul 1978	32,664	25,569	24,134	1,435	7,095	78.3	73.9	5.6	21.7
Jun-Aug 1978	32,686	25,585	24,150	1,435	7,101	78.3	73.9	5.6	21.7
Jul-Sep 1978	32,710	25,603	24,172	1,431	7,106	78.3	73.9	5.6	21.7
Aug-Oct 1978	32,734	25,627	24,202	1,425	7,107	78.3	73.9	5.6	21.7
Sep-Nov 1978	32,758	25,649	24,238	1,410	7,109	78.3	74.0	5.5	21.7
Oct-Dec 1978	32,782	25,671	24,275	1,397	7,111	78.3	74.0	5.4	21.7
Nov-Jan 1979	32,806	25,696	24,308	1,388	7,110	78.3	74.1	5.4	21.7
Dec-Feb 1979	32,830	25,713	24,322	1,391	7,117	78.3	74.1	5.4	21.7
Jan-Mar 1979	32,854	25,724	24,329	1,395	7,131	78.3	74.1	5.4	21.7
Feb-Apr 1979	32,879	25,721	24,332	1,389	7,157	78.2	74.0	5.4	21.8
Mar-May 1979	32,903	25,730	24,350	1,380	7,173	78.2	74.0	5.4	21.8
Apr-Jun 1979	32,927	25,749	24,369	1,380	7,177	78.2	74.0	5.4	21.8
May-Jul 1979	32,951	25,779	24,389	1,390	7,172	78.2	74.0	5.4	21.8
Jun-Aug 1979	32,975	25,803	24,406	1,396	7,172	78.2	74.0	5.4	21.8
Jul-Sep 1979	32,991	25,822	24,417	1,404	7,170	78.3	74.0	5.4	21.7
Aug-Oct 1979	33,008	25,845	24,429	1,416	7,163	78.3	74.0	5.5	21.7
Sep-Nov 1979	33,024	25,870	24,441	1,428	7,155	78.3	74.0	5.5	21.7
Oct-Dec 1979	33,041	25,890	24,444	1,446	7,151	78.4	74.0	5.6	21.6
Nov-Jan 1980	33,057	25,905	24,439	1,466	7,152	78.4	73.9	5.7	21.6
Dec-Feb 1980	33,074	25,923	24,426	1,497	7,151	78.4	73.9	5.8	21.6
Jan-Mar 1980	33,090	25,943	24,409	1,534	7,147	78.4	73.8	5.9	21.6
Feb-Apr 1980	33,107	25,962	24,383	1,579	7,145	78.4	73.6	6.1	21.6
Mar-May 1980	33,123	25,987	24,362	1,625	7,136	78.5	73.6	6.3	21.5
Apr-Jun 1980	33,140	26,009	24,332	1,677	7,131	78.5	73.4	6.4	21.5
May-Jul 1980	33,156	26,033	24,300	1,733	7,123	78.5	73.3	6.7	21.5
Jun-Aug 1980	33,173	26,056	24,251	1,805	7,116	78.5	73.1	6.9	21.5
Jul-Sep 1980	33,189	26,067	24,185	1,882	7,122	78.5	72.9	7.2	21.5
Aug-Oct 1980	33,206	26,079	24,113	1,966	7,126	78.5	72.6	7.5	21.5
Sep-Nov 1980	33,223	26,101	24,047	2,054	7,122	78.6	72.4	7.9	21.4
Oct-Dec 1980	33,239	26,122	23,976	2,146	7,117	78.6	72.1	8.2	21.4

Labour Force Survey, summary by sex United Kingdom (thousands) seasonally adjusted (Continued)

All aged 16 to 59/64	All aged 16 to 59/64	Total economically active	Total in employment	Unemployed	Economically inactive	Economic Activity rate (%)	Employment rate (%)	Unemployment rate (%)	Economic inactivity rate (%)
	10	11	12	13	14	15	16	17	18
All Persons	YBTF	YBSK	YBSE	YBSH	YBSN	MGSO	MGSU	YBTI	YBTL
Nov-Jan 1981	33,256	26,148	23,915	2,233	7,108	78.6	71.9	8.5	21.4
Dec-Feb 1981	33,273	26,157	23,849	2,308	7,116	78.6	71.7	8.8	21.4
Jan-Mar 1981	33,289	26,169	23,788	2,380	7,120	78.6	71.5	9.1	21.4
Feb-Apr 1981	33,306	26,180	23,727	2,453	7,126	78.6	71.2	9.4	21.4
Mar-May 1981	33,323	26,192	23,671	2,521	7,131	78.6	71.0	9.6	21.4
Apr-Jun 1981	33,339	26,186	23,621	2,565	7,154	78.5	70.9	9.8	21.5
May-Jul 1981	33,356	26,172	23,571	2,602	7,184	78.5	70.7	9.9	21.5
Jun-Aug 1981	33,372	26,164	23,532	2,632	7,209	78.4	70.5	10.1	21.6
Jul-Sep 1981	33,384	26,156	23,494	2,662	7,229	78.3	70.4	10.2	21.7
Aug-Oct 1981	33,396	26,140	23,451	2,689	7,256	78.3	70.2	10.3	21.7
Sep-Nov 1981	33,408	26,129	23,412	2,717	7,280	78.2	70.1	10.4	21.8
Oct-Dec 1981	33,420	26,105	23,367	2,738	7,315	78.1	69.9	10.5	21.9
Nov-Jan 1982	33,432	26,084	23,328	2,756	7,349	78.0	69.8	10.6	22.0
Dec-Feb 1982	33,444	26,067	23,299	2,768	7,377	77.9	69.7	10.6	22.1
Jan-Mar 1982	33,456	26,060	23,281	2,779	7,396	77.9	69.6	10.7	22.1
Feb-Apr 1982	33,468	26,048	23,258	2,789	7,421	77.8	69.5	10.7	22.2
Mar-May 1982	33,480	26,040	23,241	2,800	7,440	77.8	69.4	10.8	22.2
Apr-Jun 1982	33,492	26,023	23,206	2,816	7,470	77.7	69.3	10.8	22.3
May-Jul 1982	33,504	26,005	23,172	2,833	7,500	77.6	69.2	10.9	22.4
Jun-Aug 1982	33,516	25,983	23,130	2,853	7,533	77.5	69.0	11.0	22.5
Jul-Sep 1982	33,537	25,965	23,093	2,873	7,572	77.4	68.9	11.1	22.6
Aug-Oct 1982	33,558	25,942	23,049	2,893	7,616	77.3	68.7	11.2	22.7
Sep-Nov 1982	33,579	25,916	23,002	2,914	7,663	77.2	68.5	11.2	22.8
Oct-Dec 1982	33,600	25,894	22,959	2,935	7,705	77.1	68.3	11.3	22.9
Nov-Jan 1983	33,620	25,875	22,923	2,952	7,746	77.0	68.2	11.4	23.0
Dec-Feb 1983	33,641	25,857	22,892	2,965	7,785	76.9	68.0	11.5	23.1
Jan-Mar 1983	33,662	25,848	22,874	2,974	7,814	76.8	68.0	11.5	23.2
Feb-Apr 1983	33,683	25,843	22,858	2,985	7,839	76.7	67.9	11.6	23.3
Mar-May 1983	33,704	25,856	22,857	2,999	7,848	76.7	67.8	11.6	23.3
Apr-Jun 1983	33,725	25,902	22,880	3,022	7,822	76.8	67.8	11.7	23.2
May-Jul 1983	33,745	25,955	22,910	3,045	7,790	76.9	67.9	11.7	23.1
Jun-Aug 1983	33,766	26,034	22,973	3,061	7,732	77.1	68.0	11.8	22.9
Jul-Sep 1983	33,788	26,115	23,041	3,074	7,673	77.3	68.2	11.8	22.7
Aug-Oct 1983	33,810	26,197	23,109	3,088	7,613	77.5	68.3	11.8	22.5
Sep-Nov 1983	33,832	26,273	23,167	3,106	7,558	77.7	68.5	11.8	22.3
Oct-Dec 1983	33,853	26,343	23,218	3,124	7,511	77.8	68.6	11.9	22.2
Nov-Jan 1984	33,875	26,411	23,268	3,143	7,464	78.0	68.7	11.9	22.0
Dec-Feb 1984	33,897	26,477	23,310	3,167	7,420	78.1	68.8	12.0	21.9
Jan-Mar 1984	33,919	26,541	23,351	3,191	7,377	78.2	68.8	12.0	21.8
Feb-Apr 1984	33,941	26,599	23,391	3,208	7,342	78.4	68.9	12.1	21.6
Mar-May 1984	33,962	26,652	23,432	3,221	7,310	78.5	69.0	12.1	21.5
Apr-Jun 1984	33,984	26,681	23,473	3,208	7,303	78.5	69.1	12.0	21.5
May-Jul 1984	34,006	26,708	23,509	3,199	7,298	78.5	69.1	12.0	21.5
Jun-Aug 1984	34,028	26,728	23,540	3,188	7,300	78.5	69.2	11.9	21.5
Jul-Sep 1984	34,043	26,755	23,571	3,185	7,287	78.6	69.2	11.9	21.4
Aug-Oct 1984	34,058	26,793	23,613	3,180	7,265	78.7	69.3	11.9	21.3
Sep-Nov 1984	34,072	26,827	23,651	3,176	7,245	78.7	69.4	11.8	21.3
Oct-Dec 1984	34,087	26,856	23,690	3,166	7,231	78.8	69.5	11.8	21.2
Nov-Jan 1985	34,102	26,874	23,718	3,156	7,228	78.8	69.6	11.7	21.2
Dec-Feb 1985	34,117	26,896	23,750	3,146	7,221	78.8	69.6	11.7	21.2
Jan-Mar 1985	34,132	26,913	23,781	3,133	7,219	78.9	69.7	11.6	21.1
Feb-Apr 1985	34,147	26,933	23,811	3,122	7,214	78.9	69.7	11.6	21.1
Mar-May 1985	34,162	26,939	23,829	3,109	7,223	78.9	69.8	11.5	21.1
Apr-Jun 1985	34,176	26,958	23,852	3,106	7,219	78.9	69.8	11.5	21.1
May-Jul 1985	34,191	26,967	23,867	3,099	7,225	78.9	69.8	11.5	21.1
Jun-Aug 1985	34,206	26,981	23,888	3,093	7,225	78.9	69.8	11.5	21.1
Jul-Sep 1985	34,218	26,999	23,908	3,091	7,219	78.9	69.9	11.4	21.1
Aug-Oct 1985	34,231	27,017	23,927	3,090	7,214	78.9	69.9	11.4	21.1
Sep-Nov 1985	34,243	27,030	23,942	3,089	7,213	78.9	69.9	11.4	21.1
Oct-Dec 1985	34,255	27,039	23,949	3,090	7,216	78.9	69.9	11.4	21.1

Labour Force Survey, summary by sex United Kingdom (thousands) seasonally adjusted (Continued)

All aged 16 to 59/64

	All aged 16 to 59/64	Total economically active	Total in employment	Unemployed	Economically inactive	Economic Activity rate (%)	Employment rate (%)	Unemployment rate (%)	Economic inactivity rate (%)
	10	11	12	13	14	15	16	17	18
All Persons	YBTF	YBSK	YBSE	YBSH	YBSN	MGSO	MGSU	YBTI	YBTL
Nov-Jan 1986	34,268	27,048	23,955	3,093	7,220	78.9	69.9	11.4	21.1
Dec-Feb 1986	34,280	27,063	23,965	3,098	7,217	78.9	69.9	11.4	21.1
Jan-Mar 1986	34,292	27,076	23,970	3,106	7,217	79.0	69.9	11.5	21.0
Feb-Apr 1986	34,305	27,087	23,980	3,107	7,218	79.0	69.9	11.5	21.0
Mar-May 1986	34,317	27,100	23,989	3,111	7,217	79.0	69.9	11.5	21.0
Apr-Jun 1986	34,329	27,115	24,000	3,115	7,214	79.0	69.9	11.5	21.0
May-Jul 1986	34,341	27,145	24,020	3,125	7,196	79.0	69.9	11.5	21.0
Jun-Aug 1986	34,354	27,182	24,050	3,132	7,172	79.1	70.0	11.5	20.9
Jul-Sep 1986	34,367	27,214	24,080	3,134	7,153	79.2	70.1	11.5	20.8
Aug-Oct 1986	34,380	27,229	24,100	3,129	7,151	79.2	70.1	11.5	20.8
Sep-Nov 1986	34,394	27,258	24,135	3,123	7,136	79.3	70.2	11.5	20.7
Oct-Dec 1986	34,407	27,275	24,160	3,115	7,132	79.3	70.2	11.4	20.7
Nov-Jan 1987	34,420	27,294	24,185	3,109	7,126	79.3	70.3	11.4	20.7
Dec-Feb 1987	34,433	27,302	24,210	3,092	7,131	79.3	70.3	11.3	20.7
Jan-Mar 1987	34,447	27,302	24,230	3,072	7,144	79.3	70.3	11.3	20.7
Feb-Apr 1987	34,460	27,325	24,275	3,050	7,135	79.3	70.4	11.2	20.7
Mar-May 1987	34,473	27,358	24,337	3,021	7,115	79.4	70.6	11.0	20.6
Apr-Jun 1987	34,486	27,392	24,410	2,982	7,094	79.4	70.8	10.9	20.6
May-Jul 1987	34,500	27,428	24,495	2,933	7,071	79.5	71.0	10.7	20.5
Jun-Aug 1987	34,513	27,460	24,570	2,890	7,053	79.6	71.2	10.5	20.4
Jul-Sep 1987	34,523	27,497	24,650	2,847	7,026	79.6	71.4	10.4	20.4
Aug-Oct 1987	34,532	27,519	24,720	2,799	7,013	79.7	71.6	10.2	20.3
Sep-Nov 1987	34,542	27,544	24,795	2,748	6,998	79.7	71.8	10.0	20.3
Oct-Dec 1987	34,552	27,571	24,870	2,701	6,980	79.8	72.0	9.8	20.2
Nov-Jan 1988	34,561	27,603	24,945	2,658	6,958	79.9	72.2	9.6	20.1
Dec-Feb 1988	34,571	27,633	25,015	2,619	6,937	79.9	72.4	9.5	20.1
Jan-Mar 1988	34,580	27,654	25,080	2,574	6,926	80.0	72.5	9.3	20.0
Feb-Apr 1988	34,590	27,671	25,140	2,531	6,919	80.0	72.7	9.1	20.0
Mar-May 1988	34,600	27,684	25,196	2,487	6,916	80.0	72.8	9.0	20.0
Apr-Jun 1988	34,609	27,701	25,250	2,451	6,908	80.0	73.0	8.8	20.0
May-Jul 1988	34,619	27,711	25,300	2,411	6,908	80.0	73.1	8.7	20.0
Jun-Aug 1988	34,629	27,729	25,355	2,374	6,900	80.1	73.2	8.6	19.9
Jul-Sep 1988	34,637	27,763	25,420	2,343	6,874	80.2	73.4	8.4	19.8
Aug-Oct 1988	34,646	27,792	25,475	2,317	6,854	80.2	73.5	8.3	19.8
Sep-Nov 1988	34,655	27,818	25,530	2,288	6,837	80.3	73.7	8.2	19.7
Oct-Dec 1988	34,663	27,833	25,585	2,248	6,831	80.3	73.8	8.1	19.7
Nov-Jan 1989	34,672	27,856	25,650	2,206	6,816	80.3	74.0	7.9	19.7
Dec-Feb 1989	34,681	27,886	25,720	2,166	6,795	80.4	74.2	7.8	19.6
Jan-Mar 1989	34,690	27,925	25,795	2,130	6,764	80.5	74.4	7.6	19.5
Feb-Apr 1989	34,698	27,945	25,855	2,090	6,753	80.5	74.5	7.5	19.5
Mar-May 1989	34,707	27,952	25,897	2,055	6,755	80.5	74.6	7.4	19.5
Apr-Jun 1989	34,716	27,953	25,920	2,033	6,762	80.5	74.7	7.3	19.5
May-Jul 1989	34,724	27,963	25,940	2,023	6,761	80.5	74.7	7.2	19.5
Jun-Aug 1989	34,733	27,966	25,955	2,011	6,767	80.5	74.7	7.2	19.5
Jul-Sep 1989	34,739	27,980	25,980	2,000	6,759	80.5	74.8	7.1	19.5
Aug-Oct 1989	34,746	27,996	26,005	1,991	6,750	80.6	74.8	7.1	19.4
Sep-Nov 1989	34,752	28,020	26,035	1,985	6,732	80.6	74.9	7.1	19.4
Oct-Dec 1989	34,759	28,040	26,060	1,980	6,718	80.7	75.0	7.1	19.3
Nov-Jan 1990	34,765	28,043	26,070	1,973	6,723	80.7	75.0	7.0	19.3
Dec-Feb 1990	34,771	28,049	26,080	1,969	6,723	80.7	75.0	7.0	19.3
Jan-Mar 1990	34,778	28,048	26,080	1,968	6,730	80.6	75.0	7.0	19.4
Feb-Apr 1990	34,784	28,058	26,090	1,968	6,726	80.7	75.0	7.0	19.3
Mar-May 1990	34,791	28,073	26,103	1,970	6,718	80.7	75.0	7.0	19.3
Apr-Jun 1990	34,797	28,083	26,115	1,968	6,714	80.7	75.0	7.0	19.3
May-Jul 1990	34,804	28,089	26,115	1,974	6,714	80.7	75.0	7.0	19.3
Jun-Aug 1990	34,810	28,095	26,105	1,990	6,715	80.7	75.0	7.1	19.3
Jul-Sep 1990	34,815	28,083	26,070	2,013	6,732	80.7	74.9	7.2	19.3
Aug-Oct 1990	34,820	28,068	26,025	2,043	6,752	80.6	74.7	7.3	19.4
Sep-Nov 1990	34,825	28,059	25,980	2,079	6,766	80.6	74.6	7.4	19.4
Oct-Dec 1990	34,830	28,046	25,925	2,122	6,783	80.5	74.4	7.6	19.5

Labour Force Survey, summary by sex United Kingdom (thousands) seasonally adjusted (Continued)

All aged 16 to 59/64									
	All aged 16 to 59/64	Total economically active	Total in employment	Unemployed	Economically inactive	Economic Activity rate (%)	Employment rate (%)	Unemployment rate (%)	Economic inactivity rate (%)
	10	11	12	13	14	15	16	17	18
All Persons	YBTF	YBSK	YBSE	YBSH	YBSN	MGSO	MGSU	YBTI	YBTL
Nov-Jan 1991	34,835	28,018	25,860	2,158	6,816	80.4	74.2	7.7	19.6
Dec-Feb 1991	34,839	28,002	25,795	2,207	6,838	80.4	74.0	7.9	19.6
Jan-Mar 1991	34,844	27,983	25,715	2,268	6,861	80.3	73.8	8.1	19.7
Feb-Apr 1991	34,849	27,974	25,635	2,340	6,875	80.3	73.6	8.4	19.7
Mar-May 1991	34,854	27,958	25,554	2,404	6,896	80.2	73.3	8.6	19.8
Apr-Jun 1991	34,857	27,914	25,460	2,454	6,943	80.1	73.0	8.8	19.9
May-Jul 1991	34,860	27,882	25,380	2,502	6,978	80.0	72.8	9.0	20.0
Jun-Aug 1991	34,863	27,852	25,305	2,547	7,010	79.9	72.6	9.1	20.1
Jul-Sep 1991	34,865	27,817	25,230	2,587	7,048	79.8	72.4	9.3	20.2
Aug-Oct 1991	34,868	27,776	25,160	2,616	7,092	79.7	72.2	9.4	20.3
Sep-Nov 1991	34,871	27,730	25,090	2,640	7,141	79.5	72.0	9.5	20.5
Oct-Dec 1991	34,874	27,692	25,030	2,662	7,182	79.4	71.8	9.6	20.6
Nov-Jan 1992	34,877	27,655	24,975	2,680	7,221	79.3	71.6	9.7	20.7
Dec-Feb 1992	34,880	27,636	24,935	2,701	7,244	79.2	71.5	9.8	20.8
Jan-Mar 1992	34,882	27,633	24,905	2,728	7,250	79.2	71.4	9.9	20.8
Feb-Apr 1992	34,885	27,619	24,870	2,749	7,266	79.2	71.3	10.0	20.8
Mar-May 1992	34,879	27,581	24,817	2,764	7,298	79.1	71.2	10.0	20.9
Apr-Jun 1992	34,880	27,530	24,782	2,748	7,350	78.9	71.0	10.0	21.1
May-Jul 1992	34,881	27,498	24,723	2,775	7,383	78.8	70.9	10.1	21.2
Jun-Aug 1992	34,882	27,494	24,707	2,787	7,388	78.8	70.8	10.1	21.2
Jul-Sep 1992	34,882	27,483	24,696	2,787	7,400	78.8	70.8	10.1	21.2
Aug-Oct 1992	34,883	27,473	24,651	2,821	7,410	78.8	70.7	10.3	21.2
Sep-Nov 1992	34,883	27,493	24,620	2,873	7,390	78.8	70.6	10.5	21.2
Oct-Dec 1992	34,883	27,471	24,569	2,902	7,412	78.8	70.4	10.6	21.2
Nov-Jan 1993	34,884	27,491	24,534	2,957	7,393	78.8	70.3	10.8	21.2
Dec-Feb 1993	34,884	27,505	24,507	2,998	7,379	78.8	70.3	10.9	21.2
Jan-Mar 1993	34,884	27,481	24,509	2,972	7,403	78.8	70.3	10.8	21.2
Feb-Apr 1993	34,885	27,444	24,486	2,957	7,441	78.7	70.2	10.8	21.3
Mar-May 1993	34,885	27,429	24,510	2,919	7,456	78.6	70.3	10.6	21.4
Apr-Jun 1993	34,885	27,426	24,525	2,901	7,459	78.6	70.3	10.6	21.4
May-Jul 1993	34,886	27,423	24,522	2,901	7,463	78.6	70.3	10.6	21.4
Jun-Aug 1993	34,886	27,383	24,501	2,882	7,503	78.5	70.2	10.5	21.5
Jul-Sep 1993	34,890	27,408	24,538	2,871	7,481	78.6	70.3	10.5	21.4
Aug-Oct 1993	34,894	27,406	24,540	2,866	7,488	78.5	70.3	10.5	21.5
Sep-Nov 1993	34,898	27,403	24,544	2,859	7,495	78.5	70.3	10.4	21.5
Oct-Dec 1993	34,902	27,409	24,548	2,861	7,493	78.5	70.3	10.4	21.5
Nov-Jan 1993	34,906	27,403	24,536	2,867	7,503	78.5	70.3	10.5	21.5
Dec-Feb 1994	34,910	27,405	24,585	2,820	7,505	78.5	70.4	10.3	21.5
Jan-Mar 1994	34,915	27,421	24,644	2,777	7,494	78.5	70.6	10.1	21.5
Feb-Apr 1994	34,919	27,411	24,671	2,740	7,508	78.5	70.7	10.0	21.5
Mar-May 1994	34,923	27,395	24,672	2,723	7,528	78.4	70.6	9.9	21.6
Apr-Jun 1994	34,927	27,383	24,673	2,711	7,544	78.4	70.6	9.9	21.6
May-Jul 1994	34,931	27,410	24,728	2,682	7,521	78.5	70.8	9.8	21.5
Jun-Aug 1994	34,935	27,402	24,738	2,664	7,533	78.4	70.8	9.7	21.6
Jul-Sep 1994	34,944	27,393	24,779	2,615	7,551	78.4	70.9	9.5	21.6
Aug-Oct 1994	34,954	27,363	24,778	2,585	7,591	78.3	70.9	9.4	21.7
Sep-Nov 1994	34,963	27,334	24,802	2,531	7,629	78.2	70.9	9.3	21.8
Oct-Dec 1994	34,972	27,298	24,802	2,496	7,674	78.1	70.9	9.1	21.9
Nov-Jan 1994	34,981	27,266	24,790	2,475	7,716	77.9	70.9	9.1	22.1
Dec-Feb 1995	34,990	27,312	24,838	2,474	7,678	78.1	71.0	9.1	21.9
Jan-Mar 1995	35,000	27,349	24,873	2,476	7,651	78.1	71.1	9.1	21.9
Feb-Apr 1995	35,009	27,374	24,908	2,467	7,635	78.2	71.1	9.0	21.8
Mar-May 1995	35,018	27,389	24,937	2,452	7,629	78.2	71.2	9.0	21.8
Apr-Jun 1995	35,027	27,380	24,960	2,419	7,647	78.2	71.3	8.8	21.8
May-Jul 1995	35,036	27,411	24,986	2,425	7,625	78.2	71.3	8.8	21.8
Jun-Aug 1995	35,046	27,457	25,044	2,413	7,589	78.3	71.5	8.8	21.7
Jul-Sep 1995	35,057	27,477	25,055	2,422	7,580	78.4	71.5	8.8	21.6
Aug-Oct 1995	35,068	27,491	25,079	2,412	7,577	78.4	71.5	8.8	21.6
Sep-Nov 1995	35,079	27,491	25,095	2,396	7,588	78.4	71.5	8.7	21.6
Oct-Dec 1995	35,090	27,516	25,190	2,326	7,574	78.4	71.8	8.5	21.6

Labour Force Survey, summary by sex United Kingdom (thousands) seasonally adjusted (Continued)

All aged 16 to 59/64

	All aged 16 to 59/64	Total economically active	Total in employment	Unemployed	Economically inactive	Economic Activity rate (%)	Employment rate (%)	Unemployment rate (%)	Economic inactivity rate (%)
	10	11	12	13	14	15	16	17	18
All Persons	YBTF	YBSK	YBSE	YBSH	YBSN	MGSO	MGSU	YBTI	YBTL
Nov-Jan 1996	35,101	27,548	25,199	2,349	7,553	78.5	71.8	8.5	21.5
Dec-Feb 1996	35,112	27,533	25,200	2,334	7,579	78.4	71.8	8.5	21.6
Jan-Mar 1996	35,123	27,509	25,203	2,306	7,614	78.3	71.8	8.4	21.7
Feb-Apr 1996	35,135	27,532	25,206	2,326	7,603	78.4	71.7	8.4	21.6
Mar-May 1996	35,146	27,554	25,230	2,324	7,592	78.4	71.8	8.4	21.6
Apr-Jun 1996	35,157	27,563	25,248	2,315	7,594	78.4	71.8	8.4	21.6
May-Jul 1996	35,168	27,529	25,241	2,288	7,639	78.3	71.8	8.3	21.7
Jun-Aug 1996	35,179	27,544	25,291	2,252	7,635	78.3	71.9	8.2	21.7
Jul-Sep 1996	35,190	27,536	25,282	2,254	7,653	78.3	71.8	8.2	21.7
Aug-Oct 1996	35,200	27,594	25,335	2,259	7,606	78.4	72.0	8.2	21.6
Sep-Nov 1996	35,211	27,640	25,403	2,237	7,571	78.5	72.1	8.1	21.5
Oct-Dec 1996	35,221	27,638	25,435	2,203	7,583	78.5	72.2	8.0	21.5
Nov-Jan 1997	35,232	27,639	25,480	2,159	7,593	78.4	72.3	7.8	21.6
Dec-Feb 1997	35,242	27,651	25,545	2,106	7,592	78.5	72.5	7.6	21.5
Jan-Mar 1997	35,253	27,646	25,591	2,055	7,606	78.4	72.6	7.4	21.6
Feb-Apr 1997	35,263	27,660	25,635	2,025	7,603	78.4	72.7	7.3	21.6
Mar-May 1997	35,274	27,666	25,645	2,021	7,608	78.4	72.7	7.3	21.6
Apr-Jun 1997	35,284	27,734	25,707	2,027	7,550	78.6	72.9	7.3	21.4
May-Jul 1997	35,295	27,739	25,682	2,057	7,556	78.6	72.8	7.4	21.4
Jun-Aug 1997	35,305	27,697	25,702	1,995	7,609	78.4	72.8	7.2	21.6
Jul-Sep 1997	35,316	27,684	25,757	1,927	7,632	78.4	72.9	7.0	21.6
Aug-Oct 1997	35,326	27,684	25,798	1,885	7,642	78.4	73.0	6.8	21.6
Sep-Nov 1997	35,336	27,686	25,821	1,865	7,650	78.4	73.1	6.7	21.6
Oct-Dec 1997	35,346	27,690	25,848	1,842	7,656	78.3	73.1	6.7	21.7
Nov-Jan 1998	35,356	27,651	25,852	1,799	7,705	78.2	73.1	6.5	21.8
Dec-Feb 1998	35,366	27,683	25,889	1,794	7,683	78.3	73.2	6.5	21.7
Jan-Mar 1998	35,377	27,696	25,906	1,790	7,680	78.3	73.2	6.5	21.7
Feb-Apr 1998	35,387	27,707	25,933	1,774	7,680	78.3	73.3	6.4	21.7
Mar-May 1998	35,397	27,700	25,938	1,763	7,697	78.3	73.3	6.4	21.7
Apr-Jun 1998	35,407	27,709	25,944	1,765	7,698	78.3	73.3	6.4	21.7
May-Jul 1998	35,417	27,766	25,993	1,773	7,652	78.4	73.4	6.4	21.6
Jun-Aug 1998	35,427	27,831	26,053	1,778	7,597	78.6	73.5	6.4	21.4
Jul-Sep 1998	35,443	27,821	26,058	1,763	7,622	78.5	73.5	6.3	21.5
Aug-Oct 1998	35,458	27,852	26,090	1,762	7,606	78.5	73.6	6.3	21.5
Sep-Nov 1998	35,473	27,895	26,145	1,750	7,578	78.6	73.7	6.3	21.4
Oct-Dec 1998	35,488	27,897	26,150	1,747	7,591	78.6	73.7	6.3	21.4
Nov-Jan 1999	35,503	27,968	26,195	1,773	7,535	78.8	73.8	6.3	21.2
Dec-Feb 1999	35,518	28,005	26,230	1,776	7,513	78.8	73.8	6.3	21.2
Jan-Mar 1999	35,533	27,995	26,238	1,757	7,538	78.8	73.8	6.3	21.2
Feb-Apr 1999	35,548	27,985	26,232	1,753	7,563	78.7	73.8	6.3	21.3
Mar-May 1999	35,563	27,974	26,235	1,740	7,589	78.7	73.8	6.2	21.3
Apr-Jun 1999	35,579	28,001	26,278	1,724	7,577	78.7	73.9	6.2	21.3
May-Jul 1999	35,594	28,005	26,302	1,703	7,588	78.7	73.9	6.1	21.3
Jun-Aug 1999	35,609	28,032	26,352	1,681	7,576	78.7	74.0	6.0	21.3
Jul-Sep 1999	35,626	28,073	26,394	1,679	7,553	78.8	74.1	6.0	21.2
Aug-Oct 1999	35,644	28,057	26,390	1,667	7,586	78.7	74.0	5.9	21.3
Sep-Nov 1999	35,661	28,113	26,441	1,672	7,548	78.8	74.1	5.9	21.2
Oct-Dec 1999	35,678	28,138	26,474	1,664	7,540	78.9	74.2	5.9	21.1
Nov-Jan 2000	35,696	28,147	26,468	1,679	7,549	78.9	74.1	6.0	21.1
Dec-Feb 2000	35,713	28,141	26,480	1,661	7,572	78.8	74.1	5.9	21.2
Jan-Mar 2000	35,731	28,178	26,521	1,657	7,552	78.9	74.2	5.9	21.1
Feb-Apr 2000	35,748	28,194	26,559	1,635	7,554	78.9	74.3	5.8	21.1
Mar-May 2000	35,766	28,223	26,602	1,621	7,542	78.9	74.4	5.7	21.1
Apr-Jun 2000	35,783	28,212	26,630	1,582	7,571	78.8	74.4	5.6	21.2
May-Jul 2000	35,800	28,222	26,692	1,530	7,579	78.8	74.6	5.4	21.2
Jun-Aug 2000	35,818	28,236	26,729	1,507	7,581	78.8	74.6	5.3	21.2
Jul-Sep 2000	35,840	28,252	26,721	1,531	7,588	78.8	74.6	5.4	21.2
Aug-Oct 2000	35,862	28,244	26,692	1,553	7,618	78.8	74.4	5.5	21.2
Sep-Nov 2000	35,884	28,195	26,675	1,520	7,689	78.6	74.3	5.4	21.4
Oct-Dec 2000	35,906	28,206	26,705	1,502	7,700	78.6	74.4	5.3	21.4

Labour Force Survey, summary by sex United Kingdom (thousands) seasonally adjusted (Continued)

All aged 16 to 59/64

	All aged 16 to 59/64	Total economically active	Total in employment	Unemployed	Economically inactive	Economic Activity rate (%)	Employment rate (%)	Unemployment rate (%)	Economic inactivity rate (%)
	10	11	12	13	14	15	16	17	18
All Persons	YBTF	YBSK	YBSE	YBSH	YBSN	MGSO	MGSU	YBTI	YBTL
Nov-Jan 2001	35,928	28,298	26,815	1,483	7,630	78.8	74.6	5.2	21.2
Dec-Feb 2001	35,950	28,312	26,819	1,493	7,638	78.8	74.6	5.3	21.2
Jan-Mar 2001	35,972	28,277	26,824	1,453	7,695	78.6	74.6	5.1	21.4
Feb-Apr 2001	35,994	28,286	26,846	1,439	7,708	78.6	74.6	5.1	21.4
Mar-May 2001	36,016	28,288	26,872	1,416	7,729	78.5	74.6	5.0	21.5
Apr-Jun 2001	36,038	28,322	26,863	1,458	7,717	78.6	74.5	5.1	21.4
May-Jul 2001	36,061	28,291	26,835	1,456	7,770	78.5	74.4	5.1	21.5
Jun-Aug 2001	36,083	28,322	26,859	1,463	7,761	78.5	74.4	5.2	21.5
Jul-Sep 2001	36,100	28,315	26,845	1,470	7,786	78.4	74.4	5.2	21.6
Aug-Oct 2001	36,118	28,342	26,871	1,472	7,776	78.5	74.4	5.2	21.5
Sep-Nov 2001	36,136	28,378	26,901	1,477	7,758	78.5	74.4	5.2	21.5
Oct-Dec 2001	36,154	28,395	26,889	1,506	7,759	78.5	74.4	5.3	21.5
Nov-Jan 2002	36,172	28,389	26,892	1,497	7,783	78.5	74.3	5.3	21.5
Dec-Feb 2002	36,190	28,407	26,922	1,486	7,783	78.5	74.4	5.2	21.5
Jan-Mar 2002	36,208	28,396	26,901	1,495	7,812	78.4	74.3	5.3	21.6
Feb-Apr 2002	36,226	28,460	26,960	1,499	7,766	78.6	74.4	5.3	21.4
Mar-May 2002	36,244	28,494	26,983	1,511	7,749	78.6	74.4	5.3	21.4
Apr-Jun 2002	36,261	28,517	27,024	1,493	7,744	78.6	74.5	5.2	21.4
May-Jul 2002	36,279	28,503	27,004	1,499	7,776	78.6	74.4	5.3	21.4
Jun-Aug 2002	36,297	28,557	27,047	1,510	7,740	78.7	74.5	5.3	21.3
Jul-Sep 2002	36,314	28,561	27,023	1,538	7,753	78.7	74.4	5.4	21.3
Aug-Oct 2002	36,331	28,620	27,100	1,520	7,711	78.8	74.6	5.3	21.2
Sep-Nov 2002	36,348	28,640	27,130	1,510	7,708	78.8	74.6	5.3	21.2
Oct-Dec 2002	36,365	28,669	27,173	1,495	7,696	78.8	74.7	5.2	21.2
Nov-Jan 2003	36,382	28,598	27,138	1,460	7,784	78.6	74.6	5.1	21.4
Dec-Feb 2003	36,399	28,606	27,114	1,492	7,793	78.6	74.5	5.2	21.4
Jan-Mar 2003	36,416	28,656	27,148	1,508	7,759	78.7	74.6	5.3	21.3
Feb-Apr 2003	36,433	28,673	27,183	1,491	7,759	78.7	74.6	5.2	21.3
Mar-May 2003	36,449	28,697	27,239	1,459	7,752	78.7	74.7	5.1	21.3
Apr-Jun 2003	36,466	28,709	27,264	1,445	7,757	78.7	74.8	5.0	21.3
May-Jul 2003	36,483	28,751	27,267	1,484	7,732	78.8	74.7	5.2	21.2
Jun-Aug 2003	36,500	28,711	27,227	1,484	7,790	78.7	74.6	5.2	21.3
Jul-Sep 2003	36,520	28,740	27,256	1,484	7,779	78.7	74.6	5.2	21.3
Aug-Oct 2003	36,539	28,727	27,269	1,459	7,811	78.6	74.6	5.1	21.4
Sep-Nov 2003	36,558	28,718	27,273	1,445	7,840	78.6	74.6	5.0	21.4
Oct-Dec 2003	36,578	28,718	27,279	1,439	7,860	78.5	74.6	5.0	21.5
Nov-Jan 2004	36,597	28,790	27,367	1,423	7,807	78.7	74.8	4.9	21.3
Dec-Feb 2004	36,617	28,816	27,400	1,416	7,801	78.7	74.8	4.9	21.3
Jan-Mar 2004	36,636	28,826	27,412	1,414	7,810	78.7	74.8	4.9	21.3
Feb-Apr 2004	36,655	28,821	27,405	1,416	7,834	78.6	74.8	4.9	21.4
Mar-May 2004	36,675	28,827	27,418	1,409	7,848	78.6	74.8	4.9	21.4
Apr-Jun 2004	36,694	28,818	27,401	1,416	7,876	78.5	74.7	4.9	21.5
May-Jul 2004	36,714	28,814	27,417	1,397	7,899	78.5	74.7	4.8	21.5
Jun-Aug 2004	36,733	28,797	27,420	1,377	7,936	78.4	74.6	4.8	21.6
Jul-Sep 2004	36,758	28,851	27,475	1,376	7,907	78.5	74.7	4.8	21.5
Aug-Oct 2004	36,784	28,871	27,492	1,379	7,913	78.5	74.7	4.8	21.5
Sep-Nov 2004	36,809	28,936	27,546	1,390	7,873	78.6	74.8	4.8	21.4
Oct-Dec 2004	36,834	28,975	27,575	1,400	7,859	78.7	74.9	4.8	21.3
Nov-Jan 2005	36,860	29,001	27,602	1,400	7,858	78.7	74.9	4.8	21.3
Dec-Feb 2005	36,885	29,066	27,645	1,421	7,819	78.8	75.0	4.9	21.2
Jan-Mar 2005	36,910	29,021	27,630	1,390	7,890	78.6	74.9	4.8	21.4
Feb-Apr 2005	36,936	29,003	27,615	1,388	7,932	78.5	74.8	4.8	21.5
Mar-May 2005	36,961	29,027	27,618	1,408	7,934	78.5	74.7	4.9	21.5
Apr-Jun 2005	36,987	29,058	27,641	1,418	7,928	78.6	74.7	4.9	21.4
May-Jul 2005	37,012	29,094	27,695	1,400	7,918	78.6	74.8	4.8	21.4
Jun-Aug 2005	37,037	29,122	27,726	1,396	7,915	78.6	74.9	4.8	21.4
Jul-Sep 2005	37,059	29,166	27,756	1,410	7,893	78.7	74.9	4.8	21.3
Aug-Oct 2005	37,080	29,185	27,717	1,468	7,895	78.7	74.7	5.0	21.3
Sep-Nov 2005	**37,102**	**29,162**	**27,659**	**1,504**	**7,940**	**78.6**	**74.5**	**5.2**	**21.4**

Labour Force Survey, summary by sex United Kingdom (thousands) seasonally adjusted (Continued)

All aged 16 to 59/64

	All aged 16 to 59/64	Total economically active	Total in employment	Unemployed	Economically inactive	Economic Activity rate (%)	Employment rate (%)	Unemployment rate (%)	Economic inactivity rate (%)
	10	11	12	13	14	15	16	17	18
Male	YBTG	YBSL	YBSF	YBSI	YBSO	MGSP	MGSV	YBTJ	YBTM
Jan-Mar 1971	16,561	15,746	15,247	499	815	95.1	92.1	3.2	4.9
Feb-Apr 1971	16,566	15,738	15,224	514	828	95.0	91.9	3.3	5.0
Mar-May 1971	16,571	15,741	15,206	535	829	95.0	91.8	3.4	5.0
Apr-Jun 1971	16,576	15,758	15,203	555	818	95.1	91.7	3.5	4.9
May-Jul 1971	16,580	15,755	15,185	570	825	95.0	91.6	3.6	5.0
Jun-Aug 1971	16,585	15,741	15,164	576	845	94.9	91.4	3.7	5.1
Jul-Sep 1971	16,588	15,717	15,134	583	871	94.7	91.2	3.7	5.3
Aug-Oct 1971	16,591	15,698	15,104	594	893	94.6	91.0	3.8	5.4
Sep-Nov 1971	16,594	15,686	15,074	612	907	94.5	90.8	3.9	5.5
Oct-Dec 1971	16,597	15,702	15,074	628	895	94.6	90.8	4.0	5.4
Nov-Jan 1972	16,600	15,713	15,075	637	887	94.7	90.8	4.1	5.3
Dec-Feb 1972	16,602	15,739	15,096	643	864	94.8	90.9	4.1	5.2
Jan-Mar 1972	16,605	15,766	15,119	648	839	94.9	91.0	4.1	5.1
Feb-Apr 1972	16,608	15,789	15,137	652	819	95.1	91.1	4.1	4.9
Mar-May 1972	16,611	15,782	15,137	645	829	95.0	91.1	4.1	5.0
Apr-Jun 1972	16,614	15,759	15,128	630	855	94.9	91.1	4.0	5.1
May-Jul 1972	16,617	15,733	15,119	614	883	94.7	91.0	3.9	5.3
Jun-Aug 1972	16,620	15,721	15,119	602	899	94.6	91.0	3.8	5.4
Jul-Sep 1972	16,623	15,727	15,130	597	896	94.6	91.0	3.8	5.4
Aug-Oct 1972	16,626	15,730	15,141	590	896	94.6	91.1	3.7	5.4
Sep-Nov 1972	16,630	15,741	15,159	582	889	94.7	91.2	3.7	5.3
Oct-Dec 1972	16,633	15,738	15,171	567	895	94.6	91.2	3.6	5.4
Nov-Jan 1973	16,636	15,750	15,202	548	886	94.7	91.4	3.5	5.3
Dec-Feb 1973	16,640	15,760	15,234	526	880	94.7	91.6	3.3	5.3
Jan-Mar 1973	16,643	15,783	15,276	508	860	94.8	91.8	3.2	5.2
Feb-Apr 1973	16,647	15,798	15,304	494	849	94.9	91.9	3.1	5.1
Mar-May 1973	16,650	15,792	15,307	485	858	94.8	91.9	3.1	5.2
Apr-Jun 1973	16,653	15,775	15,297	478	878	94.7	91.9	3.0	5.3
May-Jul 1973	16,657	15,747	15,278	469	910	94.5	91.7	3.0	5.5
Jun-Aug 1973	16,660	15,724	15,265	458	936	94.4	91.6	2.9	5.6
Jul-Sep 1973	16,663	15,703	15,257	445	960	94.2	91.6	2.8	5.8
Aug-Oct 1973	16,666	15,683	15,249	435	982	94.1	91.5	2.8	5.9
Sep-Nov 1973	16,668	15,672	15,247	425	996	94.0	91.5	2.7	6.0
Oct-Dec 1973	16,671	15,653	15,239	414	1,018	93.9	91.4	2.6	6.1
Nov-Jan 1974	16,674	15,639	15,221	418	1,035	93.8	91.3	2.7	6.2
Dec-Feb 1974	16,677	15,637	15,209	428	1,039	93.8	91.2	2.7	6.2
Jan-Mar 1974	16,679	15,637	15,192	445	1,042	93.8	91.1	2.8	6.2
Feb-Apr 1974	16,682	15,633	15,182	451	1,049	93.7	91.0	2.9	6.3
Mar-May 1974	16,685	15,624	15,172	452	1,061	93.6	90.9	2.9	6.4
Apr-Jun 1974	16,688	15,625	15,171	454	1,062	93.6	90.9	2.9	6.4
May-Jul 1974	16,690	15,630	15,172	458	1,060	93.6	90.9	2.9	6.4
Jun-Aug 1974	16,693	15,650	15,183	467	1,043	93.8	91.0	3.0	6.2
Jul-Sep 1974	16,698	15,658	15,185	473	1,040	93.8	90.9	3.0	6.2
Aug-Oct 1974	16,702	15,665	15,184	481	1,037	93.8	90.9	3.1	6.2
Sep-Nov 1974	16,707	15,660	15,176	485	1,046	93.7	90.8	3.1	6.3
Oct-Dec 1974	16,711	15,656	15,165	491	1,055	93.7	90.8	3.1	6.3
Nov-Jan 1975	16,716	15,647	15,146	501	1,069	93.6	90.6	3.2	6.4
Dec-Feb 1975	16,720	15,641	15,126	514	1,079	93.5	90.5	3.3	6.5
Jan-Mar 1975	16,725	15,646	15,115	531	1,079	93.6	90.4	3.4	6.4
Feb-Apr 1975	16,729	15,646	15,095	551	1,083	93.5	90.2	3.5	6.5
Mar-May 1975	16,734	15,663	15,085	577	1,071	93.6	90.1	3.7	6.4
Apr-Jun 1975	16,738	15,681	15,075	606	1,057	93.7	90.1	3.9	6.3
May-Jul 1975	16,743	15,700	15,066	635	1,042	93.8	90.0	4.0	6.2
Jun-Aug 1975	16,747	15,715	15,056	659	1,032	93.8	89.9	4.2	6.2
Jul-Sep 1975	16,753	15,725	15,044	682	1,028	93.9	89.8	4.3	6.1
Aug-Oct 1975	16,760	15,739	15,035	705	1,020	93.9	89.7	4.5	6.1
Sep-Nov 1975	16,766	15,744	15,015	729	1,021	93.9	89.6	4.6	6.1
Oct-Dec 1975	16,772	15,756	15,003	753	1,016	93.9	89.5	4.8	6.1

Labour Force Survey, summary by sex United Kingdom (thousands) seasonally adjusted (Continued)

All aged 16 to 59/64

	All aged 16 to 59/64	Total economically active	Total in employment	Unemployed	Economically inactive	Economic Activity rate (%)	Employment rate (%)	Unemployment rate (%)	Economic inactivity rate (%)
	10	11	12	13	14	15	16	17	18
Male	YBTG	YBSL	YBSF	YBSI	YBSO	MGSP	MGSV	YBTJ	YBTM
Nov-Jan 1976	16,778	15,757	14,987	770	1,022	93.9	89.3	4.9	6.1
Dec-Feb 1976	16,785	15,758	14,975	783	1,027	93.9	89.2	5.0	6.1
Jan-Mar 1976	16,791	15,756	14,963	793	1,035	93.8	89.1	5.0	6.2
Feb-Apr 1976	16,797	15,746	14,946	800	1,051	93.7	89.0	5.1	6.3
Mar-May 1976	16,803	15,752	14,944	808	1,052	93.7	88.9	5.1	6.3
Apr-Jun 1976	16,810	15,746	14,933	813	1,063	93.7	88.8	5.2	6.3
May-Jul 1976	16,816	15,741	14,925	816	1,075	93.6	88.8	5.2	6.4
Jun-Aug 1976	16,822	15,740	14,924	816	1,082	93.6	88.7	5.2	6.4
Jul-Sep 1976	16,829	15,733	14,916	817	1,096	93.5	88.6	5.2	6.5
Aug-Oct 1976	16,837	15,730	14,915	815	1,107	93.4	88.6	5.2	6.6
Sep-Nov 1976	16,844	15,726	14,914	812	1,118	93.4	88.5	5.2	6.6
Oct-Dec 1976	16,851	15,725	14,914	811	1,126	93.3	88.5	5.2	6.7
Nov-Jan 1977	16,859	15,726	14,915	811	1,133	93.3	88.5	5.2	6.7
Dec-Feb 1977	16,866	15,725	14,916	810	1,140	93.2	88.4	5.1	6.8
Jan-Mar 1977	16,873	15,715	14,907	808	1,159	93.1	88.3	5.1	6.9
Feb-Apr 1977	16,880	15,706	14,898	808	1,174	93.0	88.3	5.1	7.0
Mar-May 1977	16,888	15,707	14,897	810	1,181	93.0	88.2	5.2	7.0
Apr-Jun 1977	16,895	15,705	14,888	818	1,190	93.0	88.1	5.2	7.0
May-Jul 1977	16,902	15,704	14,879	826	1,198	92.9	88.0	5.3	7.1
Jun-Aug 1977	16,910	15,711	14,877	834	1,198	92.9	88.0	5.3	7.1
Jul-Sep 1977	16,917	15,718	14,877	841	1,199	92.9	87.9	5.3	7.1
Aug-Oct 1977	16,924	15,711	14,868	843	1,213	92.8	87.8	5.4	7.2
Sep-Nov 1977	16,931	15,704	14,860	844	1,227	92.8	87.8	5.4	7.2
Oct-Dec 1977	16,939	15,698	14,858	840	1,241	92.7	87.7	5.3	7.3
Nov-Jan 1978	16,946	15,692	14,858	834	1,254	92.6	87.7	5.3	7.4
Dec-Feb 1978	16,953	15,686	14,860	826	1,267	92.5	87.7	5.3	7.5
Jan-Mar 1978	16,961	15,678	14,859	819	1,283	92.4	87.6	5.2	7.6
Feb-Apr 1978	16,968	15,665	14,853	813	1,302	92.3	87.5	5.2	7.7
Mar-May 1978	16,975	15,661	14,852	809	1,314	92.3	87.5	5.2	7.7
Apr-Jun 1978	16,982	15,648	14,844	804	1,335	92.1	87.4	5.1	7.9
May-Jul 1978	16,990	15,643	14,843	799	1,347	92.1	87.4	5.1	7.9
Jun-Aug 1978	16,997	15,642	14,845	796	1,355	92.0	87.3	5.1	8.0
Jul-Sep 1978	17,007	15,647	14,854	792	1,361	92.0	87.3	5.1	8.0
Aug-Oct 1978	17,018	15,651	14,865	786	1,367	92.0	87.3	5.0	8.0
Sep-Nov 1978	17,029	15,651	14,876	775	1,378	91.9	87.4	4.9	8.1
Oct-Dec 1978	17,039	15,652	14,888	764	1,388	91.9	87.4	4.9	8.1
Nov-Jan 1979	17,050	15,664	14,906	757	1,386	91.9	87.4	4.8	8.1
Dec-Feb 1979	17,060	15,669	14,909	760	1,392	91.8	87.4	4.8	8.2
Jan-Mar 1979	17,071	15,672	14,910	762	1,399	91.8	87.3	4.9	8.2
Feb-Apr 1979	17,081	15,665	14,909	756	1,416	91.7	87.3	4.8	8.3
Mar-May 1979	17,092	15,657	14,912	745	1,435	91.6	87.2	4.8	8.4
Apr-Jun 1979	17,103	15,654	14,910	743	1,449	91.5	87.2	4.7	8.5
May-Jul 1979	17,113	15,658	14,910	747	1,455	91.5	87.1	4.8	8.5
Jun-Aug 1979	17,124	15,662	14,912	751	1,461	91.5	87.1	4.8	8.5
Jul-Sep 1979	17,135	15,667	14,911	756	1,468	91.4	87.0	4.8	8.6
Aug-Oct 1979	17,145	15,670	14,905	764	1,476	91.4	86.9	4.9	8.6
Sep-Nov 1979	17,156	15,677	14,904	773	1,479	91.4	86.9	4.9	8.6
Oct-Dec 1979	17,167	15,678	14,893	785	1,490	91.3	86.7	5.0	8.7
Nov-Jan 1980	17,178	15,673	14,875	798	1,505	91.2	86.6	5.1	8.8
Dec-Feb 1980	17,189	15,676	14,857	820	1,513	91.2	86.4	5.2	8.8
Jan-Mar 1980	17,200	15,690	14,845	845	1,510	91.2	86.3	5.4	8.8
Feb-Apr 1980	17,211	15,701	14,823	878	1,510	91.2	86.1	5.6	8.8
Mar-May 1980	17,222	15,715	14,803	911	1,507	91.2	86.0	5.8	8.8
Apr-Jun 1980	17,233	15,724	14,774	950	1,509	91.2	85.7	6.0	8.8
May-Jul 1980	17,244	15,737	14,744	992	1,507	91.3	85.5	6.3	8.7
Jun-Aug 1980	17,255	15,750	14,704	1,046	1,504	91.3	85.2	6.6	8.7
Jul-Sep 1980	17,265	15,757	14,652	1,105	1,507	91.3	84.9	7.0	8.7
Aug-Oct 1980	17,275	15,762	14,593	1,169	1,513	91.2	84.5	7.4	8.8
Sep-Nov 1980	17,285	15,778	14,541	1,237	1,507	91.3	84.1	7.8	8.7
Oct-Dec 1980	17,295	15,788	14,482	1,306	1,507	91.3	83.7	8.3	8.7

Labour Force Survey, summary by sex United Kingdom (thousands) seasonally adjusted (Continued)

All aged 16 to 59/64

	All aged 16 to 59/64	Total economically active	Total in employment	Unemployed	Economically inactive	Economic Activity rate (%)	Employment rate (%)	Unemployment rate (%)	Economic inactivity rate (%)
	10	11	12	13	14	15	16	17	18
Male	YBTG	YBSL	YBSF	YBSI	YBSO	MGSP	MGSV	YBTJ	YBTM
Nov-Jan 1981	17,305	15,805	14,432	1,372	1,500	91.3	83.4	8.7	8.7
Dec-Feb 1981	17,315	15,809	14,380	1,429	1,506	91.3	83.0	9.0	8.7
Jan-Mar 1981	17,326	15,815	14,331	1,484	1,511	91.3	82.7	9.4	8.7
Feb-Apr 1981	17,336	15,822	14,281	1,541	1,514	91.3	82.4	9.7	8.7
Mar-May 1981	17,346	15,832	14,237	1,595	1,514	91.3	82.1	10.1	8.7
Apr-Jun 1981	17,356	15,827	14,200	1,628	1,529	91.2	81.8	10.3	8.8
May-Jul 1981	17,366	15,816	14,160	1,656	1,550	91.1	81.5	10.5	8.9
Jun-Aug 1981	17,376	15,807	14,129	1,678	1,570	91.0	81.3	10.6	9.0
Jul-Sep 1981	17,384	15,797	14,098	1,699	1,588	90.9	81.1	10.8	9.1
Aug-Oct 1981	17,392	15,777	14,060	1,717	1,615	90.7	80.8	10.9	9.3
Sep-Nov 1981	17,400	15,765	14,029	1,736	1,635	90.6	80.6	11.0	9.4
Oct-Dec 1981	17,408	15,742	13,991	1,751	1,666	90.4	80.4	11.1	9.6
Nov-Jan 1982	17,415	15,725	13,961	1,765	1,690	90.3	80.2	11.2	9.7
Dec-Feb 1982	17,423	15,715	13,940	1,774	1,709	90.2	80.0	11.3	9.8
Jan-Mar 1982	17,431	15,711	13,930	1,782	1,720	90.1	79.9	11.3	9.9
Feb-Apr 1982	17,439	15,698	13,911	1,788	1,741	90.0	79.8	11.4	10.0
Mar-May 1982	17,447	15,694	13,900	1,794	1,753	90.0	79.7	11.4	10.0
Apr-Jun 1982	17,455	15,678	13,872	1,807	1,776	89.8	79.5	11.5	10.2
May-Jul 1982	17,462	15,669	13,849	1,820	1,794	89.7	79.3	11.6	10.3
Jun-Aug 1982	17,470	15,655	13,820	1,835	1,816	89.6	79.1	11.7	10.4
Jul-Sep 1982	17,484	15,647	13,799	1,848	1,837	89.5	78.9	11.8	10.5
Aug-Oct 1982	17,497	15,631	13,770	1,861	1,866	89.3	78.7	11.9	10.7
Sep-Nov 1982	17,510	15,614	13,739	1,875	1,897	89.2	78.5	12.0	10.8
Oct-Dec 1982	17,523	15,599	13,710	1,889	1,924	89.0	78.2	12.1	11.0
Nov-Jan 1983	17,537	15,589	13,689	1,900	1,948	88.9	78.1	12.2	11.1
Dec-Feb 1983	17,550	15,575	13,669	1,906	1,975	88.7	77.9	12.2	11.3
Jan-Mar 1983	17,563	15,569	13,658	1,910	1,995	88.6	77.8	12.3	11.4
Feb-Apr 1983	17,577	15,556	13,641	1,915	2,021	88.5	77.6	12.3	11.5
Mar-May 1983	17,590	15,551	13,630	1,921	2,039	88.4	77.5	12.4	11.6
Apr-Jun 1983	17,603	15,556	13,630	1,926	2,047	88.4	77.4	12.4	11.6
May-Jul 1983	17,617	15,559	13,630	1,929	2,058	88.3	77.4	12.4	11.7
Jun-Aug 1983	17,630	15,585	13,659	1,926	2,045	88.4	77.5	12.4	11.6
Jul-Sep 1983	17,644	15,611	13,690	1,921	2,033	88.5	77.6	12.3	11.5
Aug-Oct 1983	17,657	15,636	13,720	1,916	2,021	88.6	77.7	12.3	11.4
Sep-Nov 1983	17,671	15,653	13,741	1,912	2,018	88.6	77.8	12.2	11.4
Oct-Dec 1983	17,685	15,669	13,761	1,909	2,015	88.6	77.8	12.2	11.4
Nov-Jan 1984	17,698	15,688	13,781	1,907	2,010	88.6	77.9	12.2	11.4
Dec-Feb 1984	17,712	15,709	13,800	1,909	2,003	88.7	77.9	12.2	11.3
Jan-Mar 1984	17,725	15,730	13,820	1,911	1,995	88.7	78.0	12.1	11.3
Feb-Apr 1984	17,739	15,750	13,840	1,910	1,989	88.8	78.0	12.1	11.2
Mar-May 1984	17,753	15,768	13,860	1,908	1,985	88.8	78.1	12.1	11.2
Apr-Jun 1984	17,766	15,778	13,879	1,899	1,988	88.8	78.1	12.0	11.2
May-Jul 1984	17,780	15,785	13,890	1,894	1,995	88.8	78.1	12.0	11.2
Jun-Aug 1984	17,794	15,790	13,900	1,890	2,004	88.7	78.1	12.0	11.3
Jul-Sep 1984	17,798	15,800	13,910	1,891	1,998	88.8	78.2	12.0	11.2
Aug-Oct 1984	17,803	15,819	13,929	1,890	1,984	88.9	78.2	11.9	11.1
Sep-Nov 1984	17,808	15,830	13,940	1,890	1,978	88.9	78.3	11.9	11.1
Oct-Dec 1984	17,813	15,835	13,950	1,885	1,978	88.9	78.3	11.9	11.1
Nov-Jan 1985	17,818	15,831	13,951	1,881	1,987	88.8	78.3	11.9	11.2
Dec-Feb 1985	17,823	15,837	13,960	1,877	1,986	88.9	78.3	11.9	11.1
Jan-Mar 1985	17,828	15,841	13,970	1,872	1,987	88.9	78.4	11.8	11.1
Feb-Apr 1985	17,833	15,847	13,980	1,867	1,987	88.9	78.4	11.8	11.1
Mar-May 1985	17,838	15,836	13,977	1,859	2,002	88.8	78.4	11.7	11.2
Apr-Jun 1985	17,843	15,835	13,979	1,856	2,008	88.7	78.3	11.7	11.3
May-Jul 1985	17,848	15,822	13,971	1,850	2,026	88.6	78.3	11.7	11.4
Jun-Aug 1985	17,853	15,817	13,971	1,846	2,036	88.6	78.3	11.7	11.4
Jul-Sep 1985	17,857	15,814	13,971	1,843	2,043	88.6	78.2	11.7	11.4
Aug-Oct 1985	17,860	15,812	13,971	1,841	2,048	88.5	78.2	11.6	11.5
Sep-Nov 1985	17,864	15,809	13,969	1,840	2,055	88.5	78.2	11.6	11.5
Oct-Dec 1985	17,867	15,801	13,960	1,841	2,066	88.4	78.1	11.6	11.6

Labour Force Survey, summary by sex United Kingdom (thousands) seasonally adjusted (Continued)

All aged 16 to 59/64

	All aged 16 to 59/64	Total economically active	Total in employment	Unemployed	Economically inactive	Economic Activity rate (%)	Employment rate (%)	Unemployment rate (%)	Economic inactivity rate (%)
	10	11	12	13	14	15	16	17	18
Male	YBTG	YBSL	YBSF	YBSI	YBSO	MGSP	MGSV	YBTJ	YBTM
Nov-Jan 1986	17,871	15,796	13,952	1,844	2,075	88.4	78.1	11.7	11.6
Dec-Feb 1986	17,874	15,793	13,948	1,846	2,081	88.4	78.0	11.7	11.6
Jan-Mar 1986	17,878	15,792	13,940	1,852	2,086	88.3	78.0	11.7	11.7
Feb-Apr 1986	17,881	15,782	13,930	1,852	2,099	88.3	77.9	11.7	11.7
Mar-May 1986	17,885	15,779	13,925	1,854	2,106	88.2	77.9	11.8	11.8
Apr-Jun 1986	17,889	15,773	13,920	1,853	2,115	88.2	77.8	11.8	11.8
May-Jul 1986	17,892	15,777	13,920	1,857	2,115	88.2	77.8	11.8	11.8
Jun-Aug 1986	17,896	15,789	13,930	1,859	2,107	88.2	77.8	11.8	11.8
Jul-Sep 1986	17,900	15,797	13,940	1,857	2,103	88.3	77.9	11.8	11.7
Aug-Oct 1986	17,905	15,792	13,940	1,852	2,113	88.2	77.9	11.7	11.8
Sep-Nov 1986	17,910	15,796	13,948	1,849	2,114	88.2	77.9	11.7	11.8
Oct-Dec 1986	17,915	15,795	13,950	1,845	2,120	88.2	77.9	11.7	11.8
Nov-Jan 1987	17,920	15,795	13,952	1,843	2,124	88.1	77.9	11.7	11.9
Dec-Feb 1987	17,924	15,795	13,960	1,835	2,129	88.1	77.9	11.6	11.9
Jan-Mar 1987	17,929	15,794	13,970	1,824	2,135	88.1	77.9	11.6	11.9
Feb-Apr 1987	17,934	15,804	13,992	1,812	2,129	88.1	78.0	11.5	11.9
Mar-May 1987	17,939	15,818	14,024	1,794	2,120	88.2	78.2	11.3	11.8
Apr-Jun 1987	17,943	15,832	14,060	1,772	2,112	88.2	78.4	11.2	11.8
May-Jul 1987	17,948	15,845	14,102	1,742	2,103	88.3	78.6	11.0	11.7
Jun-Aug 1987	17,953	15,866	14,150	1,716	2,087	88.4	78.8	10.8	11.6
Jul-Sep 1987	17,957	15,880	14,190	1,690	2,077	88.4	79.0	10.6	11.6
Aug-Oct 1987	17,960	15,890	14,230	1,660	2,070	88.5	79.2	10.4	11.5
Sep-Nov 1987	17,964	15,897	14,268	1,629	2,067	88.5	79.4	10.2	11.5
Oct-Dec 1987	17,968	15,899	14,300	1,599	2,068	88.5	79.6	10.1	11.5
Nov-Jan 1988	17,971	15,912	14,342	1,570	2,059	88.5	79.8	9.9	11.5
Dec-Feb 1988	17,975	15,925	14,382	1,543	2,050	88.6	80.0	9.7	11.4
Jan-Mar 1988	17,979	15,943	14,430	1,513	2,036	88.7	80.3	9.5	11.3
Feb-Apr 1988	17,982	15,946	14,460	1,486	2,036	88.7	80.4	9.3	11.3
Mar-May 1988	17,986	15,949	14,489	1,460	2,037	88.7	80.6	9.2	11.3
Apr-Jun 1988	17,990	15,946	14,510	1,436	2,043	88.6	80.7	9.0	11.4
May-Jul 1988	17,993	15,940	14,530	1,410	2,053	88.6	80.8	8.8	11.4
Jun-Aug 1988	17,997	15,939	14,552	1,387	2,058	88.6	80.9	8.7	11.4
Jul-Sep 1988	18,001	15,948	14,580	1,368	2,053	88.6	81.0	8.6	11.4
Aug-Oct 1988	18,004	15,955	14,602	1,353	2,049	88.6	81.1	8.5	11.4
Sep-Nov 1988	18,008	15,965	14,630	1,335	2,043	88.7	81.2	8.4	11.3
Oct-Dec 1988	18,011	15,961	14,652	1,308	2,050	88.6	81.4	8.2	11.4
Nov-Jan 1989	18,015	15,960	14,680	1,280	2,055	88.6	81.5	8.0	11.4
Dec-Feb 1989	18,018	15,974	14,720	1,254	2,044	88.7	81.7	7.9	11.3
Jan-Mar 1989	18,022	15,995	14,762	1,232	2,027	88.8	81.9	7.7	11.2
Feb-Apr 1989	18,025	16,001	14,792	1,208	2,024	88.8	82.1	7.6	11.2
Mar-May 1989	18,029	16,010	14,821	1,189	2,019	88.8	82.2	7.4	11.2
Apr-Jun 1989	18,032	16,017	14,840	1,177	2,015	88.8	82.3	7.3	11.2
May-Jul 1989	18,036	16,022	14,850	1,172	2,014	88.8	82.3	7.3	11.2
Jun-Aug 1989	18,039	16,022	14,858	1,165	2,017	88.8	82.4	7.3	11.2
Jul-Sep 1989	18,042	16,028	14,870	1,158	2,014	88.8	82.4	7.2	11.2
Aug-Oct 1989	18,045	16,031	14,878	1,153	2,015	88.8	82.4	7.2	11.2
Sep-Nov 1989	18,049	16,037	14,888	1,149	2,012	88.9	82.5	7.2	11.1
Oct-Dec 1989	18,052	16,038	14,890	1,148	2,014	88.8	82.5	7.2	11.2
Nov-Jan 1990	18,055	16,034	14,890	1,144	2,021	88.8	82.5	7.1	11.2
Dec-Feb 1990	18,058	16,032	14,890	1,142	2,026	88.8	82.5	7.1	11.2
Jan-Mar 1990	18,061	16,034	14,890	1,144	2,028	88.8	82.4	7.1	11.2
Feb-Apr 1990	18,064	16,035	14,890	1,145	2,029	88.8	82.4	7.1	11.2
Mar-May 1990	18,068	16,034	14,887	1,147	2,033	88.7	82.4	7.2	11.3
Apr-Jun 1990	18,071	16,029	14,882	1,146	2,042	88.7	82.4	7.2	11.3
May-Jul 1990	18,074	16,025	14,872	1,153	2,049	88.7	82.3	7.2	11.3
Jun-Aug 1990	18,077	16,029	14,862	1,166	2,048	88.7	82.2	7.3	11.3
Jul-Sep 1990	18,078	16,022	14,835	1,187	2,056	88.6	82.1	7.4	11.4
Aug-Oct 1990	18,078	16,014	14,802	1,212	2,064	88.6	81.9	7.6	11.4
Sep-Nov 1990	18,079	16,005	14,765	1,241	2,074	88.5	81.7	7.8	11.5
Oct-Dec 1990	18,080	15,987	14,712	1,274	2,093	88.4	81.4	8.0	11.6

Labour Force Survey, summary by sex United Kingdom (thousands) seasonally adjusted (Continued)

All aged 16 to 59/64

	All aged 16 to 59/64	Total economically active	Total in employment	Unemployed	Economically inactive	Economic Activity rate (%)	Employment rate (%)	Unemployment rate (%)	Economic inactivity rate (%)
	10	11	12	13	14	15	16	17	18
Male	YBTG	YBSL	YBSF	YBSI	YBSO	MGSP	MGSV	YBTJ	YBTM
Nov-Jan 1991	18,081	15,967	14,665	1,302	2,114	88.3	81.1	8.2	11.7
Dec-Feb 1991	18,081	15,953	14,612	1,341	2,128	88.2	80.8	8.4	11.8
Jan-Mar 1991	18,082	15,950	14,562	1,388	2,132	88.2	80.5	8.7	11.8
Feb-Apr 1991	18,083	15,944	14,502	1,442	2,139	88.2	80.2	9.0	11.8
Mar-May 1991	18,084	15,935	14,444	1,491	2,149	88.1	79.9	9.4	11.9
Apr-Jun 1991	18,084	15,904	14,370	1,534	2,180	87.9	79.5	9.6	12.1
May-Jul 1991	18,085	15,878	14,300	1,578	2,207	87.8	79.1	9.9	12.2
Jun-Aug 1991	18,085	15,856	14,238	1,618	2,229	87.7	78.7	10.2	12.3
Jul-Sep 1991	18,086	15,834	14,180	1,654	2,251	87.6	78.4	10.4	12.4
Aug-Oct 1991	18,086	15,812	14,130	1,682	2,274	87.4	78.1	10.6	12.6
Sep-Nov 1991	18,087	15,787	14,080	1,707	2,299	87.3	77.8	10.8	12.7
Oct-Dec 1991	18,087	15,761	14,030	1,731	2,326	87.1	77.6	11.0	12.9
Nov-Jan 1992	18,087	15,738	13,988	1,751	2,349	87.0	77.3	11.1	13.0
Dec-Feb 1992	18,088	15,730	13,958	1,772	2,358	87.0	77.2	11.3	13.0
Jan-Mar 1992	18,088	15,718	13,918	1,800	2,371	86.9	76.9	11.5	13.1
Feb-Apr 1992	18,089	15,704	13,880	1,824	2,385	86.8	76.7	11.6	13.2
Mar-May 1992	18,080	15,670	13,831	1,839	2,410	86.7	76.5	11.7	13.3
Apr-Jun 1992	18,078	15,640	13,818	1,822	2,439	86.5	76.4	11.6	13.5
May-Jul 1992	18,077	15,624	13,784	1,840	2,453	86.4	76.3	11.8	13.6
Jun-Aug 1992	18,076	15,617	13,764	1,852	2,459	86.4	76.1	11.9	13.6
Jul-Sep 1992	18,074	15,605	13,744	1,861	2,469	86.3	76.0	11.9	13.7
Aug-Oct 1992	18,073	15,595	13,704	1,891	2,478	86.3	75.8	12.1	13.7
Sep-Nov 1992	18,071	15,584	13,657	1,927	2,487	86.2	75.6	12.4	13.8
Oct-Dec 1992	18,070	15,560	13,613	1,947	2,509	86.1	75.3	12.5	13.9
Nov-Jan 1993	18,068	15,569	13,592	1,976	2,499	86.2	75.2	12.7	13.8
Dec-Feb 1993	18,067	15,580	13,578	2,002	2,487	86.2	75.2	12.9	13.8
Jan-Mar 1993	18,065	15,577	13,576	2,000	2,489	86.2	75.2	12.8	13.8
Feb-Apr 1993	18,064	15,526	13,538	1,988	2,537	86.0	74.9	12.8	14.0
Mar-May 1993	18,062	15,506	13,549	1,957	2,556	85.8	75.0	12.6	14.2
Apr-Jun 1993	18,061	15,493	13,570	1,923	2,568	85.8	75.1	12.4	14.2
May-Jul 1993	18,059	15,486	13,560	1,926	2,573	85.8	75.1	12.4	14.2
Jun-Aug 1993	18,057	15,457	13,552	1,905	2,600	85.6	75.0	12.3	14.4
Jul-Sep 1993	18,057	15,459	13,548	1,911	2,598	85.6	75.0	12.4	14.4
Aug-Oct 1993	18,057	15,446	13,559	1,887	2,611	85.5	75.1	12.2	14.5
Sep-Nov 1993	18,056	15,460	13,575	1,885	2,597	85.6	75.2	12.2	14.4
Oct-Dec 1993	18,056	15,461	13,572	1,889	2,595	85.6	75.2	12.2	14.4
Nov-Jan 1993	18,056	15,461	13,566	1,894	2,595	85.6	75.1	12.3	14.4
Dec-Feb 1994	18,055	15,456	13,609	1,847	2,600	85.6	75.4	11.9	14.4
Jan-Mar 1994	18,055	15,443	13,624	1,819	2,612	85.5	75.5	11.8	14.5
Feb-Apr 1994	18,055	15,447	13,647	1,800	2,608	85.6	75.6	11.7	14.4
Mar-May 1994	18,055	15,434	13,639	1,795	2,621	85.5	75.5	11.6	14.5
Apr-Jun 1994	18,054	15,422	13,628	1,795	2,632	85.4	75.5	11.6	14.6
May-Jul 1994	18,054	15,440	13,661	1,779	2,614	85.5	75.7	11.5	14.5
Jun-Aug 1994	18,054	15,436	13,671	1,765	2,617	85.5	75.7	11.4	14.5
Jul-Sep 1994	18,058	15,428	13,710	1,718	2,630	85.4	75.9	11.1	14.6
Aug-Oct 1994	18,062	15,419	13,724	1,695	2,642	85.4	76.0	11.0	14.6
Sep-Nov 1994	18,066	15,398	13,735	1,663	2,668	85.2	76.0	10.8	14.8
Oct-Dec 1994	18,070	15,380	13,741	1,640	2,689	85.1	76.0	10.7	14.9
Nov-Jan 1994	18,074	15,356	13,732	1,623	2,718	85.0	76.0	10.6	15.0
Dec-Feb 1995	18,078	15,357	13,740	1,616	2,721	84.9	76.0	10.5	15.1
Jan-Mar 1995	18,082	15,363	13,754	1,608	2,719	85.0	76.1	10.5	15.0
Feb-Apr 1995	18,086	15,362	13,772	1,590	2,724	84.9	76.1	10.4	15.1
Mar-May 1995	18,090	15,385	13,803	1,582	2,705	85.0	76.3	10.3	15.0
Apr-Jun 1995	18,094	15,379	13,807	1,572	2,715	85.0	76.3	10.2	15.0
May-Jul 1995	18,098	15,382	13,812	1,570	2,716	85.0	76.3	10.2	15.0
Jun-Aug 1995	18,102	15,399	13,838	1,561	2,703	85.1	76.4	10.1	14.9
Jul-Sep 1995	18,107	15,408	13,843	1,565	2,699	85.1	76.5	10.2	14.9
Aug-Oct 1995	18,112	15,406	13,838	1,568	2,705	85.1	76.4	10.2	14.9
Sep-Nov 1995	18,116	15,399	13,858	1,541	2,717	85.0	76.5	10.0	15.0
Oct-Dec 1995	18,121	15,404	13,905	1,499	2,717	85.0	76.7	9.7	15.0

Labour Force Survey, summary by sex United Kingdom (thousands) seasonally adjusted (Continued)

All aged 16 to 59/64

	All aged 16 to 59/64	Total economically active	Total in employment	Unemployed	Economically inactive	Economic Activity rate (%)	Employment rate (%)	Unemployment rate (%)	Economic inactivity rate (%)
	10	11	12	13	14	15	16	17	18
Male	YBTG	YBSL	YBSF	YBSI	YBSO	MGSP	MGSV	YBTJ	YBTM
Nov-Jan 1996	18,126	15,413	13,880	1,534	2,712	85.0	76.6	10.0	15.0
Dec-Feb 1996	18,131	15,411	13,879	1,532	2,720	85.0	76.6	9.9	15.0
Jan-Mar 1996	18,135	15,403	13,877	1,526	2,732	84.9	76.5	9.9	15.1
Feb-Apr 1996	18,140	15,413	13,887	1,526	2,727	85.0	76.6	9.9	15.0
Mar-May 1996	18,145	15,409	13,897	1,512	2,736	84.9	76.6	9.8	15.1
Apr-Jun 1996	18,150	15,406	13,901	1,506	2,743	84.9	76.6	9.8	15.1
May-Jul 1996	18,154	15,395	13,912	1,483	2,759	84.8	76.6	9.6	15.2
Jun-Aug 1996	18,159	15,401	13,940	1,461	2,758	84.8	76.8	9.5	15.2
Jul-Sep 1996	18,163	15,391	13,933	1,457	2,773	84.7	76.7	9.5	15.3
Aug-Oct 1996	18,168	15,406	13,946	1,460	2,762	84.8	76.8	9.5	15.2
Sep-Nov 1996	18,172	15,420	13,994	1,427	2,752	84.9	77.0	9.3	15.1
Oct-Dec 1996	18,176	15,388	14,000	1,388	2,789	84.7	77.0	9.0	15.3
Nov-Jan 1997	18,181	15,390	14,038	1,353	2,790	84.7	77.2	8.8	15.3
Dec-Feb 1997	18,185	15,394	14,076	1,318	2,791	84.7	77.4	8.6	15.3
Jan-Mar 1997	18,189	15,407	14,124	1,283	2,782	84.7	77.7	8.3	15.3
Feb-Apr 1997	18,194	15,410	14,156	1,254	2,784	84.7	77.8	8.1	15.3
Mar-May 1997	18,198	15,408	14,137	1,271	2,790	84.7	77.7	8.2	15.3
Apr-Jun 1997	18,202	15,429	14,173	1,256	2,773	84.8	77.9	8.1	15.2
May-Jul 1997	18,207	15,429	14,151	1,278	2,778	84.7	77.7	8.3	15.3
Jun-Aug 1997	18,211	15,408	14,180	1,228	2,803	84.6	77.9	8.0	15.4
Jul-Sep 1997	18,216	15,392	14,203	1,189	2,823	84.5	78.0	7.7	15.5
Aug-Oct 1997	18,220	15,401	14,239	1,162	2,819	84.5	78.1	7.5	15.5
Sep-Nov 1997	18,225	15,397	14,248	1,148	2,828	84.5	78.2	7.5	15.5
Oct-Dec 1997	18,230	15,391	14,259	1,132	2,839	84.4	78.2	7.4	15.6
Nov-Jan 1998	18,234	15,375	14,278	1,097	2,859	84.3	78.3	7.1	15.7
Dec-Feb 1998	18,239	15,394	14,308	1,086	2,845	84.4	78.4	7.1	15.6
Jan-Mar 1998	18,244	15,382	14,290	1,091	2,862	84.3	78.3	7.1	15.7
Feb-Apr 1998	18,249	15,366	14,285	1,081	2,882	84.2	78.3	7.0	15.8
Mar-May 1998	18,253	15,365	14,298	1,067	2,889	84.2	78.3	6.9	15.8
Apr-Jun 1998	18,258	15,363	14,302	1,061	2,895	84.1	78.3	6.9	15.9
May-Jul 1998	18,263	15,393	14,327	1,066	2,870	84.3	78.5	6.9	15.7
Jun-Aug 1998	18,267	15,434	14,358	1,076	2,833	84.5	78.6	7.0	15.5
Jul-Sep 1998	18,275	15,427	14,345	1,081	2,848	84.4	78.5	7.0	15.6
Aug-Oct 1998	18,283	15,424	14,340	1,084	2,859	84.4	78.4	7.0	15.6
Sep-Nov 1998	18,291	15,448	14,374	1,074	2,843	84.5	78.6	7.0	15.5
Oct-Dec 1998	18,299	15,458	14,387	1,071	2,841	84.5	78.6	6.9	15.5
Nov-Jan 1999	18,306	15,470	14,378	1,091	2,837	84.5	78.5	7.1	15.5
Dec-Feb 1999	18,314	15,503	14,415	1,088	2,811	84.7	78.7	7.0	15.3
Jan-Mar 1999	18,322	15,479	14,408	1,071	2,843	84.5	78.6	6.9	15.5
Feb-Apr 1999	18,330	15,474	14,406	1,068	2,856	84.4	78.6	6.9	15.6
Mar-May 1999	18,338	15,480	14,418	1,062	2,858	84.4	78.6	6.9	15.6
Apr-Jun 1999	18,346	15,495	14,444	1,051	2,851	84.5	78.7	6.8	15.5
May-Jul 1999	18,353	15,496	14,466	1,031	2,857	84.4	78.8	6.7	15.6
Jun-Aug 1999	18,361	15,505	14,490	1,015	2,856	84.4	78.9	6.5	15.6
Jul-Sep 1999	18,370	15,519	14,504	1,016	2,850	84.5	79.0	6.5	15.5
Aug-Oct 1999	18,378	15,507	14,513	994	2,871	84.4	79.0	6.4	15.6
Sep-Nov 1999	18,387	15,541	14,537	1,004	2,845	84.5	79.1	6.5	15.5
Oct-Dec 1999	18,395	15,540	14,545	995	2,855	84.5	79.1	6.4	15.5
Nov-Jan 2000	18,404	15,556	14,547	1,009	2,847	84.5	79.0	6.5	15.5
Dec-Feb 2000	18,412	15,538	14,550	988	2,874	84.4	79.0	6.4	15.6
Jan-Mar 2000	18,420	15,550	14,572	978	2,870	84.4	79.1	6.3	15.6
Feb-Apr 2000	18,429	15,576	14,605	970	2,853	84.5	79.3	6.2	15.5
Mar-May 2000	18,437	15,590	14,623	968	2,847	84.6	79.3	6.2	15.4
Apr-Jun 2000	18,446	15,568	14,618	951	2,878	84.4	79.2	6.1	15.6
May-Jul 2000	18,454	15,549	14,645	904	2,905	84.3	79.4	5.8	15.7
Jun-Aug 2000	18,463	15,545	14,648	896	2,918	84.2	79.3	5.8	15.8
Jul-Sep 2000	18,474	15,550	14,645	905	2,924	84.2	79.3	5.8	15.8
Aug-Oct 2000	18,486	15,557	14,641	915	2,929	84.2	79.2	5.9	15.8
Sep-Nov 2000	18,497	15,547	14,639	907	2,951	84.0	79.1	5.8	16.0
Oct-Dec 2000	18,509	15,569	14,666	903	2,940	84.1	79.2	5.8	15.9

Labour Force Survey, summary by sex United Kingdom (thousands) seasonally adjusted (Continued)

All aged 16 to 59/64	All aged 16 to 59/64	Total economically active	Total in employment	Unemployed	Economically inactive	Economic Activity rate (%)	Employment rate (%)	Unemployment rate (%)	Economic inactivity rate (%)
	10	11	12	13	14	15	16	17	18
Male	YBTG	YBSL	YBSF	YBSI	YBSO	MGSP	MGSV	YBTJ	YBTM
Nov-Jan 2001	18,520	15,607	14,713	894	2,913	84.3	79.4	5.7	15.7
Dec-Feb 2001	18,532	15,631	14,720	911	2,901	84.3	79.4	5.8	15.7
Jan-Mar 2001	18,543	15,625	14,748	877	2,918	84.3	79.5	5.6	15.7
Feb-Apr 2001	18,555	15,607	14,746	861	2,948	84.1	79.5	5.5	15.9
Mar-May 2001	18,566	15,596	14,755	840	2,970	84.0	79.5	5.4	16.0
Apr-Jun 2001	18,578	15,595	14,720	875	2,983	83.9	79.2	5.6	16.1
May-Jul 2001	18,589	15,601	14,721	880	2,989	83.9	79.2	5.6	16.1
Jun-Aug 2001	18,601	15,641	14,752	889	2,960	84.1	79.3	5.7	15.9
Jul-Sep 2001	18,611	15,640	14,749	891	2,971	84.0	79.3	5.7	16.0
Aug-Oct 2001	18,620	15,642	14,747	895	2,979	84.0	79.2	5.7	16.0
Sep-Nov 2001	18,630	15,651	14,757	894	2,979	84.0	79.2	5.7	16.0
Oct-Dec 2001	18,640	15,655	14,748	906	2,985	84.0	79.1	5.8	16.0
Nov-Jan 2002	18,649	15,642	14,737	905	3,007	83.9	79.0	5.8	16.1
Dec-Feb 2002	18,659	15,658	14,760	899	3,001	83.9	79.1	5.7	16.1
Jan-Mar 2002	18,669	15,643	14,733	910	3,025	83.8	78.9	5.8	16.2
Feb-Apr 2002	18,678	15,659	14,751	908	3,020	83.8	79.0	5.8	16.2
Mar-May 2002	18,688	15,673	14,764	909	3,015	83.9	79.0	5.8	16.1
Apr-Jun 2002	18,698	15,676	14,776	900	3,022	83.8	79.0	5.7	16.2
May-Jul 2002	18,708	15,682	14,776	906	3,026	83.8	79.0	5.8	16.2
Jun-Aug 2002	18,717	15,698	14,790	908	3,019	83.9	79.0	5.8	16.1
Jul-Sep 2002	18,727	15,704	14,769	935	3,023	83.9	78.9	6.0	16.1
Aug-Oct 2002	18,738	15,754	14,840	913	2,984	84.1	79.2	5.8	15.9
Sep-Nov 2002	18,748	15,766	14,861	905	2,982	84.1	79.3	5.7	15.9
Oct-Dec 2002	18,758	15,798	14,913	885	2,960	84.2	79.5	5.6	15.8
Nov-Jan 2003	18,768	15,758	14,893	865	3,009	84.0	79.4	5.5	16.0
Dec-Feb 2003	18,778	15,750	14,845	905	3,028	83.9	79.1	5.7	16.1
Jan-Mar 2003	18,788	15,773	14,854	919	3,015	84.0	79.1	5.8	16.0
Feb-Apr 2003	18,798	15,792	14,886	906	3,006	84.0	79.2	5.7	16.0
Mar-May 2003	18,808	15,819	14,924	895	2,990	84.1	79.3	5.7	15.9
Apr-Jun 2003	18,819	15,838	14,961	876	2,981	84.2	79.5	5.5	15.8
May-Jul 2003	18,829	15,853	14,958	895	2,975	84.2	79.4	5.6	15.8
Jun-Aug 2003	18,839	15,830	14,938	892	3,009	84.0	79.3	5.6	16.0
Jul-Sep 2003	18,850	15,837	14,950	887	3,014	84.0	79.3	5.6	16.0
Aug-Oct 2003	18,862	15,821	14,941	880	3,041	83.9	79.2	5.6	16.1
Sep-Nov 2003	18,874	15,803	14,935	867	3,071	83.7	79.1	5.5	16.3
Oct-Dec 2003	18,885	15,797	14,928	869	3,088	83.6	79.0	5.5	16.4
Nov-Jan 2004	18,897	15,820	14,970	851	3,077	83.7	79.2	5.4	16.3
Dec-Feb 2004	18,909	15,839	14,999	840	3,069	83.8	79.3	5.3	16.2
Jan-Mar 2004	18,920	15,846	15,014	832	3,074	83.8	79.4	5.2	16.2
Feb-Apr 2004	18,932	15,845	15,011	834	3,087	83.7	79.3	5.3	16.3
Mar-May 2004	18,944	15,847	15,029	819	3,096	83.7	79.3	5.2	16.3
Apr-Jun 2004	18,955	15,846	15,014	833	3,109	83.6	79.2	5.3	16.4
May-Jul 2004	18,967	15,847	15,025	822	3,120	83.5	79.2	5.2	16.5
Jun-Aug 2004	18,979	15,848	15,033	815	3,130	83.5	79.2	5.1	16.5
Jul-Sep 2004	18,994	15,862	15,055	807	3,132	83.5	79.3	5.1	16.5
Aug-Oct 2004	19,009	15,859	15,061	798	3,150	83.4	79.2	5.0	16.6
Sep-Nov 2004	19,025	15,912	15,090	822	3,113	83.6	79.3	5.2	16.4
Oct-Dec 2004	19,040	15,928	15,104	823	3,112	83.7	79.3	5.2	16.3
Nov-Jan 2005	19,055	15,944	15,121	823	3,111	83.7	79.4	5.2	16.3
Dec-Feb 2005	19,071	15,950	15,124	826	3,121	83.6	79.3	5.2	16.4
Jan-Mar 2005	19,086	15,953	15,132	821	3,133	83.6	79.3	5.1	16.4
Feb-Apr 2005	19,101	15,941	15,122	819	3,160	83.5	79.2	5.1	16.5
Mar-May 2005	19,117	15,937	15,104	834	3,179	83.4	79.0	5.2	16.6
Apr-Jun 2005	19,132	15,954	15,127	827	3,178	83.4	79.1	5.2	16.6
May-Jul 2005	19,147	15,969	15,142	827	3,179	83.4	79.1	5.2	16.6
Jun-Aug 2005	19,163	15,983	15,151	832	3,179	83.4	79.1	5.2	16.6
Jul-Sep 2005	19,177	16,003	15,164	839	3,174	83.4	79.1	5.2	16.6
Aug-Oct 2005	19,191	16,031	15,158	873	3,160	83.5	79.0	5.4	16.5
Sep-Nov 2005	**19,205**	**16,037**	**15,148**	**889**	**3,168**	**83.5**	**78.9**	**5.5**	**16.5**

Labour Force Survey, summary by sex United Kingdom (thousands) seasonally adjusted (Continued)

All aged 16 to 59/64

	All aged 16 to 59/64	Total economically active	Total in employment	Unemployed	Economically inactive	Economic Activity rate (%)	Employment rate (%)	Unemployment rate (%)	Economic inactivity rate (%)
	10	11	12	13	14	15	16	17	18
Female	YBTG	YBSL	YBSF	YBSI	YBSO	MGSP	MGSV	YBTJ	YBTM
Jan-Mar 1971	15,283	9,076	8,617	459	6,207	59.4	56.4	5.1	40.6
Feb-Apr 1971	15,284	9,069	8,607	462	6,215	59.3	56.3	5.1	40.7
Mar-May 1971	15,284	9,074	8,609	465	6,211	59.4	56.3	5.1	40.6
Apr-Jun 1971	15,285	9,076	8,609	467	6,209	59.4	56.3	5.1	40.6
May-Jul 1971	15,286	9,081	8,611	470	6,205	59.4	56.3	5.2	40.6
Jun-Aug 1971	15,286	9,074	8,605	470	6,212	59.4	56.3	5.2	40.6
Jul-Sep 1971	15,286	9,066	8,595	471	6,220	59.3	56.2	5.2	40.7
Aug-Oct 1971	15,286	9,061	8,587	474	6,226	59.3	56.2	5.2	40.7
Sep-Nov 1971	15,287	9,063	8,585	479	6,223	59.3	56.2	5.3	40.7
Oct-Dec 1971	15,287	9,070	8,588	482	6,217	59.3	56.2	5.3	40.7
Nov-Jan 1972	15,287	9,085	8,602	483	6,202	59.4	56.3	5.3	40.6
Dec-Feb 1972	15,287	9,103	8,619	484	6,183	59.6	56.4	5.3	40.4
Jan-Mar 1972	15,287	9,126	8,641	485	6,161	59.7	56.5	5.3	40.3
Feb-Apr 1972	15,287	9,142	8,656	487	6,145	59.8	56.6	5.3	40.2
Mar-May 1972	15,287	9,153	8,666	488	6,134	59.9	56.7	5.3	40.1
Apr-Jun 1972	15,287	9,159	8,672	487	6,129	59.9	56.7	5.3	40.1
May-Jul 1972	15,288	9,164	8,680	485	6,123	59.9	56.8	5.3	40.1
Jun-Aug 1972	15,288	9,173	8,691	482	6,114	60.0	56.9	5.3	40.0
Jul-Sep 1972	15,289	9,188	8,707	481	6,100	60.1	57.0	5.2	39.9
Aug-Oct 1972	15,290	9,204	8,724	480	6,085	60.2	57.1	5.2	39.8
Sep-Nov 1972	15,290	9,220	8,740	481	6,070	60.3	57.2	5.2	39.7
Oct-Dec 1972	15,291	9,242	8,762	480	6,049	60.4	57.3	5.2	39.6
Nov-Jan 1973	15,292	9,267	8,789	478	6,025	60.6	57.5	5.2	39.4
Dec-Feb 1973	15,293	9,298	8,823	475	5,995	60.8	57.7	5.1	39.2
Jan-Mar 1973	15,294	9,330	8,858	472	5,964	61.0	57.9	5.1	39.0
Feb-Apr 1973	15,295	9,354	8,883	471	5,941	61.2	58.1	5.0	38.8
Mar-May 1973	15,296	9,373	8,904	469	5,923	61.3	58.2	5.0	38.7
Apr-Jun 1973	15,297	9,381	8,913	468	5,916	61.3	58.3	5.0	38.7
May-Jul 1973	15,298	9,386	8,921	466	5,912	61.4	58.3	5.0	38.6
Jun-Aug 1973	15,299	9,391	8,928	463	5,908	61.4	58.4	4.9	38.6
Jul-Sep 1973	15,299	9,402	8,943	459	5,897	61.5	58.5	4.9	38.5
Aug-Oct 1973	15,299	9,415	8,958	456	5,884	61.5	58.6	4.8	38.5
Sep-Nov 1973	15,298	9,426	8,972	454	5,872	61.6	58.6	4.8	38.4
Oct-Dec 1973	15,298	9,438	8,987	452	5,860	61.7	58.7	4.8	38.3
Nov-Jan 1974	15,298	9,452	9,000	452	5,846	61.8	58.8	4.8	38.2
Dec-Feb 1974	15,298	9,460	9,007	453	5,838	61.8	58.9	4.8	38.2
Jan-Mar 1974	15,298	9,474	9,018	456	5,824	61.9	58.9	4.8	38.1
Feb-Apr 1974	15,298	9,485	9,027	458	5,813	62.0	59.0	4.8	38.0
Mar-May 1974	15,298	9,497	9,039	459	5,800	62.1	59.1	4.8	37.9
Apr-Jun 1974	15,297	9,512	9,051	461	5,786	62.2	59.2	4.8	37.8
May-Jul 1974	15,297	9,528	9,067	461	5,770	62.3	59.3	4.8	37.7
Jun-Aug 1974	15,297	9,545	9,083	462	5,752	62.4	59.4	4.8	37.6
Jul-Sep 1974	15,299	9,561	9,099	462	5,738	62.5	59.5	4.8	37.5
Aug-Oct 1974	15,300	9,572	9,109	462	5,728	62.6	59.5	4.8	37.4
Sep-Nov 1974	15,301	9,578	9,116	462	5,723	62.6	59.6	4.8	37.4
Oct-Dec 1974	15,303	9,579	9,116	463	5,723	62.6	59.6	4.8	37.4
Nov-Jan 1975	15,304	9,581	9,115	466	5,723	62.6	59.6	4.9	37.4
Dec-Feb 1975	15,305	9,583	9,113	470	5,722	62.6	59.5	4.9	37.4
Jan-Mar 1975	15,307	9,584	9,109	476	5,722	62.6	59.5	5.0	37.4
Feb-Apr 1975	15,308	9,589	9,107	482	5,719	62.6	59.5	5.0	37.4
Mar-May 1975	15,309	9,597	9,107	490	5,713	62.7	59.5	5.1	37.3
Apr-Jun 1975	15,311	9,605	9,107	497	5,706	62.7	59.5	5.2	37.3
May-Jul 1975	15,312	9,612	9,106	505	5,701	62.8	59.5	5.3	37.2
Jun-Aug 1975	15,314	9,616	9,106	511	5,697	62.8	59.5	5.3	37.2
Jul-Sep 1975	15,320	9,618	9,102	516	5,702	62.8	59.4	5.4	37.2
Aug-Oct 1975	15,327	9,624	9,099	525	5,703	62.8	59.4	5.5	37.2
Sep-Nov 1975	15,334	9,632	9,098	534	5,702	62.8	59.3	5.5	37.2
Oct-Dec 1975	15,341	9,636	9,093	543	5,705	62.8	59.3	5.6	37.2

Labour Force Survey, summary by sex United Kingdom (thousands) seasonally adjusted (Continued)

All aged 16 to 59/64

	All aged 16 to 59/64	Total economically active	Total in employment	Unemployed	Economically inactive	Economic Activity rate (%)	Employment rate (%)	Unemployment rate (%)	Economic inactivity rate (%)
	10	11	12	13	14	15	16	17	18
Female	YBTG	YBSL	YBSF	YBSI	YBSO	MGSP	MGSV	YBTJ	YBTM
Nov-Jan 1976	15,348	9,643	9,093	550	5,705	62.8	59.2	5.7	37.2
Dec-Feb 1976	15,355	9,645	9,089	556	5,710	62.8	59.2	5.8	37.2
Jan-Mar 1976	15,362	9,647	9,084	563	5,715	62.8	59.1	5.8	37.2
Feb-Apr 1976	15,369	9,653	9,085	568	5,716	62.8	59.1	5.9	37.2
Mar-May 1976	15,376	9,656	9,083	573	5,720	62.8	59.1	5.9	37.2
Apr-Jun 1976	15,383	9,661	9,084	576	5,722	62.8	59.1	6.0	37.2
May-Jul 1976	15,390	9,669	9,088	580	5,721	62.8	59.1	6.0	37.2
Jun-Aug 1976	15,396	9,675	9,090	585	5,722	62.8	59.0	6.0	37.2
Jul-Sep 1976	15,407	9,685	9,095	590	5,722	62.9	59.0	6.1	37.1
Aug-Oct 1976	15,417	9,692	9,098	594	5,725	62.9	59.0	6.1	37.1
Sep-Nov 1976	15,428	9,698	9,103	596	5,730	62.9	59.0	6.1	37.1
Oct-Dec 1976	15,438	9,708	9,111	598	5,730	62.9	59.0	6.2	37.1
Nov-Jan 1977	15,449	9,719	9,118	601	5,730	62.9	59.0	6.2	37.1
Dec-Feb 1977	15,459	9,729	9,126	603	5,730	62.9	59.0	6.2	37.1
Jan-Mar 1977	15,470	9,737	9,132	605	5,733	62.9	59.0	6.2	37.1
Feb-Apr 1977	15,480	9,744	9,138	606	5,736	62.9	59.0	6.2	37.1
Mar-May 1977	15,491	9,750	9,142	607	5,741	62.9	59.0	6.2	37.1
Apr-Jun 1977	15,501	9,761	9,149	611	5,741	63.0	59.0	6.3	37.0
May-Jul 1977	15,512	9,774	9,157	617	5,738	63.0	59.0	6.3	37.0
Jun-Aug 1977	15,522	9,785	9,162	623	5,737	63.0	59.0	6.4	37.0
Jul-Sep 1977	15,536	9,800	9,171	629	5,737	63.1	59.0	6.4	36.9
Aug-Oct 1977	15,550	9,811	9,180	631	5,739	63.1	59.0	6.4	36.9
Sep-Nov 1977	15,564	9,826	9,191	635	5,738	63.1	59.1	6.5	36.9
Oct-Dec 1977	15,578	9,833	9,198	636	5,745	63.1	59.0	6.5	36.9
Nov-Jan 1978	15,592	9,844	9,208	635	5,748	63.1	59.1	6.5	36.9
Dec-Feb 1978	15,606	9,856	9,222	634	5,750	63.2	59.1	6.4	36.8
Jan-Mar 1978	15,619	9,867	9,235	632	5,753	63.2	59.1	6.4	36.8
Feb-Apr 1978	15,633	9,886	9,253	633	5,748	63.2	59.2	6.4	36.8
Mar-May 1978	15,647	9,899	9,265	634	5,748	63.3	59.2	6.4	36.7
Apr-Jun 1978	15,661	9,916	9,280	635	5,745	63.3	59.3	6.4	36.7
May-Jul 1978	15,675	9,927	9,291	636	5,748	63.3	59.3	6.4	36.7
Jun-Aug 1978	15,689	9,943	9,305	638	5,746	63.4	59.3	6.4	36.6
Jul-Sep 1978	15,702	9,957	9,318	639	5,745	63.4	59.3	6.4	36.6
Aug-Oct 1978	15,716	9,976	9,337	639	5,740	63.5	59.4	6.4	36.5
Sep-Nov 1978	15,729	9,998	9,362	636	5,732	63.6	59.5	6.4	36.4
Oct-Dec 1978	15,743	10,020	9,387	633	5,723	63.6	59.6	6.3	36.4
Nov-Jan 1979	15,756	10,032	9,401	631	5,724	63.7	59.7	6.3	36.3
Dec-Feb 1979	15,770	10,045	9,413	632	5,725	63.7	59.7	6.3	36.3
Jan-Mar 1979	15,784	10,051	9,418	633	5,732	63.7	59.7	6.3	36.3
Feb-Apr 1979	15,797	10,056	9,423	633	5,741	63.7	59.7	6.3	36.3
Mar-May 1979	15,811	10,072	9,438	634	5,738	63.7	59.7	6.3	36.3
Apr-Jun 1979	15,824	10,096	9,459	637	5,729	63.8	59.8	6.3	36.2
May-Jul 1979	15,838	10,121	9,478	643	5,716	63.9	59.8	6.4	36.1
Jun-Aug 1979	15,851	10,141	9,495	646	5,711	64.0	59.9	6.4	36.0
Jul-Sep 1979	15,857	10,155	9,506	649	5,702	64.0	60.0	6.4	36.0
Aug-Oct 1979	15,862	10,175	9,524	652	5,687	64.1	60.0	6.4	35.9
Sep-Nov 1979	15,868	10,192	9,537	655	5,676	64.2	60.1	6.4	35.8
Oct-Dec 1979	15,874	10,213	9,552	661	5,661	64.3	60.2	6.5	35.7
Nov-Jan 1980	15,879	10,232	9,564	668	5,647	64.4	60.2	6.5	35.6
Dec-Feb 1980	15,885	10,247	9,569	678	5,638	64.5	60.2	6.6	35.5
Jan-Mar 1980	15,890	10,253	9,564	689	5,637	64.5	60.2	6.7	35.5
Feb-Apr 1980	15,896	10,261	9,560	701	5,635	64.6	60.1	6.8	35.4
Mar-May 1980	15,901	10,272	9,559	714	5,629	64.6	60.1	6.9	35.4
Apr-Jun 1980	15,907	10,285	9,559	727	5,622	64.7	60.1	7.1	35.3
May-Jul 1980	15,913	10,296	9,556	740	5,616	64.7	60.1	7.2	35.3
Jun-Aug 1980	15,918	10,306	9,547	759	5,612	64.7	60.0	7.4	35.3
Jul-Sep 1980	15,925	10,310	9,533	777	5,615	64.7	59.9	7.5	35.3
Aug-Oct 1980	15,931	10,318	9,520	797	5,614	64.8	59.8	7.7	35.2
Sep-Nov 1980	15,938	10,323	9,506	817	5,615	64.8	59.6	7.9	35.2
Oct-Dec 1980	15,944	10,334	9,494	840	5,610	64.8	59.5	8.1	35.2

Labour Force Survey, summary by sex United Kingdom (thousands) seasonally adjusted (Continued)

All aged 16 to 59/64

	All aged 16 to 59/64	Total economically active	Total in employment	Unemployed	Economically inactive	Economic Activity rate (%)	Employment rate (%)	Unemployment rate (%)	Economic inactivity rate (%)
	10	11	12	13	14	15	16	17	18
Female	YBTG	YBSL	YBSF	YBSI	YBSO	MGSP	MGSV	YBTJ	YBTM
Nov-Jan 1981	15,951	10,343	9,483	860	5,608	64.8	59.4	8.3	35.2
Dec-Feb 1981	15,957	10,347	9,469	879	5,610	64.8	59.3	8.5	35.2
Jan-Mar 1981	15,964	10,354	9,458	896	5,610	64.9	59.2	8.7	35.1
Feb-Apr 1981	15,970	10,358	9,446	912	5,612	64.9	59.1	8.8	35.1
Mar-May 1981	15,977	10,360	9,434	926	5,616	64.8	59.1	8.9	35.2
Apr-Jun 1981	15,983	10,358	9,422	937	5,625	64.8	58.9	9.0	35.2
May-Jul 1981	15,990	10,356	9,411	945	5,633	64.8	58.9	9.1	35.2
Jun-Aug 1981	15,996	10,357	9,403	954	5,639	64.7	58.8	9.2	35.3
Jul-Sep 1981	16,000	10,359	9,396	963	5,641	64.7	58.7	9.3	35.3
Aug-Oct 1981	16,004	10,364	9,391	972	5,641	64.8	58.7	9.4	35.2
Sep-Nov 1981	16,009	10,364	9,383	981	5,645	64.7	58.6	9.5	35.3
Oct-Dec 1981	16,013	10,363	9,376	987	5,650	64.7	58.6	9.5	35.3
Nov-Jan 1982	16,017	10,358	9,367	991	5,659	64.7	58.5	9.6	35.3
Dec-Feb 1982	16,021	10,353	9,359	994	5,668	64.6	58.4	9.6	35.4
Jan-Mar 1982	16,025	10,349	9,351	997	5,676	64.6	58.4	9.6	35.4
Feb-Apr 1982	16,029	10,349	9,348	1,002	5,680	64.6	58.3	9.7	35.4
Mar-May 1982	16,034	10,346	9,341	1,005	5,687	64.5	58.3	9.7	35.5
Apr-Jun 1982	16,038	10,344	9,335	1,010	5,693	64.5	58.2	9.8	35.5
May-Jul 1982	16,042	10,336	9,322	1,014	5,706	64.4	58.1	9.8	35.6
Jun-Aug 1982	16,046	10,329	9,310	1,019	5,717	64.4	58.0	9.9	35.6
Jul-Sep 1982	16,054	10,319	9,294	1,025	5,735	64.3	57.9	9.9	35.7
Aug-Oct 1982	16,061	10,311	9,279	1,032	5,750	64.2	57.8	10.0	35.8
Sep-Nov 1982	16,069	10,303	9,263	1,040	5,766	64.1	57.6	10.1	35.9
Oct-Dec 1982	16,076	10,295	9,249	1,046	5,781	64.0	57.5	10.2	36.0
Nov-Jan 1983	16,084	10,286	9,234	1,052	5,798	64.0	57.4	10.2	36.0
Dec-Feb 1983	16,091	10,282	9,223	1,059	5,809	63.9	57.3	10.3	36.1
Jan-Mar 1983	16,099	10,279	9,215	1,064	5,819	63.9	57.2	10.4	36.1
Feb-Apr 1983	16,106	10,288	9,218	1,070	5,818	63.9	57.2	10.4	36.1
Mar-May 1983	16,114	10,305	9,227	1,078	5,808	64.0	57.3	10.5	36.0
Apr-Jun 1983	16,121	10,346	9,250	1,096	5,775	64.2	57.4	10.6	35.8
May-Jul 1983	16,129	10,396	9,280	1,116	5,732	64.5	57.5	10.7	35.5
Jun-Aug 1983	16,136	10,449	9,314	1,135	5,687	64.8	57.7	10.9	35.2
Jul-Sep 1983	16,144	10,504	9,351	1,153	5,640	65.1	57.9	11.0	34.9
Aug-Oct 1983	16,153	10,561	9,389	1,172	5,592	65.4	58.1	11.1	34.6
Sep-Nov 1983	16,161	10,620	9,426	1,195	5,541	65.7	58.3	11.2	34.3
Oct-Dec 1983	16,169	10,673	9,458	1,216	5,496	66.0	58.5	11.4	34.0
Nov-Jan 1984	16,177	10,724	9,487	1,237	5,453	66.3	58.6	11.5	33.7
Dec-Feb 1984	16,185	10,768	9,510	1,258	5,417	66.5	58.8	11.7	33.5
Jan-Mar 1984	16,193	10,811	9,531	1,280	5,382	66.8	58.9	11.8	33.2
Feb-Apr 1984	16,202	10,849	9,551	1,298	5,353	67.0	58.9	12.0	33.0
Mar-May 1984	16,210	10,885	9,572	1,313	5,325	67.1	59.1	12.1	32.9
Apr-Jun 1984	16,218	10,903	9,594	1,309	5,315	67.2	59.2	12.0	32.8
May-Jul 1984	16,226	10,924	9,618	1,305	5,302	67.3	59.3	11.9	32.7
Jun-Aug 1984	16,234	10,938	9,640	1,298	5,296	67.4	59.4	11.9	32.6
Jul-Sep 1984	16,244	10,955	9,661	1,294	5,289	67.4	59.5	11.8	32.6
Aug-Oct 1984	16,254	10,974	9,684	1,290	5,280	67.5	59.6	11.8	32.5
Sep-Nov 1984	16,264	10,997	9,711	1,286	5,267	67.6	59.7	11.7	32.4
Oct-Dec 1984	16,274	11,021	9,740	1,281	5,253	67.7	59.9	11.6	32.3
Nov-Jan 1985	16,284	11,043	9,768	1,275	5,241	67.8	60.0	11.5	32.2
Dec-Feb 1985	16,294	11,059	9,790	1,269	5,235	67.9	60.1	11.5	32.1
Jan-Mar 1985	16,304	11,072	9,811	1,261	5,232	67.9	60.2	11.4	32.1
Feb-Apr 1985	16,314	11,087	9,832	1,255	5,227	68.0	60.3	11.3	32.0
Mar-May 1985	16,323	11,103	9,853	1,250	5,221	68.0	60.4	11.3	32.0
Apr-Jun 1985	16,333	11,123	9,873	1,250	5,211	68.1	60.4	11.2	31.9
May-Jul 1985	16,343	11,145	9,896	1,249	5,198	68.2	60.6	11.2	31.8
Jun-Aug 1985	16,353	11,164	9,917	1,247	5,189	68.3	60.6	11.2	31.7
Jul-Sep 1985	16,362	11,185	9,937	1,248	5,177	68.4	60.7	11.2	31.6
Aug-Oct 1985	16,371	11,205	9,956	1,248	5,166	68.4	60.8	11.1	31.6
Sep-Nov 1985	16,379	11,221	9,972	1,249	5,158	68.5	60.9	11.1	31.5
Oct-Dec 1985	16,388	11,238	9,989	1,249	5,150	68.6	61.0	11.1	31.4

Labour Force Survey, summary by sex United Kingdom (thousands) seasonally adjusted (Continued)

All aged 16 to 59/64

	All aged 16 to 59/64	Total economically active	Total in employment	Unemployed	Economically inactive	Economic Activity rate (%)	Employment rate (%)	Unemployment rate (%)	Economic inactivity rate (%)
	10	11	12	13	14	15	16	17	18
Female	YBTG	YBSL	YBSF	YBSI	YBSO	MGSP	MGSV	YBTJ	YBTM
Nov-Jan 1986	16,397	11,251	10,002	1,249	5,145	68.6	61.0	11.1	31.4
Dec-Feb 1986	16,406	11,269	10,018	1,252	5,136	68.7	61.1	11.1	31.3
Jan-Mar 1986	16,414	11,283	10,030	1,253	5,131	68.7	61.1	11.1	31.3
Feb-Apr 1986	16,423	11,305	10,050	1,255	5,118	68.8	61.2	11.1	31.2
Mar-May 1986	16,432	11,321	10,064	1,256	5,111	68.9	61.2	11.1	31.1
Apr-Jun 1986	16,441	11,342	10,080	1,262	5,099	69.0	61.3	11.1	31.0
May-Jul 1986	16,449	11,368	10,100	1,268	5,082	69.1	61.4	11.2	30.9
Jun-Aug 1986	16,458	11,393	10,120	1,273	5,065	69.2	61.5	11.2	30.8
Jul-Sep 1986	16,467	11,416	10,140	1,276	5,050	69.3	61.6	11.2	30.7
Aug-Oct 1986	16,475	11,437	10,160	1,277	5,038	69.4	61.7	11.2	30.6
Sep-Nov 1986	16,484	11,461	10,188	1,274	5,022	69.5	61.8	11.1	30.5
Oct-Dec 1986	16,492	11,480	10,210	1,270	5,012	69.6	61.9	11.1	30.4
Nov-Jan 1987	16,501	11,498	10,232	1,266	5,002	69.7	62.0	11.0	30.3
Dec-Feb 1987	16,509	11,507	10,250	1,257	5,002	69.7	62.1	10.9	30.3
Jan-Mar 1987	16,518	11,508	10,260	1,248	5,009	69.7	62.1	10.8	30.3
Feb-Apr 1987	16,526	11,520	10,282	1,238	5,006	69.7	62.2	10.7	30.3
Mar-May 1987	16,535	11,540	10,314	1,227	4,994	69.8	62.4	10.6	30.2
Apr-Jun 1987	16,543	11,560	10,350	1,210	4,983	69.9	62.6	10.5	30.1
May-Jul 1987	16,552	11,584	10,392	1,191	4,968	70.0	62.8	10.3	30.0
Jun-Aug 1987	16,560	11,595	10,420	1,175	4,965	70.0	62.9	10.1	30.0
Jul-Sep 1987	16,566	11,617	10,460	1,157	4,949	70.1	63.1	10.0	29.9
Aug-Oct 1987	16,572	11,629	10,490	1,139	4,943	70.2	63.3	9.8	29.8
Sep-Nov 1987	16,578	11,647	10,527	1,119	4,931	70.3	63.5	9.6	29.7
Oct-Dec 1987	16,584	11,672	10,570	1,102	4,912	70.4	63.7	9.4	29.6
Nov-Jan 1988	16,590	11,691	10,603	1,088	4,899	70.5	63.9	9.3	29.5
Dec-Feb 1988	16,596	11,708	10,632	1,076	4,887	70.5	64.1	9.2	29.5
Jan-Mar 1988	16,602	11,711	10,650	1,061	4,891	70.5	64.1	9.1	29.5
Feb-Apr 1988	16,608	11,725	10,680	1,045	4,883	70.6	64.3	8.9	29.4
Mar-May 1988	16,614	11,735	10,707	1,028	4,879	70.6	64.4	8.8	29.4
Apr-Jun 1988	16,620	11,755	10,740	1,015	4,865	70.7	64.6	8.6	29.3
May-Jul 1988	16,626	11,771	10,770	1,001	4,855	70.8	64.8	8.5	29.2
Jun-Aug 1988	16,632	11,789	10,802	987	4,842	70.9	65.0	8.4	29.1
Jul-Sep 1988	16,637	11,815	10,840	975	4,822	71.0	65.2	8.3	29.0
Aug-Oct 1988	16,642	11,837	10,872	964	4,805	71.1	65.3	8.1	28.9
Sep-Nov 1988	16,647	11,853	10,900	953	4,794	71.2	65.5	8.0	28.8
Oct-Dec 1988	16,652	11,872	10,932	939	4,780	71.3	65.7	7.9	28.7
Nov-Jan 1989	16,658	11,896	10,970	926	4,761	71.4	65.9	7.8	28.6
Dec-Feb 1989	16,663	11,912	11,000	912	4,751	71.5	66.0	7.7	28.5
Jan-Mar 1989	16,668	11,931	11,032	898	4,737	71.6	66.2	7.5	28.4
Feb-Apr 1989	16,673	11,944	11,062	882	4,729	71.6	66.3	7.4	28.4
Mar-May 1989	16,678	11,942	11,075	867	4,736	71.6	66.4	7.3	28.4
Apr-Jun 1989	16,684	11,937	11,080	857	4,747	71.5	66.4	7.2	28.5
May-Jul 1989	16,689	11,941	11,090	851	4,747	71.6	66.5	7.1	28.4
Jun-Aug 1989	16,694	11,944	11,098	846	4,750	71.5	66.5	7.1	28.5
Jul-Sep 1989	16,697	11,953	11,110	843	4,745	71.6	66.5	7.0	28.4
Aug-Oct 1989	16,700	11,966	11,127	838	4,735	71.6	66.6	7.0	28.4
Sep-Nov 1989	16,704	11,983	11,148	836	4,720	71.7	66.7	7.0	28.3
Oct-Dec 1989	16,707	12,003	11,170	833	4,704	71.8	66.9	6.9	28.2
Nov-Jan 1990	16,710	12,009	11,180	829	4,701	71.9	66.9	6.9	28.1
Dec-Feb 1990	16,713	12,016	11,190	826	4,697	71.9	67.0	6.9	28.1
Jan-Mar 1990	16,717	12,014	11,190	824	4,703	71.9	66.9	6.9	28.1
Feb-Apr 1990	16,720	12,023	11,200	823	4,697	71.9	67.0	6.8	28.1
Mar-May 1990	16,723	12,039	11,216	823	4,684	72.0	67.1	6.8	28.0
Apr-Jun 1990	16,726	12,054	11,232	822	4,672	72.1	67.2	6.8	27.9
May-Jul 1990	16,730	12,064	11,242	822	4,666	72.1	67.2	6.8	27.9
Jun-Aug 1990	16,733	12,066	11,242	823	4,667	72.1	67.2	6.8	27.9
Jul-Sep 1990	16,737	12,061	11,235	826	4,676	72.1	67.1	6.9	27.9
Aug-Oct 1990	16,741	12,054	11,222	832	4,687	72.0	67.0	6.9	28.0
Sep-Nov 1990	16,745	12,053	11,215	838	4,692	72.0	67.0	7.0	28.0
Oct-Dec 1990	16,750	12,060	11,212	847	4,690	72.0	66.9	7.0	28.0

Labour Force Survey, summary by sex United Kingdom (thousands) seasonally adjusted (Continued)

All aged 16 to 59/64

	All aged 16 to 59/64	Total economically active	Total in employment	Unemployed	Economically inactive	Economic Activity rate (%)	Employment rate (%)	Unemployment rate (%)	Economic inactivity rate (%)
	10	11	12	13	14	15	16	17	18
Female	YBTG	YBSL	YBSF	YBSI	YBSO	MGSP	MGSV	YBTJ	YBTM
Nov-Jan 1991	16,754	12,051	11,195	856	4,703	71.9	66.8	7.1	28.1
Dec-Feb 1991	16,758	12,049	11,182	866	4,709	71.9	66.7	7.2	28.1
Jan-Mar 1991	16,762	12,033	11,152	880	4,729	71.8	66.5	7.3	28.2
Feb-Apr 1991	16,766	12,030	11,132	898	4,736	71.8	66.4	7.5	28.2
Mar-May 1991	16,770	12,023	11,110	913	4,748	71.7	66.2	7.6	28.3
Apr-Jun 1991	16,773	12,010	11,090	920	4,763	71.6	66.1	7.7	28.4
May-Jul 1991	16,775	12,004	11,080	924	4,771	71.6	66.1	7.7	28.4
Jun-Aug 1991	16,778	11,996	11,068	929	4,781	71.5	66.0	7.7	28.5
Jul-Sep 1991	16,780	11,983	11,050	933	4,797	71.4	65.9	7.8	28.6
Aug-Oct 1991	16,782	11,964	11,030	934	4,818	71.3	65.7	7.8	28.7
Sep-Nov 1991	16,785	11,943	11,010	933	4,842	71.2	65.6	7.8	28.8
Oct-Dec 1991	16,787	11,931	11,000	931	4,855	71.1	65.5	7.8	28.9
Nov-Jan 1992	16,789	11,917	10,988	930	4,872	71.0	65.4	7.8	29.0
Dec-Feb 1992	16,792	11,906	10,978	929	4,885	70.9	65.4	7.8	29.1
Jan-Mar 1992	16,794	11,915	10,988	928	4,879	70.9	65.4	7.8	29.1
Feb-Apr 1992	16,796	11,915	10,990	925	4,881	70.9	65.4	7.8	29.1
Mar-May 1992	16,800	11,911	10,987	924	4,889	70.9	65.4	7.8	29.1
Apr-Jun 1992	16,802	11,891	10,964	927	4,911	70.8	65.3	7.8	29.2
May-Jul 1992	16,804	11,874	10,939	935	4,930	70.7	65.1	7.9	29.3
Jun-Aug 1992	16,806	11,877	10,942	935	4,929	70.7	65.1	7.9	29.3
Jul-Sep 1992	16,808	11,878	10,951	927	4,930	70.7	65.2	7.8	29.3
Aug-Oct 1992	16,810	11,878	10,948	930	4,932	70.7	65.1	7.8	29.3
Sep-Nov 1992	16,812	11,909	10,963	946	4,903	70.8	65.2	7.9	29.2
Oct-Dec 1992	16,814	11,911	10,956	955	4,902	70.8	65.2	8.0	29.2
Nov-Jan 1993	16,815	11,922	10,942	980	4,893	70.9	65.1	8.2	29.1
Dec-Feb 1993	16,817	11,925	10,930	995	4,892	70.9	65.0	8.3	29.1
Jan-Mar 1993	16,819	11,905	10,932	972	4,915	70.8	65.0	8.2	29.2
Feb-Apr 1993	16,821	11,917	10,948	969	4,904	70.8	65.1	8.1	29.2
Mar-May 1993	16,823	11,923	10,961	962	4,900	70.9	65.2	8.1	29.1
Apr-Jun 1993	16,825	11,933	10,955	978	4,892	70.9	65.1	8.2	29.1
May-Jul 1993	16,827	11,937	10,962	975	4,889	70.9	65.1	8.2	29.1
Jun-Aug 1993	16,828	11,926	10,949	977	4,902	70.9	65.1	8.2	29.1
Jul-Sep 1993	16,833	11,949	10,989	960	4,883	71.0	65.3	8.0	29.0
Aug-Oct 1993	16,837	11,960	10,981	979	4,877	71.0	65.2	8.2	29.0
Sep-Nov 1993	16,842	11,944	10,969	975	4,898	70.9	65.1	8.2	29.1
Oct-Dec 1993	16,846	11,948	10,976	973	4,898	70.9	65.2	8.1	29.1
Nov-Jan 1993	16,851	11,943	10,970	973	4,908	70.9	65.1	8.1	29.1
Dec-Feb 1994	16,855	11,949	10,976	973	4,906	70.9	65.1	8.1	29.1
Jan-Mar 1994	16,859	11,978	11,020	958	4,882	71.0	65.4	8.0	29.0
Feb-Apr 1994	16,864	11,964	11,024	940	4,900	70.9	65.4	7.9	29.1
Mar-May 1994	16,868	11,961	11,033	928	4,907	70.9	65.4	7.8	29.1
Apr-Jun 1994	16,873	11,961	11,045	916	4,912	70.9	65.5	7.7	29.1
May-Jul 1994	16,877	11,970	11,067	903	4,907	70.9	65.6	7.5	29.1
Jun-Aug 1994	16,882	11,966	11,067	899	4,916	70.9	65.6	7.5	29.1
Jul-Sep 1994	16,887	11,966	11,069	897	4,921	70.9	65.5	7.5	29.1
Aug-Oct 1994	16,892	11,944	11,054	890	4,948	70.7	65.4	7.4	29.3
Sep-Nov 1994	16,897	11,936	11,068	868	4,961	70.6	65.5	7.3	29.4
Oct-Dec 1994	16,902	11,918	11,062	856	4,985	70.5	65.4	7.2	29.5
Nov-Jan 1994	16,907	11,910	11,058	852	4,998	70.4	65.4	7.2	29.6
Dec-Feb 1995	16,913	11,956	11,098	858	4,957	70.7	65.6	7.2	29.3
Jan-Mar 1995	16,918	11,986	11,119	867	4,932	70.8	65.7	7.2	29.2
Feb-Apr 1995	16,923	12,012	11,136	876	4,911	71.0	65.8	7.3	29.0
Mar-May 1995	16,928	12,004	11,134	869	4,924	70.9	65.8	7.2	29.1
Apr-Jun 1995	16,933	12,001	11,153	847	4,933	70.9	65.9	7.1	29.1
May-Jul 1995	16,938	12,029	11,174	855	4,910	71.0	66.0	7.1	29.0
Jun-Aug 1995	16,944	12,058	11,206	851	4,886	71.2	66.1	7.1	28.8
Jul-Sep 1995	16,950	12,069	11,212	858	4,881	71.2	66.1	7.1	28.8
Aug-Oct 1995	16,956	12,085	11,240	844	4,872	71.3	66.3	7.0	28.7
Sep-Nov 1995	16,963	12,092	11,238	854	4,871	71.3	66.3	7.1	28.7
Oct-Dec 1995	16,969	12,112	11,285	827	4,857	71.4	66.5	6.8	28.6

Labour Force Survey, summary by sex United Kingdom (thousands) seasonally adjusted (Continued)

All aged 16 to 59/64

	All aged 16 to 59/64	Total economically active	Total in employment	Unemployed	Economically inactive	Economic Activity rate (%)	Employment rate (%)	Unemployment rate (%)	Economic inactivity rate (%)
	10	11	12	13	14	15	16	17	18
Female	YBTG	YBSL	YBSF	YBSI	YBSO	MGSP	MGSV	YBTJ	YBTM
Nov-Jan 1996	16,975	12,135	11,319	815	4,841	71.5	66.7	6.7	28.5
Dec-Feb 1996	16,982	12,123	11,321	802	4,859	71.4	66.7	6.6	28.6
Jan-Mar 1996	16,988	12,106	11,326	780	4,882	71.3	66.7	6.4	28.7
Feb-Apr 1996	16,994	12,119	11,319	800	4,876	71.3	66.6	6.6	28.7
Mar-May 1996	17,001	12,145	11,333	812	4,856	71.4	66.7	6.7	28.6
Apr-Jun 1996	17,007	12,157	11,348	809	4,851	71.5	66.7	6.7	28.5
May-Jul 1996	17,013	12,133	11,329	804	4,880	71.3	66.6	6.6	28.7
Jun-Aug 1996	17,020	12,143	11,351	791	4,877	71.3	66.7	6.5	28.7
Jul-Sep 1996	17,026	12,146	11,349	797	4,880	71.3	66.7	6.6	28.7
Aug-Oct 1996	17,032	12,188	11,389	799	4,844	71.6	66.9	6.6	28.4
Sep-Nov 1996	17,038	12,219	11,409	810	4,819	71.7	67.0	6.6	28.3
Oct-Dec 1996	17,045	12,251	11,435	816	4,794	71.9	67.1	6.7	28.1
Nov-Jan 1997	17,051	12,248	11,442	806	4,803	71.8	67.1	6.6	28.2
Dec-Feb 1997	17,057	12,257	11,469	788	4,800	71.9	67.2	6.4	28.1
Jan-Mar 1997	17,063	12,239	11,467	772	4,824	71.7	67.2	6.3	28.3
Feb-Apr 1997	17,070	12,250	11,480	771	4,819	71.8	67.3	6.3	28.2
Mar-May 1997	17,076	12,258	11,508	750	4,818	71.8	67.4	6.1	28.2
Apr-Jun 1997	17,082	12,305	11,534	771	4,777	72.0	67.5	6.3	28.0
May-Jul 1997	17,088	12,310	11,531	779	4,779	72.0	67.5	6.3	28.0
Jun-Aug 1997	17,095	12,289	11,522	767	4,806	71.9	67.4	6.2	28.1
Jul-Sep 1997	17,100	12,292	11,554	738	4,808	71.9	67.6	6.0	28.1
Aug-Oct 1997	17,105	12,283	11,560	723	4,823	71.8	67.6	5.9	28.2
Sep-Nov 1997	17,111	12,289	11,572	717	4,822	71.8	67.6	5.8	28.2
Oct-Dec 1997	17,116	12,299	11,589	710	4,818	71.9	67.7	5.8	28.1
Nov-Jan 1998	17,122	12,276	11,574	702	4,846	71.7	67.6	5.7	28.3
Dec-Feb 1998	17,127	12,289	11,581	708	4,838	71.8	67.6	5.8	28.2
Jan-Mar 1998	17,133	12,315	11,616	699	4,818	71.9	67.8	5.7	28.1
Feb-Apr 1998	17,138	12,340	11,647	693	4,798	72.0	68.0	5.6	28.0
Mar-May 1998	17,144	12,336	11,640	696	4,808	72.0	67.9	5.6	28.0
Apr-Jun 1998	17,149	12,346	11,642	704	4,803	72.0	67.9	5.7	28.0
May-Jul 1998	17,155	12,373	11,666	707	4,782	72.1	68.0	5.7	27.9
Jun-Aug 1998	17,160	12,397	11,695	701	4,764	72.2	68.2	5.7	27.8
Jul-Sep 1998	17,167	12,394	11,713	682	4,773	72.2	68.2	5.5	27.8
Aug-Oct 1998	17,175	12,428	11,750	678	4,747	72.4	68.4	5.5	27.6
Sep-Nov 1998	17,182	12,447	11,771	676	4,735	72.4	68.5	5.4	27.6
Oct-Dec 1998	17,189	12,440	11,764	676	4,749	72.4	68.4	5.4	27.6
Nov-Jan 1999	17,197	12,498	11,817	681	4,698	72.7	68.7	5.5	27.3
Dec-Feb 1999	17,204	12,502	11,815	687	4,702	72.7	68.7	5.5	27.3
Jan-Mar 1999	17,211	12,516	11,830	686	4,695	72.7	68.7	5.5	27.3
Feb-Apr 1999	17,218	12,511	11,826	685	4,707	72.7	68.7	5.5	27.3
Mar-May 1999	17,226	12,494	11,817	678	4,731	72.5	68.6	5.4	27.5
Apr-Jun 1999	17,233	12,506	11,834	673	4,727	72.6	68.7	5.4	27.4
May-Jul 1999	17,240	12,509	11,836	673	4,731	72.6	68.7	5.4	27.4
Jun-Aug 1999	17,247	12,528	11,862	666	4,720	72.6	68.8	5.3	27.4
Jul-Sep 1999	17,256	12,554	11,890	664	4,703	72.7	68.9	5.3	27.3
Aug-Oct 1999	17,265	12,550	11,877	673	4,715	72.7	68.8	5.4	27.3
Sep-Nov 1999	17,274	12,572	11,904	668	4,703	72.8	68.9	5.3	27.2
Oct-Dec 1999	17,283	12,598	11,929	669	4,685	72.9	69.0	5.3	27.1
Nov-Jan 2000	17,292	12,591	11,921	670	4,701	72.8	68.9	5.3	27.2
Dec-Feb 2000	17,301	12,603	11,930	673	4,698	72.8	69.0	5.3	27.2
Jan-Mar 2000	17,310	12,628	11,949	679	4,682	73.0	69.0	5.4	27.0
Feb-Apr 2000	17,319	12,618	11,954	664	4,701	72.9	69.0	5.3	27.1
Mar-May 2000	17,328	12,633	11,979	654	4,695	72.9	69.1	5.2	27.1
Apr-Jun 2000	17,337	12,643	12,012	631	4,694	72.9	69.3	5.0	27.1
May-Jul 2000	17,346	12,672	12,047	625	4,674	73.1	69.5	4.9	26.9
Jun-Aug 2000	17,355	12,692	12,081	611	4,664	73.1	69.6	4.8	26.9
Jul-Sep 2000	17,366	12,702	12,076	626	4,664	73.1	69.5	4.9	26.9
Aug-Oct 2000	17,376	12,688	12,050	637	4,689	73.0	69.3	5.0	27.0
Sep-Nov 2000	17,387	12,648	12,036	613	4,739	72.7	69.2	4.8	27.3
Oct-Dec 2000	17,397	12,637	12,038	599	4,760	72.6	69.2	4.7	27.4

Labour Force Survey, summary by sex United Kingdom (thousands) seasonally adjusted (Continued)

All aged 16 to 59/64

	All aged 16 to 59/64	Total economically active	Total in employment	Unemployed	Economically inactive	Economic Activity rate (%)	Employment rate (%)	Unemployment rate (%)	Economic inactivity rate (%)
	10	11	12	13	14	15	16	17	18
Female	YBTG	YBSL	YBSF	YBSI	YBSO	MGSP	MGSV	YBTJ	YBTM
Nov-Jan 2001	17,408	12,691	12,102	589	4,717	72.9	69.5	4.6	27.1
Dec-Feb 2001	17,418	12,681	12,099	582	4,738	72.8	69.5	4.6	27.2
Jan-Mar 2001	17,429	12,652	12,076	576	4,777	72.6	69.3	4.6	27.4
Feb-Apr 2001	17,440	12,679	12,101	578	4,760	72.7	69.4	4.6	27.3
Mar-May 2001	17,450	12,692	12,116	576	4,758	72.7	69.4	4.5	27.3
Apr-Jun 2001	17,461	12,727	12,143	584	4,734	72.9	69.5	4.6	27.1
May-Jul 2001	17,471	12,690	12,114	576	4,781	72.6	69.3	4.5	27.4
Jun-Aug 2001	17,482	12,681	12,107	574	4,801	72.5	69.3	4.5	27.5
Jul-Sep 2001	17,490	12,675	12,096	579	4,815	72.5	69.2	4.6	27.5
Aug-Oct 2001	17,498	12,701	12,124	577	4,797	72.6	69.3	4.5	27.4
Sep-Nov 2001	17,506	12,727	12,144	583	4,779	72.7	69.4	4.6	27.3
Oct-Dec 2001	17,514	12,740	12,140	600	4,774	72.7	69.3	4.7	27.3
Nov-Jan 2002	17,523	12,747	12,155	592	4,775	72.7	69.4	4.6	27.3
Dec-Feb 2002	17,531	12,749	12,162	587	4,782	72.7	69.4	4.6	27.3
Jan-Mar 2002	17,539	12,753	12,168	584	4,786	72.7	69.4	4.6	27.3
Feb-Apr 2002	17,547	12,801	12,209	591	4,746	73.0	69.6	4.6	27.0
Mar-May 2002	17,555	12,821	12,219	602	4,734	73.0	69.6	4.7	27.0
Apr-Jun 2002	17,564	12,841	12,248	593	4,722	73.1	69.7	4.6	26.9
May-Jul 2002	17,572	12,822	12,228	593	4,750	73.0	69.6	4.6	27.0
Jun-Aug 2002	17,580	12,859	12,257	602	4,721	73.1	69.7	4.7	26.9
Jul-Sep 2002	17,587	12,857	12,254	603	4,730	73.1	69.7	4.7	26.9
Aug-Oct 2002	17,594	12,867	12,260	607	4,727	73.1	69.7	4.7	26.9
Sep-Nov 2002	17,600	12,874	12,269	605	4,726	73.1	69.7	4.7	26.9
Oct-Dec 2002	17,607	12,871	12,261	610	4,736	73.1	69.6	4.7	26.9
Nov-Jan 2003	17,614	12,839	12,245	594	4,774	72.9	69.5	4.6	27.1
Dec-Feb 2003	17,621	12,856	12,269	587	4,764	73.0	69.6	4.6	27.0
Jan-Mar 2003	17,627	12,883	12,294	589	4,745	73.1	69.7	4.6	26.9
Feb-Apr 2003	17,634	12,881	12,296	585	4,753	73.0	69.7	4.5	27.0
Mar-May 2003	17,641	12,879	12,315	563	4,762	73.0	69.8	4.4	27.0
Apr-Jun 2003	17,648	12,872	12,303	569	4,776	72.9	69.7	4.4	27.1
May-Jul 2003	17,655	12,898	12,309	589	4,757	73.1	69.7	4.6	26.9
Jun-Aug 2003	17,661	12,881	12,289	592	4,781	72.9	69.6	4.6	27.1
Jul-Sep 2003	17,669	12,903	12,307	597	4,766	73.0	69.7	4.6	27.0
Aug-Oct 2003	17,677	12,907	12,328	579	4,770	73.0	69.7	4.5	27.0
Sep-Nov 2003	17,685	12,916	12,338	578	4,769	73.0	69.8	4.5	27.0
Oct-Dec 2003	17,692	12,921	12,351	570	4,772	73.0	69.8	4.4	27.0
Nov-Jan 2004	17,700	12,969	12,397	572	4,731	73.3	70.0	4.4	26.7
Dec-Feb 2004	17,708	12,976	12,401	575	4,731	73.3	70.0	4.4	26.7
Jan-Mar 2004	17,716	12,980	12,398	582	4,736	73.3	70.0	4.5	26.7
Feb-Apr 2004	17,723	12,977	12,394	583	4,747	73.2	69.9	4.5	26.8
Mar-May 2004	17,731	12,979	12,389	590	4,752	73.2	69.9	4.5	26.8
Apr-Jun 2004	17,739	12,971	12,388	584	4,768	73.1	69.8	4.5	26.9
May-Jul 2004	17,747	12,968	12,393	575	4,779	73.1	69.8	4.4	26.9
Jun-Aug 2004	17,755	12,949	12,387	562	4,806	72.9	69.8	4.3	27.1
Jul-Sep 2004	17,764	12,989	12,421	569	4,775	73.1	69.9	4.4	26.9
Aug-Oct 2004	17,775	13,011	12,430	581	4,763	73.2	69.9	4.5	26.8
Sep-Nov 2004	17,785	13,024	12,456	569	4,760	73.2	70.0	4.4	26.8
Oct-Dec 2004	17,795	13,047	12,471	576	4,747	73.3	70.1	4.4	26.7
Nov-Jan 2005	17,805	13,057	12,481	577	4,747	73.3	70.1	4.4	26.7
Dec-Feb 2005	17,815	13,116	12,521	595	4,698	73.6	70.3	4.5	26.4
Jan-Mar 2005	17,825	13,068	12,498	569	4,757	73.3	70.1	4.4	26.7
Feb-Apr 2005	17,835	13,062	12,494	568	4,772	73.2	70.1	4.4	26.8
Mar-May 2005	17,845	13,090	12,515	575	4,755	73.4	70.1	4.4	26.6
Apr-Jun 2005	17,855	13,104	12,513	591	4,750	73.4	70.1	4.5	26.6
May-Jul 2005	17,865	13,126	12,553	573	4,739	73.5	70.3	4.4	26.5
Jun-Aug 2005	17,875	13,139	12,575	564	4,736	73.5	70.4	4.3	26.5
Jul-Sep 2005	17,882	13,163	12,592	571	4,719	73.6	70.4	4.3	26.4
Aug-Oct 2005	17,889	13,154	12,559	595	4,736	73.5	70.2	4.5	26.5
Sep-Nov 2005	**17,897**	**13,125**	**12,510**	**615**	**4,772**	**73.3**	**69.9**	**4.7**	**26.7**

Relationship between columns: 1 = 2 + 5; 2 = 3 + 4; 6 = 2/1; 7 = 3/1; 8 = 4/2;
9 = 5/1; 10 = 11 + 14; 11 = 12 + 13; 15 = 11/10; 16 = 12/10; 17 = 13/11; 18 = 14/10
.. Data not available.

Source: Labour Force Survey
Labour Market Statistics Helpline 020-7533 6094

Further information
Periods prior to Winter (Dec - Feb) 1994/5, data for Northern Ireland have been backcast, except for Spring (Mar - May) quarters. The Labour Force Survey is a survey of the population of private households, student halls of residence and NHS accommodation. Details of standard error and confidence intervals for the LFS are available in the LFS User Guide Volume 1

Recent developments in labour market statistics

Appendix

A

This chapter covers the wide range of new developments in labour market statistics during 2004 and 2005. It includes:

- Improvements to the Labour Market Statistics First Release
- Improvements to Labour Market Statistics Regional First Releases
- Improvements to the Work and worklessness among households First Release
- Improvements to Nomis®
- Modelled local area unemployment
- The Annual Population Survey (APS) and publication of sub-national labour market data
- New publication on labour market statistics for local authorities and parliamentary constituencies
- Historical time series
- Improving public sector employment statistics
- Labour force projections
- National Statistics Quality Review of Employment and Jobs Statistics
- Annual Survey of Hours and Earnings
- Low pay methodology
- Average Weekly Earnings
- Index of Labour Costs per Hour

There have been a number of notable developments in labour market statistics over the past few years, covering data collection, statistical methodology and published outputs. Key developments in 2004 and 2005 are covered in this chapter.

A.1 Improvements to the Labour Market Statistics First Release

There have been a number of improvements to the Labour Market Statistics First Release for the UK since the beginning of 2004.

- Data from the **Vacancy Survey** are presented in Tables 21 and 22 as seasonally adjusted, thus allowing for greater comparisons to be made over time.
- Two new tables have been introduced showing information on **redundancies**. Table 23 shows seasonally adjusted time series of both levels and rates, analysed by sex. Table 24, which is currently updated quarterly, provides a breakdown of redundancies by industry group.
- There have been some changes to the presentation of data on **economic inactivity**. Categories in the release table were changed to include reasons for inactivity for those who say they want a job and those who say they don't. Improvements to the interviewing process have enabled ONS to provide a more relevant breakdown of the reasons why people are inactive. Further analysis will be available during 2006.
- Table 11, which analyses the **claimant count** according to age and duration of claim, is now shown seasonally adjusted.
- Table 8, which covers **usual hours of work**, shows comparisons with data from both the previous quarter and previous year instead of a single point in time.
- On **international comparisons**, Table 19 has been expanded to show all 25 countries of the enlarged European Union and the source data has been reviewed to provide greater comparability between countries.
- In common with all ONS First Releases, the Labour Market Statistics First Release now includes **revisions analyses** for key series.

A.2 Improvement to Labour Market Statistics Regional First Releases

Each month ONS also publishes Labour Market Statistics First Releases for each region and country of Great Britain (Northern Ireland publishes its own release). The following improvements have been incorporated during 2004 and 2005.

- Table 6 now shows usual **hours of work** as well as actual hours of work, while **economic inactivity** rates have been included in table 10 in each of these First Releases.
- More data have been included in the Labour Force Survey estimates for **parliamentary constituencies** and **travel-to-work areas** in Tables 14 and 15.
- As in the national release, each of the First Releases for the regions and countries of the UK now include **revisions analyses** for key series.

A.3 Improvements to the Work and worklessness among households First Release

A number of improvements have been made to the biannual household news release. In addition to the release of Census reweighted household data during 2004, new tables and improved metadata have also been introduced. All figures in the release tables have been weighted to the post-Census population estimates published in February/March 2003. Additionally, a time-series is now being published on the National Statistics website, in Excel format. In response to requests from customers, new tables showing estimates of children in workless households by region and children in workless households by ethnic group were added and all of the tables in the release now consistently include data by households, people and children.

In the spring Release (published in July 2005) a new table was included showing employment rates by parental status.

A.4 Improvements to Nomis®

Labour Market profiles were introduced on Nomis® in early 2004. They present data from different datasets for an area, in the format of the labour market framework (labour demand, labour supply, benefits, and so on). The profiles allow time series data to be viewed, where appropriate, and can be downloaded to a PDF file, which includes comprehensive metadata and definitions.

Department for Work and Pensions data on working-age benefits were published on Nomis® in early 2005. Data are available for both client group and individual benefits. The smallest geographies for which data are available are local authorities and parliamentary constituencies. A range of data from the 2001 Census of Population was also made available on Nomis® in early 2005. These data included standard table cross-tabulations and census area statistics and are available down to output area level.

The claimant count series for 1991 wards was replaced by a series for 2003 Census Area Statistics (CAS) wards (overall counts for 1991 wards continue to be published to allow continuity, but the full breakdowns are now available only for CAS wards). This allows the ward claimant count to be published as a percentage of the working-age population, by using ward population estimates produced by the Small Area Population Estimates project. For local authorities, the claimant count as a percentage of the working-age population was extended back to 1992 (previously this series had gone back only to 1996).

A.5 Modelled Local Area unemployment

Following the publication of an experimental series of model-based estimates of local area unemployment levels and rates (*see* pp37–43, *Labour Market Trends* January 2003), a new random effects model has been developed which was found to produce better quality estimates than a fixed effects model. The external quality assurance phase of the project was completed in April 2005 and the National Statistician has approved these statistics for National Statistics status, subject to resolving issues relating to their presentation. As an interim solution ONS has updated the existing experimental fixed effects model for 1996/97 to 1999/2000 to be consistent with the post-2001 Census population estimates published in February 2003 and extended this model for the years 2000/01 and 2002/03 to allow users access to seven years of data. Work is continuing to extend the methodology to develop a multivariate model estimating two of the three activity statuses.

More information is available on the National Statistics website:
www.statistics.gov.uk/StatBase/Product.asp?vlnk=13574

A.6 The Annual Population Survey (APS) and publication of sub-national labour market data

A new survey, the Annual Population Survey (APS) has been launched, which includes results from the annual Labour Force Survey (LFS) and associated sample boosts. It will provide better annual information for Neighbourhood Statistics (NeSS) on key social and socio-economic variables, such as housing, employment, education and ethnicity, particularly at local area level, providing annual updates to key Census variables. A wide range of labour market information from the survey is disseminated via Nomis®. The target sample for the extra boost in 2004 was 65,000 households in England.

The fieldwork started in January 2004, and the first set of results for the period January–December 2004 were initially made available in July 2005 in the form of microdata and in a limited number of NeSS tables. Data was published in the regional labour market First Releases for the first time on 14 September 2005. Data was launched on Nomis® and in the new local area labour market web publication on 28 September 2005.

A.7 New publication on labour market statistics for local authorities and parliamentary constituencies

On 28 September 2005, ONS launched a new web based publication on local labour markets (local authorities and parliamentary constituencies). It describes the local area labour market framework, presents topic summaries, includes some summary local area data and has links to more detailed data on Nomis® (and to the Nomis local area profiles). The APS is used as the source of labour supply data for the new publication, which will be updated quarterly, as new periods of APS data are released although some data, for example population estimates and jobs densities, are annual estimates and will, therefore, be updated annually.

Previously a summary publication was published on the National Statistics web site when annual LFS were published on Nomis. The new publication follows a similar format, but will be a more analytical publication rather than simply describe one source of local data. The publication provides an overall picture of the labour market in local areas by presenting data on labour supply (from the APS), labour demand (jobs and jobs densities), earning (from ASHE) and benefits. Future updates of the publication will also include model-based estimates of unemployment and data on local Jobcentre vacancies.

The publication explains the concept of the local area framework and describes sources of data, and presents analyses of individual topics, looking at differences between and within Government Office Regions. The topic analyses contain regional summary tables, and summary local area data are also available but, for access to detailed data, links are provided to take users to the Nomis local area profiles and to the main Nomis® datasets. The new publication will aim to guide the user in using these data to understand the local labour market, but Nomis® will remain the main source of detailed local labour market data (for as long as the service continues to be funded). The volume and detail of data available on Nomis® and the range of geographies covered is beyond the scope of the new publication.

A.8 Historical time series

In December 2004 ONS published a new set of consistent series of historical labour market data on a National Statistics basis. This release covered the period 1971–1991, producing historical estimates of headline LFS series, on a consistent basis with post-1992 LFS data. These series are shown after Chapter 6 in this publication.

Full details of the way in which the historical series were produced are available on the National Statistics website (www.statistics.gov.uk). However, the key point is that estimates prior to 1992 were estimated using econometric modelling techniques, as opposed to being taken directly from the LFS.

There are two stages to the estimation of the historical time series. For 1971–79, there are no useable LFS data. The estimation of the data for this period is based on the relationship between the LFS series and other labour market measures over the period 1979–2003. For example, employment was modelled against workforce jobs and unemployment was modelled against the claimant count. Using these estimated relationships and the historical data on workforce jobs and the claimant count, it was possible to produce estimates of the employment and unemployment series for the period 1971–1979. Inactivity was then calculated as the population minus employment minus unemployment.

For 1979–1991, there are existing LFS data; however, they are not consistent with post-1992 data. The quarterly LFS was introduced in 1992; prior to this, the survey was annual (1984–1991) or biennial (1979–1983). The introduction of the quarterly survey appears to have introduced a discontinuity. In addition, there were discontinuities arising from changes in the classification of unpaid family workers, changes in the survey sampling frame, and differences in the weighting between the annual and biennial surveys. Attempts had been made in the past to quantify some of these discontinuities and estimates for the size of the discontinuities have been published (see *LFS User Guide, Vol. 1: Background and Methodology*, www.statistics.gov.uk/StatBase/Product.asp/vlnk=1537); however, no adjustments had ever been made to the headline LFS series. The consistent historical series work adjusted the headline series to allow for the discontinuities, producing ONS's best estimate of a consistent series. This created adjusted annual LFS data points. A rolling three-month series was created by interpolation, using the same modelling process which produced 1971–79 data.

Only the key headline series were estimated, those covering rates and levels for:

- Employment
- Unemployment
- Inactivity

For each of these there were two age breakdowns (working age and 16 and over) and a breakdown by sex. A total weekly hours worked series was also calculated. No further disaggregations (for example, industrial, regional or more detailed age breakdowns) were calculated on the grounds that the samples would be too small and the standard errors associated with modelling would become too large.

More detailed methodology underlying the estimates is available on the National Statistics website: www.statistics.gov.uk/cci/article.asp?ID=424

historical LFS-consistent time series

A.9 Improving public sector employment statistics

There is a greater demand than ever for good quality estimates of employment in the public sector. A number of government reviews have flagged up the need for improved public sector data, including the Atkinson Review of Measurement of Government Output and the Allsopp Review of Statistics for Economic Policymaking. More generally, users' desire for better data has been highlighted as part of ONS's Employment and Jobs Review and the Government's need for accurate and timely data to assess the workforce implications of its efficiency programme as announced at the 2004 Spending Review (Pre-Budget Report). ONS has been leading cross-departmental work over the last year to improve the quality of public sector employment (PSE) statistics in the UK.

- A new survey, the Quarterly Public Sector Employees Survey (QPSES), extends the coverage of the existing quarterly local authority survey for England and Wales to include government departments, their agencies and public sector bodies (mainly non-departmental public bodies (NDPBs) and public corporations) in Great Britain. The data collected are the number of permanent and temporary/casual employees in full- and part-time jobs by sex, on a headcount and FTE basis. Additionally, for local authorities only, ONS is testing the inclusion of a question on employees in the education sector rather than using information from the IDBR as now. Standardised definitions for sources of public sector employment have now been agreed.
- In March 2005 ONS produced estimates on a full-time equivalent (FTE) basis for the first time, by converting part-time employees' hours into a full-time equivalent. Where FTE estimates are not available directly from the sources these have been calculated using hours information from the ASHE. A quarterly time series back to the first quarter of 1999 was introduced.
- There were significant improvements to the coverage of the estimates as well as methodological changes to the way local authority data were produced. As well as the inclusion of figures for Northern Ireland, employment data was re-referenced to March 2004, calculating the historic path from growth estimates and using standard interpolation procedures to estimate data for unavailable quarters. A new method of disaggregating local authority data was also introduced. Estimates are now allocated purely on the ONS's Inter Departmental Business Register (IDBR) that classifies data according to the United Kingdom Standard Industrial Classification (SIC) 2003, rather than producing estimates on a functional basis as before.
- ONS also provided comparisons with key occupational groups produced by other departments, highlighting the differences in levels of employment and the reasons for these.
- In October 2005 an annual publication *Public Sector Employment Trends* was published. This provided detailed analysis of trends in public sector employment, drawing together departmental data for key occupational groups within the public sector. It also used LFS data to examine the characteristics of public sector workers.

Public sector jobs

A.10 Labour Force Projections

In January 2006, ONS published projections of the UK labour force, covering the period between 2006 and 2020. These updated the previous set of labour force projections published by ONS in 1998. The labour force projections refer to the number and proportion of economically active people and are disaggregated by age, sex and, for younger age groups, student status.

Projections of the labour force are based on two key components:

(a) Projections of the UK population. These capture the purely demographic factors that affect the future size and composition of the labour force. They are based on the Government Actuary's Department 2004-based National Population Projections, adjusted to refer only to household population and, thus, maintain consistency with the LFS sampling frame.

(b) Projections of economic activity rates. These capture long-term trends in labour market participation of various population subgroups, due to a number of structural socio-economic factors. They are produced using econometric modelling techniques to show the future pattern of economic activity rates indicated by past trends.

By applying the projections of economic activity rates to projections of the population, the total number of economically active people in the future is estimated.

More detailed methodology underlying the estimates is available on the National Statistics website: www.statistics.gov.uk/StatBase/Product.asp?vlnk=1945

A.11 National Statistics Quality Review of Employment and Jobs Statistics

A report on the *Quality Review of Employment and Jobs Statistics* was published in January 2006. The Review addressed a very wide range of issues relating to the reliability and coherence of employment and jobs statistics. This included detailed analysis of the differences in the estimated levels of jobs obtained respectively from the LFS and from business surveys. As well as this reconciliation analysis, the report contains detailed recommendations for statistical improvements including discussion of the desirability of a single set of jobs estimates. The report also reflects a number of statistical developments which have taken place since an emerging findings report was published in March 2004.

The report is available on the National Statistics website:
www.statistics.gov.uk/about/data/methodology/quality/reviews/labour.asp

A.12 Annual Survey of Hours and Earnings

A new annual earnings survey, the ASHE has been developed to replace the New Earnings Survey (NES). It is the first major survey redesign as part of ONS's statistical modernisation programme. The main changes that have been made to the ASHE methodology are:

- Improved coverage
- Imputation for item non-response
- Applying weighting to all estimates

The re-engineering of the NES and the subsequent ASHE methodology take forward recommendations made in the *National Statistics Quality Review of the Distribution of Earnings Statistics* for improving the collection of earnings statistics.

A comprehensive description is given in the article *Methodology for the Annual Survey of Hours and Earnings.*

For further information see the following National Statistics web pages:
www.statistics.gov.uk/CCI/article.asp?ID=356
www.statistics.gov.uk/CCI/article.asp?ID=985

Annual survey of hours and earnings

A.13 Low pay methodology

A new methodology has been created for low pay estimates that uses data from the ASHE (see above). From 2004 supplementary surveys were included in the ASHE to improve coverage at the low end of the pay distribution, so that the ASHE can appropriately be used as the sole basis for low pay estimates. The ASHE methodology includes imputation and a weighting methodology that provides more accurate weights than those previously used for low pay estimates derived from the NES.

The ASHE provides better estimates of the number of jobs affected by low pay. Accurate estimates of earnings at the low end of the pay distribution have been required in particular since the introduction of the national minimum wage in 1999. This need was met initially by using the average of estimates taken from the NES and the LFS, which were the best available sources at the time. However, the need to improve the methodology has always been recognised, and the ASHE has been developed in response.

The redesign has led to significant improvements in the methodology for low pay estimates. The ASHE includes imputation of missing earnings and hour information in individual questionnaires, and weighting by categories defined by age band, gender, occupation and region. It also introduces additional samples likely to include a higher proportion of low paid employees.

The low pay estimates for spring 2005 were issued in November 2005 and are available on the national statistics website:
www.statistics.gov.uk/CCI/nugget.asp?ID=591

Methodological details on how the estimates are derived are also available:
www.nationalstatistics.gov.uk/CCI/nugget.asp/ID=188

Jobs paid below the national minimum wage

UK legislation covering minimum wages for employees over the age of 18 was introduced on 1 April 1999. In October 2004 this was extended to introduce a national minimum wage for 16- and 17-year-olds. Estimates of the number of people in low paid jobs, and specifically those paid less than he national minimum wage, are published by the ONS annually in October.

National minimum wage rates per hour: April 1999–October 2005

	Aged 16–17	Aged 18–21	Aged 22 and over
Apr 1999 – May 2000		£3.00	£3.60
Jun 2000 – Sept 2000		£3.20	£3.60
Oct 2000 – Sep 2001		£3.20	£3.70
Oct 2001 – Sept 2002		£3.50	£4.10
Oct 2002 – Sept 2003		£3.60	£4.20
Oct 2003 – Sept 2004		£3.80	£4.50
Oct 2004 – Sept 2005	£3.00	£4.10	£4.85
Oct 2005 -	£3.00	£4.25	£5.05

Low pay estimates

A.14 Average Weekly Earnings

The Average Weekly Earnings (AWE) has been developed to complement the current Average Earnings Index (AEI) as a short-term earnings indicator.

AWE uses the same data source as AEI, the Monthly Wages and Salaries Survey (MWSS), but has improved methodology for estimation, imputation and outlier identification.

AWE is the first monthly earnings measure to give a pounds and pence figure for average weekly earnings. It also provides information on the proportion of earnings accounted for by bonuses and arrears of pay.

AWE methodology allows the effect of changes in employment between industries to be identified. For example, if the number of employees in low paying industries increases, then average pay will decrease.

Publication of results

The results of the AWE are published monthly on the National Statistics website: www.statistics.gov.uk/downloads/theme_labour/AWE_Tables_Updated.xls

AWE

A.15 Index of Labour Costs per Hour

The Index of Labour Costs per Hour (ILCH) is a new experimental statistic that measures changes in the cost of an hour of labour. As well as the wages and salaries paid to employees it measures changes in other costs to employers, such as pension contributions and benefits in kind. The ILCH will complement the AEI and new AWE, and will be used alongside the AEI as a timely short-term indicator of earnings.

The results of the ILCH are published quarterly on the National Statistics website. www.statistics.gov.uk/downloads/theme_labour/ILCH_Tables.xls

Further information on the series is given in: www.statistics.gov.uk/CCI/article.asp?ID=1183

ILCH

Sources of labour market statistics

A comprehensive Guide to Labour Market Statistics Releases is available on the National Statistics Website.
www.statistics.gov.uk/downloads/theme_labour/guide_to_LMS_FR1.pdf

This provides full details of the content of the key labour market First Releases. The national, regional and household releases aim to give a coherent picture of the main features of the labour market. They bring together statistics from a range of sources including the Labour Force Survey (LFS), employer surveys and administrative records.

The latest First Release is available on the National Statistics website at:
www.statistics.gov.uk/statbase/Product.asp/vlnk=1944

Labour Market Statistics
National Release

A user guide to regional and local labour market statistics has also been published by ONS. It is intended to help users of regional and local labour market statistics find out what is available and where to obtain the data. The Guide to Regional and local Labour Market Statistics is available on the National Statistics website:
www.statistics.gov.uk/statbase//product.asp/vlnk=4752

The latest Regional Releases are available on the National Statistics website at:
www.statistics.gov.uk/onlineproducts/lms_regional.asp

Labour Market Statistics
Regional Releases

The *Work and Worklessness among Households First Release* gives information about the labour market characteristics of working-age households, categorised into households where all adult members are working; households where no adults are working (workless households); and those containing both working and workless members. It also gives information about the employment status of parents. The data in the First Release are from the LFS Household Datasets.

The latest Work and Worklessness among Households First Release is available on the National Statistics website at: www.statistics.gov.uk/statbase/product.asp/vlnk=8552

Work and worklessness among households

Public sector employment estimates are available in the quarterly PSE Release on the National Statistics Website: www.statistics.gov.uk/STATBASE/Product.asp?vlnk=13615

Public Sector Employment

Key statistics are also available in the Labour Force Survey Historical Quarterly Supplement: www.statistics.gov.uk/onlineproducts/lms_hqs.asp

Summary of key data sources

Sources

Household survey data

Household surveys

Labour Force Survey

Labour Force Survey

The LFS is the largest regular household survey in the UK and much of the labour market data published are measured by the LFS. The concepts and definitions used in the LFS are agreed by the International Labour Organisation (ILO), an agency of the United Nations. The definitions are used by European Union member countries and members of the Organisation for Economic Co-operation and Development.

Census

Census

The primary use of the Census within labour market statistics is to assist in the weighting of sample household surveys, such as the LFS. The fact that the Census is a complete count of people also makes it a valuable source of information on small sub-groups of the population, such as some ethnic groups. For the same reason, the Census is a key source for producing analysis of small geographical areas.

Annual Population Survey

Annual Population Survey

The Annual Population Survey (APS) is a combined survey of households in Great Britain. Its purpose is to provide information on key social and socio-economic variables between the 10-yearly censuses, with particular emphasis on providing information relating to small geographical areas.

The APS comprises the annual LFS (waves one and five), plus data from the Annual Local Area Labour Force Survey (ALALFS), and a further sample boost, the APS boost.

Business surveys

Business surveys are completed by businesses and collect information such as business activity, number of employees, earnings and vacancies. It is compulsory for these surveys to be completed.

Business surveys | Compound sources

Annual Business Inquiry

The Annual Business Inquiry (ABI) is conducted in December to measure amongst other things the number of employee jobs. The survey samples around 78,000 reporting units of workplaces situated in the UK. As well as measuring employee jobs, the ABI also collects financial information from the same set of units. Therefore, figures derived from both parts of the survey, for example turnover per head, are comparable.

ABI

Annual Survey of Hours and Earnings

The ASHE has replaced the New Earnings Survey (NES) as ONS's main source for information on the distribution of earnings. See section A.12 of Appendix A.

ASHE

European Labour Costs Survey

As part of EU regulations ONS produces a survey of labour costs at regular intervals, the European Labour Costs Survey (ELCS). The purpose of the survey is to provide information about total labour costs and in particular the non-wage elements of these costs. This component of labour costs is not readily available from other sources, and is important both as a macroeconomic variable and to employers in their assessment of overall costs. The prohibitive cost and burden on businesses of running a dedicated survey mean that the UK estimates are produced from existing sources. The main source used is the Annual Survey of Hours and Earnings.

Further information is available on the National Statistics website:
www.statistics.gov.uk/CCI/nugget.asp?ID=315

European Labour Costs Survey

Monthly Wages and Salaries Survey

The Monthly Wages and Salary Survey covers a sample of firms in Great Britain. The survey obtains details of the gross wages and salaries paid to employees, in respect of the last pay week for the weekly paid, and for the calendar month for the monthly paid. The sample covers the wage bill for some 9 million employees. It is used to calculate the Average Earnings Index and the Average weekly earnings.

Monthly wages and salary survey

New Earnings Survey

From October 2004 the New Earnings Survey (NES) has been replaced by the Annual Survey of Hours and Earnings (ASHE). Results using ASHE methodology applied to NES data are available from 1998 to 2003.

NES

The ONS Vacancy Survey

The ONS Vacancy Survey is a monthly business survey that provides comprehensive estimates of job vacancies across the economy. Vacancies are defined as positions for which employers are actively seeking recruits from outside their business. Each month's headline estimates are based on three-month rolling averages, with analysis by broad industry sector and by size of business. Monthly estimates of total vacancies are also published.

Vacancy Survey

Quarterly Public Sector Employees Survey (QPSES)

The QPSES was introduced in the third quarter of 2004 and builds on the existing quarterly local authority survey (for England and Wales) by extending its coverage to include GB government departments, their agencies and public sector bodies (mainly Non-Departmental Public Bodies (NDPBs) and Public Corporations). The GB civil service component of QPSES is conducted in conjunction with the Cabinet Office, which retains responsibility for the detailed analysis and publication of estimates of employment within each department.

Short-Term Employment Surveys (STES)

These are smaller surveys that are conducted monthly for production industries and quarterly for services, with a total sample of around 39,000 reporting units per quarter. Around 9,000 production enterprises are sampled each month. The surveys are used to provide estimates of change in the number of jobs between the annual surveys.

Short-term employment surveys

National Employers Skills Survey 2004

The National Employers Skills Survey 2004 (NESS 2004) is the second national employers skills survey commissioned by the Learning and Skills Council (LSC) together with the Department for Education and Skills (DfES) and the Sector Skills Development Agency (SSDA), and shares the aims of the 2003 study, namely to provide detailed analysis of the extent and nature of employers' recruitment problems, skills gaps and training activity.

Further information is available on the Learning and Skills Council website: www.lsc.gov.uk/National/Documents/SubjectListing/Research/LSCcommissionedresearch/NESS2003Findings.htm

Administrative records

Benefits Statistics

Administrative sources of labour market statistics provide data on those claiming working-age benefits and on jobcentre vacancies. The Department for Work and Pensions (DWP) supply data on claimants of working-age benefits, which includes Jobseeker's Allowance. Jobcentre Plus, which handles a major share of all vacancies advertised by employers, supplies data on jobcentre vacancies.

Benefits statistics and general information on benefits are available from the DWP website: www.dwp.gov.uk

DWP data

Information on the key working-age benefits of Incapacity Benefit, Income Support and Jobseeker's Allowance is summarised below:

Incapacity Benefit

Incapacity Benefit (IB) replaced Sickness Benefit and Invalidity Benefit from 13 April 1995. It is paid to people who are assessed as being incapable of work and who meet certain contribution conditions.

Further information can be found at: www.dwp.gov.uk/asd/ib_sda.asp

Income Support

Income Support (IS) is intended to help people on low incomes who do not have to be available for employment. The Income Support Quarterly Statistical Enquiry (IS QSE) is a sample survey that collects information on the number and characteristics of claimants receiving IS in Great Britain. This is used to produce estimates for the whole of the population of IS claimants. Samples are taken at the end of February, May, August and November each year.

Further information can be found at: www.dwp.gov.uk/asd/isqse.asp

Jobseeker's Allowance Claimant Count

The Jobseeker's Allowance (JSA) claimant count, which is often referred to just as the claimant count, is a prominent indicator published monthly by ONS. The claimant count normally refers to the second Thursday of each month.

The data on which the count is based are derived from the Jobcentre Plus administrative system for paying JSA. They relate to all JSA claimants, including people who do not receive any benefit payment but who sign on for national insurance credits to preserve their eligibility for state pension. Claimants must declare that they are out of work, capable of, available for and actively seeking work during the week in which their claim is made. They enter into a Jobseeker's agreement setting out the action they will take to find work or improve their prospects of finding employment.

The claimant count is not the same as unemployment, which is officially measured using the LFS. The count just measures the number of people claiming benefits. It is occasionally affected by changes to rules or procedures for paying JSA. Nevertheless it provides a useful labour market indicator.

Various analyses of the claimant count are available: by sex, age, duration of claims and occupation. Similar analysis is available on monthly inflows and outflows to and from the count. The outflows can also be analysed by destination from the reasons for leaving the count. All the figures are available for a variety of geographies, down to the level of wards or super output areas via Nomis®.

Nomis®

A comparison of the claimant count and ILO unemployment is available on the National Statistics website: www.statistics.gov.uk/CCI/article.asp?ID=746

Jobseeker's Allowance

Inter-Departmental Business Register

The Inter-Departmental Business Register (IDBR) is the comprehensive list of United Kingdom businesses that is used by government for statistical purposes. It provides a sampling frame for surveys of businesses carried out by the ONS and other government departments. It is also a key data source for analyses of business activity.

It is based on inputs from three administrative sources: traders registered with HM Revenue and Customs for Value Added Tax (VAT) purposes; employers operating a pay as you earn (PAYE) scheme; and incorporated businesses registered at Companies House. The ONS Annual Register Inquiry and other surveys supplement these administrative sources, identifying and maintaining the business structures necessary to produce detailed industry and small area statistics.

The IDBR covers businesses in all parts of the economy, other than some very small businesses (self-employed, without employees and low turnover) and some non-profit making organisations.

IDBR

Indicators

Average Earnings Index

The Average Earnings Index is designed to measure changes in earnings in Great Britain. Monthly Wages and Salaries Survey data are used to produce the change in average weekly wages per employee from the previous month. Average earnings are obtained by dividing total gross pay by the total number of employees paid, including those on strike. The three-month average is the change in the average seasonally-adjusted index values for the last three months compared with the same period a year ago.

AEI

Average Weekly Earnings

Average Weekly Earnings (AWE) is an experimental monthly measure of average weekly earnings per employee. Further information is given in section A.14 of Appendix A.

AWE

Index of Labour Costs per Hour

The Index of Labour Costs per Hour (ILCH) is an experimental quarterly measure to estimate the changes in the cost incurred for an hourly unit of labour provided by an employee to an employer. Further information is available in section A.15 of Appendix A.

ILCH

Workforce jobs and employee jobs

The workforce jobs series is the source recommended by ONS for the number of jobs in the UK. Estimates consist of employee estimates from business surveys, LFS data on self employment, and administrative data on the armed forces and government supported trainees. Employee job estimates account for approximately 85 per cent of all jobs.

Workforce jobs

Appendix C

Concepts and definitions

A

Actual hours: (*see* also **Basic hours, Total hours, Usual hours**). The number of hours actually worked in the reference week including (and excluding) paid overtime. This is measured in the Labour Force Survey (LFS) and Annual Survey of Hours and Earning (ASHE). Unpaid overtime can only be included if the Labour Force Survey is being used.

Average (Mean): The result obtained by adding two or more amounts together and dividing the total by the number of amounts.

B

Base year: (*see* also **Index**). The time period from which relative levels are measured usually allocated the value of 100 in an index.

Basic hours: (*see* also **Actual hours, Total hours, Usual hours**). Collected through the LFS and the ASHE. In ASHE, basic hours are the number of guaranteed hours worked at the base rate of pay in the reference week, regardless of whether the hours were actually worked. LFS collects basic hours in two ways, usual hours and actual hours. For actual hours, the respondent is asked how many hours they have worked over the reference week excluding meal breaks. For usual hours, the respondent is asked how many hours they usually work excluding meal breaks and overtime. Respondents can be employees or self-employed and the questions are asked for all jobs undertaken by the respondent.

C

Children: Children refers to everyone aged under 16.

Civilian workforce jobs: Workforce jobs excluding those in HM Forces.

Claimant count: The number of people claiming Jobseeker's Allowance benefits.

Claimant count rate at national or regional level: The number of claimants resident in an area as a percentage of the sum of claimants and workforce jobs in the country or region.

Claimant count proportion: The number of claimants resident in an area as a percentage of the working age population resident in that area.

Consumer Prices Index: (see also Retail Price Index). The Consumer Prices Index (CPI) is the main UK domestic measure of inflation for macroeconomic purposes. It measures the average change from month to month in the prices of consumer goods and services purchased in the UK. The CPI is similar to the Retail Prices Index (RPI), but there are differences in coverage and methodology. Since December 2003 the inflation target for the UK is defined in terms of the CPI measure of inflation.

D

Dependent children: Those aged under 16 and those aged 16–18 who have not married and are in full-time education.

Disability: Labour Force Survey respondents defined as having a current long-term disability covered by the Disability Discrimination Act (DDA) or a work-limiting disability, or both. DDA disabled (current disability) includes people who have a long-term disability that substantially limits their day-to-day activities. Work-limiting disability is a long-term problem that affects the kind of work and the amount of work that a person can do.

Discouraged worker: A sub-group of the economically inactive population who said although they would like a job their main reason for not seeking work was because they believed there were no jobs available.

E

Earnings: A measure of the money people receive in return for work done, gross of tax. It includes salaries and, unless otherwise stated, bonuses but not unearned income, benefits in kind or arrears of pay. Figures are shown both including and excluding bonuses and are seasonally adjusted.

Economically active: People aged 16 or over who are either in employment or unemployed.

Economically inactive: People who are neither in employment nor unemployed. These include those who want a job but have not been seeking work in the last four weeks, those who want a job and are seeking work but not available to start, and those who do not want a job.

Employment and jobs: There are two ways of looking at employment: the number of people with jobs, or the number of jobs. The two concepts are not the same as a person can have more than one job.

The number of people with jobs is measured by the LFS and includes people aged 16 or over who did paid work (as an employee or self-employed), those who had a job that they were temporarily away from, those on government-supported training and employment programmes, and those doing unpaid family work.

The number of jobs is measured by workforce jobs and is the sum of employee jobs (as measured by surveys of employers), self-employment jobs from the LFS, those in HM Forces, and government-supported trainees. Vacant jobs are not included.

Employment rate: (*see* also Rates). The number of people in employment expressed as a percentage of the relevant population. For example, the working-age employment rate is the number of people in employment aged 16–59/64 as a percentage of the population aged 16–59/64).

EU-12 or **Eurozone:** European member states that have adopted the Euro currency – Austria, Belgium, Finland, France, Germany, Greece, Ireland, Italy, Luxembourg, The Netherlands, Portugal and Spain.

EU-15: Eurozone plus Denmark, Sweden and the UK.

EU-25: All of the European Union member states, that is the EU15 plus Cyprus, Czech Republic, Estonia, Hungary, Latvia, Lithuania, Malta, Poland, Slovak Republic and Slovenia.

F

Frictional unemployment: This type of unemployment reflects job turnover in the labour market. Even when there are plenty of vacancies, it takes time to search and find new employment and workers will remain frictionally unemployed between jobs.

Full time: In the LFS, the respondents classify themselves as either full time or part-time. However, people on government supported training and employment programmes that are at college in the reference survey week are classified, by convention, as part time. In employer surveys, people are generally classed as part time if they work for less than 30 hours per week.

Full-time education: In the LFS, this is defined to include people over the age of 16 who state that they are still at school or in some other form of full-time education, including sandwich courses. People on part-time courses, day or block-release courses, or government employment and training schemes are not included.

G

Government-supported trainees: Those on government supported training programmes are included in the employee jobs estimate, within Workforce Jobs, if they have a contract of employment– otherwise they are included in the Workforce Jobs estimate as Government Supported Trainees.

Gross domestic product (GDP): A measure of the total economic activity occurring in the UK. It can be measured in three ways:

1. Production: Measures the gross domestic product as the sum of all the value added by all activities that produce goods and services, (*see* also **Gross value added**).

2. Income: Gross domestic product (income) (GDP(I)) measures GDP as the total of incomes earned from the production of goods and services.

3. Expenditure: Gross domestic product (expenditure) (GDP(E)) measures GDP as the total of all expenditures made either in consuming finished goods and services or adding to wealth, less the cost of imports.

Gross value added: Gross value added is the difference between the value of the output produced by a sector or industry and its intermediate consumption. Intermediate consumption is the cost of raw materials and other inputs that are used up in the production process.

G7: The group of seven major economies: Canada, France, Germany, Italy, Japan, UK, and United States.

G8: The group of eight major economies: The G7 plus Russia.

H

Household: A household is defined as a single person or a group of people living at the same address who have the address as their only or main residence and either share one main meal a day or share living accommodation (or both).

Household reference person: Sometimes it is necessary to select one person in a household to indicate general characteristics of the household. For this purpose the household reference person (HRP) has replaced the head of household in all government-sponsored household surveys after 2000–01. The HRP is the person who owns, or is legally responsible for the rent of, the household accommodation; or whose employer provides the accommodation; or has the accommodation by virtue of some relationship to the owner who is not a member of the household. If there are joint householders the HRP will be the one with the higher income. If their incomes are the same, then the eldest householder is taken as the HRP.

I

Inactivity: (*see* **Economically inactive**).

Index: A number giving the value of a quantity relative to a base year, where the value of the base year is set at 100. Index numbers are used to indicate trends in prices, production, employment and other economic variables.

Inflows (and Outflows): The claimant count records are analysed to provide information about inflows onto the count and outflows from the count on a monthly basis. To make comparisons over time consistent, these figures are standardised to a 4 and a third week month before seasonal adjustment. These figures for people starting to or ceasing to claim Jobseeker's Allowance can be helpful towards interpreting changes in the claimant count.

Involuntary job separation: (*see* also **Job separation, Voluntary job separation**). The termination, by the employer, of the relationship between employee and employer. This includes both voluntary and involuntary redundancies and temporary jobs ending.

J

Jobs density: The total number of filled jobs in an area divided by the resident working-age population in that area.

Job separation: The termination of the relationship between an employee and employer, either by the employee or the employer.

L

Labour costs: The whole range of costs that employers incur when employing workers. These include wages and salaries paid to employees, social contributions, redundancy payments, benefits in kind and other non-wage components.

Labour demand: The demand side of the labour market comprises the number of jobs and vacancies.

Labour disputes: Disputes connected with terms and conditions of employment. These statistics relate to persons both directly and indirectly involved at the establishments where the disputes occurred.

Labour market attachment: A concept relating to a person's proximity to the labour force. It covers a spectrum from fully attached workers, those in employment at the one extreme, to those who do not want a job at the other extreme. The latter group, which includes economically inactive retired people, might be considered to be completely detached from the labour market.

Labour supply: People who are employed or unemployed form the actual labour supply. Economically inactive people are considered a potential source of labour supply.

M

Mean (Average): The result obtained by adding two or more amounts together and dividing the total by the number of amounts.

Median: Describes the value that is the middle one in a set of values arranged in order of size.

N

National minimum wage: An employer must pay their employees a minimum amount as defined by law.

NUTS areas: The classification of areas for European Union (EU) purposes is known as the 'Nomenclature des Unites Territorales Statistique' (NUTS). They provide a breakdown of the EU territory for producing regional statistics.

O

Outflows: (*see* **Inflows and Outflows**).

Overtime (paid): The ASHE asks employers to report the number of employee hours worked at overtime rates of pay during the reference week. The LFS requests information on actual and usual paid overtime on the same basis as basic pay.

Overtime (unpaid): This is only measured in the LFS. Respondents are asked about their actual and usual unpaid overtime in the same way as basic pay and paid overtime.

P

Part time: (*see* **Full time**)

Productivity: Whole economy output per worker is the ratio of Gross Value Added (GVA) at basic prices and LFS total employment. Manufacturing output per filled job is the ratio of manufacturing output (from the Index of Production) and productivity jobs for manufacturing (constrained to LFS jobs at the whole economy level).

Private sector employment: (*see* Public sector/private sector employment).

Public sector/private sector employment: Public sector employment comprises employment in central government, local government and public corporations as defined for the UK National Accounts. Data are collected from public sector organisations via the ONS Quarterly Public Sector Employees Survey and other sources. Employment estimates for the private sector are derived as the difference between LFS employment estimates for the whole economy (not seasonally adjusted) and the public sector employment estimates.

R

Rates: (*see* also **Employment rate, Unemployment rate, and Working-age inactivity rate**). Rates represent the proportion of the population or subgroup of the population with a certain characteristic. They are used to interpret changes in the labour market in a wider context, allowing for changes in the overall population or the number of people who are economically active. Rates can be calculated for different age groups. For employment, economic activity and economic inactivity, the most widely quoted rates are those for the working-age population (males aged 16–64 and females aged 16–59). These are shown on the front page of the releases. For unemployment, headline rates are expressed as a percentage of the economically active population aged 16 and over. Those over retirement age who continue to be economically active will therefore be included in the base while those who are economically inactive will not.

Redundancies: The number of people who were not in employment during the LFS interview reference week and who reported that they had been made redundant in the month of the reference week or in the two-calendar months prior to this; plus the number of people who were in employment during the reference week who started their job in the same calendar month as, or the two calendar months prior to, the reference week, and who reported that they had been made redundant in the month of the reference week or in the two calendar months prior to this.

Redundancy rate: The ratio of the number of redundancies in one quarter to the number of employees in the previous quarter, measured as redundancies per 1,000 employees.

Retail Price Index: (*see* also Consumer Price Index). An important domestic indicator of inflation in the UK. It measures the average change from month to month in the prices of goods and services purchased in the UK. In addition, there are two commonly used RPI aggregates:

1. RPIX – All items excluding mortgage interest payments
2. RPIY – All items excluding mortgage interest payments and indirect taxes

S

Sampling variability: Data based on statistical samples are subject to sampling variability. If many samples were drawn, each would give a different result. The ranges shown for ONS' series typically represent 95 per cent confidence intervals; that is, it is expected that in 95 per cent of samples the range would contain the true value.

Seasonal adjustment: A process of estimating regularly occurring seasonal effects and removing them from the data.

Second jobs: Jobs which LFS respondents hold in addition to a main full-time or part-time job.

Self-employed people: Those who, in their main job, work on their own account, whether or not they have employees.

Self-employment jobs: Part of the total workforce jobs, includes self-employed people in their main job and people who are employees in their main job who are self-employed in their second job. This is taken from the LFS.

Skill gap: (*see* also Skill shortage). Deficiencies in skills of an employer's existing workforce, both at the individual level and overall, which prevent the firm from achieving its business objectives.

Skill shortage: (*see* also Skill gap). Recruitment difficulties caused by a shortage of individuals with the required skills in the accessible labour market.

Standard Industrial Classification (SIC): A Standard Industrial Classification was first introduced into the UK in 1948 for use in classifying business establishments and other statistical units by the type of economic activity in which they are engaged. The SIC was last revised in 2003 and is due for further revision in 2007.

Standard Occupational Classification (SOC): The classification system used to provide a consistent occupational breakdown for UK official statistics. This system was introduced in 1991 and was updated in 2000.

T

Temporary employees: In the LFS these are defined as those employees who say that their main job is non-permanent in one of the following ways: fixed period contract, agency temping, casual work, seasonal work, other temporary work.

Total hours: (*see* also Actual hours, Basic hours, Usual hours). The hours worked plus any paid and unpaid overtime.

Trends: Trends are used to describe the long-term movement in a time series.

U

Underemployment: This is usually defined as when someone wants to work extra hours, is available to start within two weeks and has worked less than an average number of hours for their sex.

Unemployment: The number of unemployed people in the UK is measured through the LFS following the internationally agreed definition recommended by the International Labour Organisation (ILO), an agency of the United Nations. Unemployed people are:

1. Without a job, want a job, have actively sought work in the last four weeks and are available to start work in the next two weeks or
2. Out of work, have found a job and are waiting to start it in the next two weeks.

Unemployment rate: (*see* also Rates). The percentage of economically active people who are unemployed. A rate can be calculated for any population group.

Unit wage costs: A measure of the cost of wages and salaries per unit of output.

Unpaid family workers: Persons doing unpaid work for a business they own or for a business that a relative owns.

Usual hours: (*see* also Actual hours, Basic hours, Total hours). The number of hours usually worked each week including (and excluding) paid and unpaid overtime.

V

Vacancies: The number of positions for which an employer is actively seeking a recruit from outside their business or organisation.

Voluntary job separation: (*see* also Job separation, Involuntary job separation). An employee choosing to terminate their relationship with an employer, for example through resignations or retirement.

W

Working age: A female aged 16–59 or a male aged 16–64.

Working-age household: A working-age household is a household that includes at least one person of working age.

Working-age inactivity rate: (*see* also Rates). People who are economically inactive as a percentage of the working-age population.

Workless household: A workless household is a household that includes at least one person of working age where no one aged 16 or over is in employment.

Appendix D

Enquiry points

Labour Market Statistics Helpline *labour.market@ons.gov.uk*	020 7533 6094
Earnings Customer Helpline *earnings@ons.gov.uk*	01633 819024
National Statistics Enquiry Service *info@statistics.gov.uk*	0845 601 3034
Skills and Education Network senet@lsc.gov.uk	024 7682 3439
DfES Public Enquiry Unit	0870 000 2288

For statistical information on:

Average Earnings Index (monthly)	01633 819024
Claimant count	020 7533 6094
Consumer Prices Index	020 7533 5874
Earnings	01633 819024
Annual Survey of Hours and Earnings (annual):levels of earnings and hours worked for groups of workers (males and females, industries, occupations, regions, agreements, pension categories, age, part-time and full-time);distribution of earnings; composition of earnings; hours worked	
Basic wage rates and hours for manual workers with a collective agreement	01633 819008
Low-paid workers *lowpay@ons.gov.uk*	01633 819024
Labour Force Survey (quarterly): weekly and hourly earnings; distribution; men and women, occupation, region *labour.market@ons.gov.uk*	020 7533 6094
Economic activity and inactivity	020 7533 6094

Employment	020 7533 6094
Labour Force Survey: full-time and part-time; self-employment; temporary work; second jobs; occupations; men and women; ethnicity; region;people with disabilities; hours worked (usualand actual for groups of workers)	
Employee jobs by industry	01633 812318
Total workforce hours worked per week *productivity@ons.gov.uk*	01633 812766
Workforce jobs series – short-term estimates *workforce.jobs@ons.gov.uk*	01633 812318
Labour costs	01633 819024
Labour disputes	01633 819205
Labour Force Survey	020 7533 6094
Labour Force Survey Data Service *lfs.dataservice@ons.gov.uk*	020 7533 5614
New Deal (DWP)	0114 209 8228
Productivity and unit wage costs	01633 812766
Public sector employment	
General enquiries	020 7533 6178
Source and methodology enquiries	01633 812362
Qualifications (DfES)	0870 000 2288
Redundancy statistics	020 7533 6094
Retail Prices Index	020 7533 5874
Recorded announcement of latest RPI *rpi@ons.gov.uk*	020 7533 5866
Skills (DfES) Skill needs surveys and research into skill shortages	0114 259 4407
Small firms (DTI) Small Business Service (SBS)	0114 279 4439
Subregional estimates Annual employment statistics *annual.employment.figures@ons.gov.uk*	01633 812038
Annual Population Survey, local area statistics	020 7533 6130
Trade unions (DTI) Employment relations	020 7215 5934
Training	
Adult learning – work-based training (DWP)	0114 209 8236
Employer-provided training (DfES)	0114 259 4407
Travel-to-Work Areas	
Composition and review	020 7533 6114
Unemployment	020 7533 6094
Vacancies **Vacancy Survey: total stocks of vacancies**	020 7533 6162
Youth Cohort Study (DfES)	0114 259 3639